11981

*The Civilization of the American Indian Series*

[Complete list on page 229]

# Indians of the High Plains

FROM THE PREHISTORIC PERIOD TO THE COMING OF EUROPEANS

# Indians
# of the High Plains

## FROM THE PREHISTORIC PERIOD
## TO THE COMING OF EUROPEANS

George E. Hyde

NORMAN : UNIVERSITY OF OKLAHOMA PRESS

By George E. Hyde

*Corn Among the Indians of the Upper Missouri*
(Cedar Rapids, Iowa, 1917), with George F. Will
*Red Cloud's Folk* (Norman, 1937)
*The Pawnee Indians* (Denver, 1951)
*Rangers & Regulars* (Columbus, 1953)
*A Sioux Chronicle* (Norman, 1956)
*Indians of the High Plains* (Norman, 1959)

LIBRARY OF CONGRESS CATALOG CARD NUMBER: 59–7963

Copyright 1959 by the University of Oklahoma Press, Publishing Division of the University. Composed and printed at Norman, Oklahoma, U.S.A., by the University of Oklahoma Press. First edition.

To the memory of
*Asa T. Hill*
1871–1953
*Nebraska archaeologist and discoverer*
*of the ruined villages of the Padouca Nation*

# Preface

THIS BOOK is intended to present a coherent picture of the Indians of the western high plains from the earliest times of which we have a record down to the beginning of the modern period, after the year 1800. The book explores the whole of the high plains area, dealing with many tribes; thus the narrative shifts back and forth, all the way from the plains of western Canada to those of Texas and northern Mexico. For the early period, 1300 to 1700, the Apaches and their Navaho cousins have the pivotal roles; but with the fall of Apache power after 1700 the Comanches and their northern kinsmen, the Gens du Serpent, come to the fore and take the leadership in the high plains, until they in their turn are broken or swept aside by the advance of new and more powerful tribes.

The presentation of the Plains Apaches as the nation known before 1750 or 1800 as the Padoucas is an outstanding feature of the book. It has been the custom of historians to identify the Padoucas as Comanches; but in the past thirty years new evidence, in the form of Spanish and French documents hitherto unknown and new archaeological investigations, has made the old view untenable. It is thus necessary to make adjustments and alterations in early plains history; for, if the Apaches and not the Comanches were the great Padouca Nation, the whole course of early plains history is changed, and the Apaches must be given the credit for being the first great tribe that attempted to form settlements and undertake to grow crops in the heart of the plains in historic times. The present volume sets forth in detail this Apache-Padouca achievement and records the locations of many of the little villages or *rancherías* in which these people lived, extending all the way from Dakota down into Texas. The story of the rise and fall of the Gens du Serpent is another important feature of the book. Up to the present time, most of our historians and anthropologists have not troubled to piece together the Indian traditions and other evidence of former Gens du Serpent or Snake power in the northern plains. This has been done in the present volume, and it indicates that from before 1700 to about 1770 the Snakes dominated the plains, from the Platte to the Saskatchewan.

The author has made considerable use of modern archaeology, a science that has made surprising advances during the past thirty years in uncovering hitherto unknown features of early Indian life in the western high plains. By combining this new archaeological material with evidence taken from Spanish and French documents, it has been possible to clear up many points in early plains history and to give them rational explanations.

This book is intended for general reading, and I have refrained from pinning down every little statement by adding a footnote to indicate the source of information. Archaeologists and anthropologists will know the sources; the general reader probably will not care to know, and he has my sympathy. This is a reading book, not a treatise.

My gratitude is due to my sister Mabel L. Reed for aid and comfort in the writing of this book. I wish to thank Marvin F. Kivett, director of the Nebraska Historical Society Museum, for aid, advice, and photographs; Roger T. Grange, Jr., curator of the Fort Robinson, Nebraska, Museum, for photographs, and Miss Doris Quick for drawing the maps for the book.

George E. Hyde

*Omaha, Nebraska*
*June 3, 1959*

# Contents

# Illustrations

# Indians of the High Plains

FROM THE PREHISTORIC PERIOD TO THE COMING OF EUROPEANS

# 1. The Early Apaches

SOME TIME in the late prehistoric period eastern Woodland Indians pushed out into the plains as far at least as the forks of the Platte and the upper branches of the Kansas River. And, although there are traces of very early peoples, whose identity is unknown, the story of the early Indian inhabitants of the western high plains may properly begin with mention of these Woodland Indians. Following them came the Basket Maker Folk, who entered the plains of Oklahoma from the west. Both of the primitive peoples here referred to grew maize in small patches at favorable points in the vast territory through which their sparse population was spread. This period, as far as the Woodland Indians were concerned, would appear to have been a time of penetration rather than of occupation, so small were their camps and so vast the areas of wilderness that separated one small camp from its nearest neighbor.

After the year 1200 a new and more extensive penetration of the region occurred, with groups of Caddoan Indians advancing into the plains of Kansas and Nebraska (also, perhaps into western Oklahoma), where they formed small communities, dwelling in rectangular earth lodges and supporting themselves partly by hunting and partly by raising small crops of maize, beans, squash, and some other products. These were the folk whose remains, uncovered by recent excavations, have been designated Upper Republican by archaeologists because their village ruins were first

3

discovered in the upper valley of the Republican River in south-western Nebraska. About the time that these Upper Republicans or primitive Pawnees came into the high plains, another group of Indians formed settlements on the headwaters of the Canadian River in the Texas Panhandle. Here the people, whoever they were, built houses of stone slabs and adobe, apparently with flat roofs, and divided into many rooms after the Pueblo fashion. They made pottery very similar to that of the Upper Republicans and also planted maize. A tentative dating has been given to both the Upper Republican and the Texas Panhandle cultures. Some sherds of Pueblo pottery (Pecos Pueblo ware) found in the Texas village ruins are said to date to the period 1300–1500, while tree-ring datings taken from pieces of charcoal at the Ash Hollow Cave near the forks of the Platte date the Upper Republican occupation to approximately the same period.[1]

This brings us almost to the time when real history begins in the southern plains: to the period when the Spanish explorers found those plains occupied by the Apaches of the great northern Athapascan linguistic family; but of this dawning of history in the southern plains we still have little solid information, and for nearly two centuries later we have almost no knowledge of the Indians who roved the northern plains.

The Spanish discovery of Apaches as far south as New Mexico, however, affords us a clue to what had been happening in the unknown north prior to 1540, and, taking into account the detailed information we have on the northern region for the period after 1670, we may assume that sometime around the date 1200 strong groups of Athapascan Indians left their old lands in the Mackenzie Basin or in the mountains to the west of that district and started their long advance southward through the great plains. It was apparently a two-pronged movement: one group of tribes

---

[1] J. L. Champe, *Ash Hollow Cave;* Waldo R. Wedel, "Culture Sequences in the Central Great Plains," *Smithsonian Miscellaneous Collections,* Vol. C; Alex D. Krieger in Fifth Plains Conference, *Notebook I.* The dating of Upper Republican seems to be fairly established. In the Texas Panhandle the dating seems doubtful, perhaps because there were several occupations, one of which should be an Apache occupation dating about 1680 to 1730.

moved down through the plains, and another migrated southward through the interior plateau country lying west of the Rockies, some of this latter group pushing as far down as the southern part of California.[2]

The Navahos were among the first Athapascans to come as far south as New Mexico; but unlike the other Apaches, they seem to have turned off from the route through the plains, passing west of the Rockies and coming into New Mexico through western Colorado. Julian H. Steward has suggested that the Promontory Point culture recently discovered in caves and other sites on the northern shores of Great Salt Lake may prove to be the remains of early Navaho occupation. This culture is late prehistoric, and the indications are that the people who brought it to Great Salt Lake came from the far north and obtruded themselves into the Promontory Point lands. Nearly two hundred specimens of northern four-piece moccasins have been found here and also fur mittens, sinew-backed bows, and beaver-tooth dice: all features of the culture of the frigid northlands. These northern invaders also brought native pottery of plains type, which suggests that they came down through the plains and then swung west to reach the Promontory Point district.[3]

Even if they were not the Promontory Point folk, the Navahos certainly migrated through this region west of the Rockies, for Richard F. Van Falkenburgh has recently discovered early Navaho remains in western Colorado, extending for a distance of one hundred miles north of the San Juan River.[4] The Spaniards of

[2] See map in John P. Harrington, "Southern Periferal Athapaskawan Origins, Divisions, and Migrations," *Smithsonian Miscellaneous Collections*, Vol. C. Harry Hoijer, "Southern Athapaskan Languages," *American Anthropologist*, N. S., Vol. XL (1938), states that the Apaches were divided into two language groups, Lipans of the plains and Arizona or western Apaches, and that a study of dialects indicates that the Navahos were the first group to break off from the western Apaches, while the Gatakas or Prairie Apaches were the first to leave the eastern group. This seems to fit nicely with the known historical and archaeological evidence.

[3] Julian H. Steward, "Native Cultures of the Intermontane (Great Basin) Area," *Smithsonian Miscellaneous Collections*, Vol. C., p. 471-74.

[4] Harrington, "Southern Periferal Athapaskawan Origins," *Smithsonian Miscellaneous Collections*, Vol. C, p. 529.

New Mexico reported in the eighteenth century the finding of extensive ruins of early Pueblo settlements in this district north of the San Juan River, and we might conjecture that these settlements were destroyed by the Navahos in their advance southward. What is known for certain is that in late prehistoric times the Navahos crossed the San Juan and drove the primitive Pueblo population out of the lands west of the upper Río Grande, the Río Chama, and Largo Canyon district, and here the Navahos remained, calling their new home Tinetxah. Part of the land they had taken lay within the eastern borders of their present reservation; wood found in the ruins of a Navaho hogan here gave a tree-ring date 1575; but archaeologists are of the opinion that the Navahos entered this neighborhood at an earlier period.[5]

In support of archaeological evidence, we have the testimony of Navaho and Pueblo tradition and of some early Spanish statements which show that the Navahos were attacking the Pueblo settlements west of the upper Río Grande in late prehistoric and early historic times. The Tewa Pueblos, the most northerly group, with villages on both sides of the Río Grande, were the principal sufferers. They had a frontier stronghold called Chipiinuinge on the high mesa south of Río Chama which they tried to defend against the Navahos, but by the opening of the historic period they had been driven from the Río Chama district and had retired southward.

To the south of the Tewas on the west side of the Río Grande were the Keres Pueblos, while on the east side of the river were the Tano towns, which at this early period were under attack by the Querechos and Teyas of the plains east of New Mexico, the Querechos being Apaches, the Teyas a group of unknown affiliation. The Pueblo tribes were facing destruction at the hands of these wild invaders and should have combined against them, but instead of presenting a united front, they were raiding each other.

[5] *Ibid.*; Dolores Gunnerson, "The Southern Athabascans: Their Arrival in the Southwest," *El Palacio*, Vol. VI (November–December, 1956), 359. Some authorities think the Navahos were in northern New Mexico as early as 1300; Frederick W. Hodge (1895) thought that Navaho tradition suggested that their arrival in New Mexico was an event of the late fifteenth century.

At the very time that they were being so hard pressed by the Navahos on the north, the Tewas were warring on their Keres neighbors to the south.

We have little information on this early period, but it is stated that the wild Teyas of the eastern plains raided the Tano pueblos south of the present Santa Fé so severely that these pueblos were depopulated and some of them abandoned about the date 1525. Similar raids by wild plains tribes were being made on Pecos and on the pueblo later known as Santo Domingo. Some of the Tewas held out at their fortress, Chipiinuinge, until the coming of Coronado (1541–42).

Up to the present time it has been impossible to determine whether the wild tribe in the plains called the Teyas, who were devastating the Pueblo districts east of the Río Grande as early as the year 1525, were Apaches or Indians of some other stock. The identity of the Teyas is a puzzle. The statement in the Coronado narratives that this tribe was warring on the Querechos, who were certainly Apaches, seems to imply that the Teyas were not Apaches. Frederick Webb Hodge held for many years that the Teyas were Caddoan Indians of Texas; but Herbert Bolton apparently refuted that. Dolores Gunnerson in a recent study identified the Teyas as Apaches, and John Harrington finds that the name Teya is still applied to Apaches of the Lipan group by the Pueblo Indians of Pecos and Jémez.

However, the Coronado documents clearly term the Apaches "Querechos" and state that this tribe visited and even spent winters at Quivira on the eastern borders of the plains, on the Arkansas River in what is now southern Kansas, and that the Querechos also visited, traded, and wintered among the Pueblo tribes in New Mexico. These statements mean that in 1542 the Apaches were in control of the southern plains across their entire width, and from northern Texas up to the Arkansas River or beyond.

What the situation was in the plains farther to the north is unknown, but, as the Apache tribes were evidently migrating southward through the plains from the great hive of Athapascan peoples in the Mackenzie Basin, it seems a fair inference that

7

Apache groups, by 1541, held the plains in Colorado, western Kansas, western Nebraska, western Dakota, eastern Wyoming, and, perhaps, as far north as the Saskatchewan. In the Ash Hollow Cave near the forks of the Platte, the Apache (Dismal River) occupation is dated by tree-ring analysis to as far back as about 1684.[6] Since this stratum contains broken pottery of Apache make, we may assume that the tribe had been in Nebraska for quite a long period, as there is little likelihood that they brought the art of pottery-making from the far north. It is difficult to see how they could have learned this art except from the Caddoan Indians of the Upper Republican River or the Pueblos of New Mexico.[7]

Harrington has stated that the migrating Athapascan tribes, on coming into the district east of New Mexico, found that there was no serious barrier toward the west and that part of these Indians swung westward, crossing the Río Grande and coming out presently in the edge of the later home of the Arizona Apaches. He has also suggested that the Gila Apaches formed a portion of these westward-moving bands. In Coronado's day Apaches were not mentioned west of the Río Grande, but by 1550 Querecho Apaches were living near Acoma, had learned to plant maize, and were alternately raiding Acoma and coming to trade deer and rabbit skins for maize and cotton mantles. Such raids and trade visits were entirely foot operations—the Indians of prehistory had no horses. When the Spaniards entered this district, these insolent Apaches boldly attacked them, throwing stones at the men in armor and then scampering up the rugged hillsides to safety, shouting defiance and making insulting gestures. At night they slipped into the Spanish camps and attempted to kill armored men and the dreaded horses with flint knives and lances. In 1583, Espejo reported that these Querechos were still near Acoma, and in 1599 Oñate encountered them in the Pueblo country and termed them *es infinita gente los Apichees que también hemos visto al-*

[6] Champe, *Ash Hollow Cave*, 55, 86. On page 27, he says the Apache or Dismal River occupation began about 1675 and ended about 1705.

[7] The Dismal River (Apache) pottery is now being studied and separated into types. It seems to show many Pawnee traits, but it has some Mandan and other upper Missouri traits.

*gunos.*[8] Fray Benavides (*ca.* 1630) termed the Apaches the largest tribe in the world, a statement that some modern ethnologists are prone to reject with the offhand assertion that the Apaches were never a large tribe. They were numerous enough in the sixteenth and seventeenth centuries to seize and hold the entire plains area, from Texas to Wyoming.

Oñate spoke of the Apaches by the name Querechos, also terming them *Vaqueros*, meaning "herdsmen," a name referring to the fact that they wandered in the buffalo country, making their living from the vast herds. The older name, Querecho, now went out of use.

In 1598 Oñate sent Záldivar with sixty-nine men into the plains. Marching by way of Pecos and on eastward, they found a rancheria (not described in detail) of Vaqueros, who begged the Spaniards to make peace for them with the Jumanos, who were raiding them. Going on to a large river, evidently the upper Canadian, Záldivar met more Vaqueros returning to the plains after a trading expedition to Picurís and Taos, where they had exchanged dried meat, tallow, hides, and salt for maize, pottery, cotton cloaks, and small green stones (turquoises). Here Záldivar saw an Apache rancheria or camp of fifty skin tipis colored red and white, "with flaps and openings, all very neat." The Spaniards had a splendid time in the plains among the friendly Apaches, hunting buffalo and visiting Vaquero rancherias. Záldivar described the Apaches as armed with Turkish bows (bone bows?) and flint-headed arrows; they hid in blinds near the watering places and killed the buffalo when they came to drink. This was in the autumn of 1598, and Záldivar returned to New Mexico early in November.[9]

Záldivar's statement that the Jumanos were warring on the Va-

[8] Herbert Eugene Bolton (ed.), *Spanish Exploration in the Southwest, 1542–1706*, 183; George E. Hyde, *Rangers and Regulars*, 35; Frank C. Lockwood, *The Apache Indians*, 8.

[9] Bolton, *Spanish Exploration*, 226; George P. Hammond and Agapito Rey, *Don Juan de Oñate, Colonizer of New Mexico, 1595–1628*. Oñate did use the old name Querecho before he went into the plains and met the Apaches. He then discarded Querecho, termed these Indians Apaches, and applied the Spanish name Vaquero to them.

quero Apaches of the Canadian River region and that the Apaches begged the Spaniards to make peace for them is very interesting, for it is an indication that in 1598 the Apaches were not having everything their own way. The identity and early history of the Jumano tribe is one of the unsolved mysteries of the southern plains. In 1535, Cabeza de Vaca had met part of the Jumanos, whom he called the People of the Cows, on the west side of the Río Grande below the present El Paso. At this date the Jumanos evidently did not plant, as they told Cabeza de Vaca that tribes to the north had maize. In 1583, Espejo found Jumanos in the same district. According to Espejo, this tribe had streaked faces (tattooed or painted). The first group he encountered lived in flat-roofed huts, but those farther on, near the Río Grande, were in grass lodges. Beyond the Jumanos, on the Río Grande below El Paso, Espejo met two other tribes, evidently the Sumas and Mansos: buffalo-hunting Indians, who had striped cotton cloaks and featherwork obtained from neighboring tribes that were more highly advanced. These buffalo-hunting neighbors of the Jumanos had grass-lodge villages but did not plant maize or other crops; they hunted buffalo and deer, caught fish, and also had mescal fruit and a supply of salt. The whole region near the lower Río Grande in 1583 was thinly populated; great spaces of uninhabited plains lay between each small grass-lodge village and the next, as far as the most southerly of the Pueblo towns near the present Socorro.[10]

These early references to the Jumanos are important, for this tribe seems to have been the only one that actually advanced northward and eastward into the high plains at the time when the Apaches were coming down from the north, and, as stated by Záldivar, by 1598 the Jumanos were raiding the Apaches with sufficient power to make that tribe anxious for peace. One suspects that at this period the Apaches of the plains were not the fierce raiders they were half a century later; for it is to be noted that from 1541 to 1620 the Spanish references are mainly to friendly trading visits of the Apaches to the Pueblo towns.

[10] Bolton, *Spanish Exploration*, 176.

But general statements are often misleading, and at the very moment of Záldivar's pleasant sojourn among the friendly Vaqueros of the upper Canadian, the Apaches on the eastern border of the plains, close to Quivira, appear to have been warring on their Caddoan neighbors. This was disclosed when Oñate crossed the plains to Quivira in 1601 with a strong force of Spaniards. On the Canadian he first met camps of friendly Indians, whom he termed *apachi*. They had no fixed abode, but were in full possession of the plains through which they roved. These people seem to have been on the western edge of the great buffalo range, through which Oñate marched in August. After leaving the Canadian and crossing the Cimarron, as Bolton suggests, the Spaniards came upon a great rancheria of Indians whom they termed *Escansaques:* a group of five thousand people living in circular lodges, some of them ninety feet in diameter, constructed of tree branches or poles, covered with tanned skins. This great camp of six hundred lodges was within eight leagues of Quivira, and the Escansaques, eager to raid their neighbors, offered to join forces with Oñate. They went along whether wanted or not, and while the Spaniards were encamped among the friendly Caddoan Indians of Quivira, the Escansaques attempted to start hostilities by setting the Quivira grass lodges aflame. Oñate ordered the troublemakers to leave, but they had achieved part of their purpose, for the Quiviras were no longer friendly, and, fearing an attack by an overwhelming force of Quivira warriors on his men, Oñate left the villages and retired toward the Escansaque rancheria. Just what happened here is obscure, but the Spaniards played their usual high-handed tricks, seizing Indian property and also women, and thus they brought on themselves an assault by fifteen hundred warriors, who did not relent from morning until dark, wounding nearly all of Oñate's men and forcing him to turn loose the Escansaque women and beat a retreat. Recrossing the plains by an unrecorded route, he reached New Mexico late in November.[11]

The Escansaques have been variously identified. Perhaps the

[11] *Ibid.*, 250–64.

most curious effort was that which termed them the Kansa tribe of Siouan Indians, who, as far as we know, were not even in Kansas in 1601 and whose western migration certainly did not bring them to the Quivira district for a century and a half after Oñate's day. The most reasonable view seems to be that the Escansaques were those plains Apaches, evidently of the Lipan group, who were termed by the Caddoan Indians Kantsi or Cantsi. An identification from similarity in name alone is not justified, but in this instance the Escansaques seem to have moved southward to upper Red River after 1600; then they are not mentioned again, but the Cantsis or Lipans take their place in the Red River region. We may also note that the "es" in Escansaque is a Spanish article sometimes prefixed to Indian names. This name, therefore, might be (Es) *Kantsi*(que), written *Escansaque*.[12]

It is impossible to obtain a correct view of the Indians of the high plains at this early period without considering the tribes that dwelt in the borders of the plains, and this is particularly true of the tribe known as the Jumanos, first seen by Cabeza de Vaca on or near the Río Grande in 1535 and then met by Espejo in the same district in 1583. Part of this tribe seems to have migrated toward the northeast to the Río Pecos country and perhaps even farther eastward. Among the Salinas Pueblos, between the Río Grande and the Río Pecos, there was a town, the Humanos Pueblo, which may have been actually inhabited by the Jumanos, though some authorities state that this tribe came here only to trade. The pueblo was a trading center to which the Plains Indians came to barter antelope skins and other articles for maize.[13] After 1600 another Jumano group established itself out in the plains on a stream which the Spanish called the Río Nueces. Bol-

---

[12] Frank Secoy in a recent study also decided that the Escansaques were probably Apaches (*Changing Military Patterns on the Great Plains*, 12). Plains Indians of this period fought on foot, rushed forward in a horde, shouting, dancing, and singing. The Escansaques came forward in this manner, then formed a great semicircle close to Oñate's men and shot clouds of arrows. They kept this up for hours, yelling and leaping about.

[13] *The Memorial of Fray Alonso de Benavides, 1630* (ed. by Frederick Webb Hodge and Charles Fletcher Lummis), 249.

ton locates these Jumanos in West Texas in the Colorado River region, but the Spanish accounts seem to make it more probable that the place was on the Canadian or Red River. With or near the Jumanos on the Río Nueces was a tribe called by the Spaniards *Aijados*, who were raiding the Quiviras of the Arkansas River in southern Kansas strongly enough to induce the Quivira chiefs to cross the whole width of the plains in 1606, to beg the Spaniards of New Mexico for aid against these Aijado enemies. In 1625 Father Salas visited the Jumano villages on Río Nueces, one hundred leagues east of Santa Fé, and in 1629 two friars visited the villages and from there exchanged friendly messages with the Aijados, who lived thirty leagues east of the Jumanos. Beyond the Aijados lay Quivira. In 1632, Salas and another missionary, Ortega, spent six months in the Jumano villages on the Nueces, which they speak of as a large river. In 1634 Captain Vaca led a small force of troops to the Jumanos and beyond, claiming that he came to the immediate vicinity of Quivira. After this date the tribes on the Nueces began to fight furiously among themselves, and when Martín and Castillo led a force of Spanish troops into that district, they found that the Escansaques were now on Río Nueces with another tribe, the Cuitoas, to the east of them, and the Aijados evidently east of the Escansaques and close to the Tejas, that Caddoan tribe in East Texas from whose name the word "Texas" was formed. In 1654, Governor Guadalajara of New Mexico with thirty Spanish soldiers and two hundred Indian allies went to the Jumano villages on the Nueces and was there informed that farther down the river the Cuitoas, Escansaques, and Aijados were all at war and that it would be dangerous to go among them. The Governor sent López with part of his force down the river, and at thirty leagues López met the Cuitoas and had a fight with them, taking some prisoners and plunder. The expedition was then given up. These southern plains Indians, who had been friendly in earlier years, were now so hostile that it was not safe for even a large Spanish expedition to venture into the plains. In 1688, Don Pedro de Posada reported that the Jumanos and other formerly friendly tribes on the Nueces had been forced to remove from that district because of Apache wars on them.[14]

Thus the first act in the Jumano drama came to an end. One may surmise that this tribe, living on the lower Río Grande in 1535, wandering on foot, and not planting crops or having permanent villages, had later obtained (either by trade with tribes in northern Mexico or by raiding the Spanish settlements) some Spanish articles, weapons and, perhaps, a few horses. The Jumanos then advanced east to Río Pecos and either established the Pueblo Humanos in the Salinas district or made that pueblo their trading center. They then began to raid the Apaches of the Vaquero group, evidently on the upper Canadian in the Texas Panhandle; and, as they made these Apaches beg for peace, it seems fair to assume that the Jumanos had some Spanish weapons and perhaps horses, which gave them an advantage over the Apaches. Finally, about 1630, the Jumanos established themselves in fixed villages on Río Nueces. By 1685 we find them trading Spanish goods and horses to the Caddoan Indians in East Texas, and presently they moved eastward and established themselves among the Caddoan Indians near the mouth of the Canadian. For one century they were known as a trading group, and they were the only southwestern Indians, as far as the records inform us, that migrated eastward across the width of the southern plains and established themselves on the eastern border.[15]

[14] Hubert Howe Bancroft's histories of Texas and New Mexico are my sources for the Spanish visits to Río Nueces. Gunnerson, "The Southern Athabascans," El Palacio, Vol. VI, 220, quotes the Posada report of 1688.

[15] I cannot refrain from pointing out the following interesting facts. The Spanish documents state that the Vaquero Apaches in 1598–1601 lived one hundred leagues east of a pueblo on the Río Grande and that after 1630 the Jumano villages were one hundred leagues east of a similar point in New Mexico. This seems to hint that the Jumanos drove out the Vaqueros and occupied their lands, which were evidently in the Canadian district in the Texas Panhandle. Here near the present town of Amarillo, Texas, there are several ruins: villages with houses of stone and adobe, flat-roofed, and built in the style of New Mexican Pueblo houses. In these ruins is found rude native pottery, made on the spot, mixed with Pecos Pueblo pottery. At Pecos, excavation disclosed numerous skin-dressing implements and other tools made of a peculiar kind of stone the Indians obtained in the Amarillo neighborhood. If it were not for the dating archaeologists have decreed (as early, some attest, as 1300), one might surmise that these

The main reason for the change in the old friendly relations of the southern plains tribes with the Spaniards, after the period 1630, was apparently the acquisition of horses and Spanish weapons by some of the tribes and particularly by the Apaches. In 1583 Espejo's expedition found no metal weapons or horses among the Indians along the lower Río Grande or in New Mexico. The first Indians in this region to obtain horses and Spanish arms were apparently the tribes on the Río Conchos, a western tributary of the Río Grande flowing through the Mexican state of Chihuahua. Early in the sixteenth century the Spaniards pushed their way into this river valley and started the usual work of enlightenment by forming missions and settlements. The friars began rounding up unwilling Indian neophytes and subjecting them to servitude under severe discipline, while the Spanish settlers openly raided the Indian villages with fire and sword, killing part of the people and carrying the rest off into slavery. A long series of bloody raids, burnings, and fierce floggings produced a spirit of desperation in the hearts of some of the Indians, who began to resist and then to make retaliatory raids on their oppressors. Soon the raiders made the discovery that an armored Spaniard could be killed by an Indian armed only with a flint knife if the attack were made with sufficient courage and skill. They also learned that the dreaded horses were not particularly dangerous, unless they had armed Spaniards on their backs. Obregón states that the Indians could not imagine how to make use of the first horses they captured, so they killed and ate the animals; but presently they learned to ride, thus greatly increasing the range and power of their raids. By 1560 these Mexican Indians had a fair supply of horses.

As far as the Indians of the plains were concerned, it would appear that they obtained their first horses and metal weapons by barter with the Indians beyond the Río Grande and later by raiding, but the Apache raids into Mexico must have been few and on a small scale until about 1690–95 when they devastated Chihuahua and Sonora, killing the settlers and running off great

village ruins were either the old Jumano villages of *ca.* 1630–50 or else that they were early villages of the Apaches who traded at Pecos.

15

numbers of horses. The country in western New Mexico and eastern Arizona, known to the Spaniards in the late eighteenth century as *Apachería*, the "Land of the Apaches," was apparently unoccupied before 1680, although there may have been some small Apache groups hidden away in the mountainous districts who did not attract the notice of the Spaniards, as they were not raiding. As we have seen, the first Apaches noted in New Mexico, west of the Río Grande and south of the Navahos, were small groups of Querechos who were near Acoma in 1550–1600. By 1600–25 the group, known even then as the Gilas, was west of the Río Grande, but not far to the west, as the rancheria of the principal Gila chief, Sanaba, was only fourteen leagues west of the pueblo of Senecu on the river. Sanaba was a sophisticated Apache, who around the year 1628 was paying frequent visits to the Senecu town, probably to feast and gamble. He pleased Father Benavides greatly by making a painting on antelope skin, in which he depicted the old Apache deities, the sun and the moon, below the new symbol of the cross; but any hopes that the friars had of converting the Gilas were soon blasted. The Gilas at this time were living near the extreme headwaters of the river that later bore their name, and they were probably the Apaches who had rancherias hidden away in the Sierra Florida, west of the Río Grande on the present southern border of New Mexico.

East of the Gilas, on the east side of the Río Grande, in the *Jornada del Muerto* district north of El Paso, were the Apaches of Perillo; and far to the east of this group, on the west side of the Río Pecos, almost in the edge of the Staked Plains, were the Apaches of the Valley of the Seven Rivers. As far as we may judge, these Apache groups all belonged to the old Querechos, known after 1600 as the Vaqueros. These seem to have been what are known today as the San Carlos–type Apaches, differing notably from the Lipan and Jicarilla Apaches, who held the plains farther toward the east and north.

In northern New Mexico west of the upper Río Grande, were the Navahos, then a small tribe but potent, holding their own lands strongly, at frequent intervals raiding the Pueblos, and always evading the Spanish efforts to gain a foothold in the Navaho lands. The Apaches of Quinia were about thirty leagues beyond the Navahos, according to Benavides. The Quinias may have been named for their chief, who was probably the great Captain Quima. The Quiviras who visited New Mexico in 1606 stated that the best route to their country led from Taos through the lands of Quima. Here we may observe that this name, given by the Spanish writers as "Quinia," may be Kinya, and that in the nineteenth century the Mescaleros called the Jicarillas *Kinya-Inde*, "Kinya People." Near the Quinias was a tribe or band called Menases, apparently another Apache group named for its chief.[16] The Jicarilla Apaches were not mentioned in Spanish documents until 1706, but "Jicarilla" is a Spanish designation for this tribe, and it is possible that they were the group first known as the Quinias.

On the whole, the Apaches of the plains were not regarded as bad Indians by the Spaniards until the period 1660, when horses and metal weapons came into the hands of these Indians. Intertribal warfare was now increased; the acquisition of a few horses and Spanish weapons gave an Apache band a great advantage over neighboring tribes who were still on foot and armed with flint weapons, and, having obtained a few horses, an Apache band was naturally eager to secure more of these invaluable animals by the simple process of sending out war parties to raid the tribes that had horses. The horse also seems to have given the Plains Indians an advantage over the Pueblos which they had formerly lacked. They could now strike swiftly and effectively. They had always been poor people wandering afoot on the plains, and they had envied the rich inhabitants of the large Pueblo towns: people who had maize, *frijoles*, and squashes, not as rare luxuries but for every meal, and whose many-roomed houses were filled with brightly-striped cotton cloaks, brilliant featherwork, handsome painted pottery, strings of turquoise beads, and other fabulous

[16] *The Memorial of Benavides*, 90, 306; Alfred Barnaby Thomas, *After Coronado*, 9. The Navahos, now the largest one-language Indian group in the United States, were stated by Spanish witnesses who had lived among them in 1700–45 to have had a population of from two thousand to, at most, four thousand.

wealth. At best, the Apaches, coming afoot from the plains with their supply of bare necessities packed on the backs of their dogs and women, were permitted at certain seasons of the year to camp for a time under the sheltering walls of the Pueblo towns. Sometimes they came to beg, sometimes to barter dried meat, dressed antelope and buffalo skins, and Apache bone bows for maize and cotton cloaks; on rare occasions they caught the fat people of the terraced houses off guard and, in a sudden burst of fury, stormed the town and plundered it. But now, with horses and metal weapons in their possession, the Apaches of the plains had power that these stay-at-home Pueblo folk lacked, and they were not backward in using that power to the full.

From 1600 on, the Apaches of the Valley of the Seven Rivers alternately traded and raided in the Albuquerque district, but neither their bartering nor their plundering was on an extensive scale. In the north the Navahos, probably aided at times by the Quinia Apaches, were raiding the Pueblos in the Santa Clara district, at the same time coming frequently to Jémez on friendly trading visits. Then the Apaches in the plains began to obtain horses and Spanish arms, and from about 1655 to 1675 the Pueblos and Spaniards of New Mexico suffered greatly, both from severe droughts and from savage Apache raids.[17] The coming of the horse is indicated as the main cause of these raids, for it was the southern Apaches, those who first obtained horses, who struck the first heavy blows. The Piro towns, the Pueblo settlements farthest down the Río Grande, melted away, and even Senecú had to be abandoned in 1675. East of the Río Grande, as the towns in the Salinas district were exposed to the full fury of Apache attacks (1669–74), one town after another was abandoned. Then, in 1675, the Salinas Indians fled west to Isleta for refuge, but the Apaches followed in their track, raiding in the Isleta and Albuquerque district.

Made desperate by savage Apache raids, great droughts, Spanish rule, and the bewildering activities of the friars, who talked

17 Alfred Barnaby Thomas, *Plains Indians and New Mexico*, 3–4; Lockwood, *The Apache Indians*, 11; Secoy, *Changing Military Patterns*, 21.

of a new faith of love while having poor Indians flogged for eating a bit of meat on a fast day, in 1680 the Pueblos revolted, rising in sudden fury and killing four hundred Spaniards, including twenty-one Franciscan friars. It was the greatest disaster in Spanish colonial history. The surviving Spaniards, with a few loyal Indians, retreated down the Río Grande and formed a settlement at a place called El Paso, where they held out, waiting for succor and reinforcements from Mexico.

Meantime the Apaches from the plains threw themselves with enthusiasm into the welter of revolt raging among the Pueblo towns. The Spaniards gone, the Pueblos fell to fighting among themselves, for they belonged to various groups, each of which had certain ancient grudges against its neighbors to settle. The Apaches allied themselves to one Pueblo faction, aided them to plunder and murder the people of other towns, then turned on their allies to plunder them. The Navahos and that little-known and distant tribe in the north, the Utes, joined in this outburst of savage raiding. The Pueblos of Taos and Pecos and the Keres Pueblos waged open war on the Tano Pueblos and on the Tewa towns west of the Río Grande, the Apaches from the plains joining in this intertribal fighting, gathering great quantities of plunder, including more horses and Spanish weapons.[18]

When Governor Vargas and his Spanish and Indian army marched up the Río Grande in 1692 to reoccupy New Mexico, he had to fight Apaches all along the way, and these wild Plains Indians succeeded in running off many horses from the army herds. Vargas found the Pueblo country in a sad condition, after twelve years of freedom and internecine war. Many Pueblo towns had been abandoned or destroyed. The Pueblos were broken up into bitterly hostile factions, and from this situation the Apaches were reaping a harvest of plunder and captives.

One suspects that during this time of anarchy part of the Apaches of the plains passed through the Pueblo country, crossing the Río Grande south of the Pueblo towns, and established

[18] Frederick W. Hodge, in *The Memorial of Benavides*, 284, gives details of these events.

themselves in or near their later homeland in western New Mexico and eastern Arizona. The Gilas seem to have made such a shift westward, and when New Mexico was reoccupied by the Spaniards in 1692, the Apache Vaqueros of the plains were no longer mentioned, but a new group, which the Spanish writers termed the Apache Hordes of Pharoah or Faraon Apaches, held the old Vaquero lands. It is to be observed, however, that all of these general designations for the Apaches east of New Mexico—Querechos from 1541 to 1600, Vaqueros from 1600 to 1692, and Faraons from that time on—are Pueblo Indian and Spanish names for Apache groups whose true identity is difficult to learn.

The Apaches of the southern plains had now reached the high tide in their career as rulers of these plains. They were no longer the friendly, rather frightened people wandering through the plains on foot, following the vast buffalo herds as a means of life, that Coronado and other early Spanish explorers had met, but had become a powerful nation of mounted Indians whose principal occupation was war. From the beginning of their history in the south they had always come to the Pueblo towns—twice each year, in the early summer and late autumn—and in the early times when they were afoot and very poor, they had come humbly, as a rule, to camp under the walls of the terraced houses, to beg or barter for a few simple needs; but now, after the Pueblo revolt of 1680–92, these Apaches came to the trading fairs at Pecos, Taos, and Picurís in strong mounted bands, haughty and fierce; and instead of begging or offering a little dried meat or some tanned antelope and buffalo skins for a small supply of the coveted maize, they now brought Indian slaves, the produce of their constant raiding, and demanded of the Pueblos and Spaniards, first of all, metal weapons: long, ugly Spanish daggers, hatchets, and sword blades, which they used as points on their lances.

Many of the slaves brought in by the Apaches were Pueblo women and children, taken in a raid on one town and brought to be traded at another; but in the main, after 1690, the slaves seem to have been Caddoan Indians, termed Quiviras and Pawnees by the Spanish writers. Raids on the Caddoan villages along the east-

ern border of the plains had now developed into a business enter-
prise among the Plains Apaches. Imitating the Spaniards, the
Apaches had made rawhide armor for their men and horses, armor
which would render flint weapons almost useless against their
mounted warriors; and as the Caddoan Indians at this time were
practically without metal weapons and still had few horses, they
were at the mercy of the big Apache raiding parties.

It is curious to find the Spanish writers referring to the Navahos
organizing great raiding parties of mounted warriors and crossing
the entire breadth of the plains to attack Caddoan villages at this
period. Harrington, an authority on the Navahos, did not refer
to these raids when he was discussing the possibility of early Navaho activities in the plains, and the most that he would venture
was a suggestion that in early times this tribe had occasionally
visited the western edge of the plains for buffalo or had traded
for buffalo meat and hides with some tribe that lived in the plains.
The Spanish statements concerning these Navaho raids across
the plains are circumstantial, but it is to be suspected that these
raids were made by the Apaches.

The "Navaho" practice, as described by the Spanish writers,
was to wait until February, a season when the Caddoan Indians
would be confined to their villages by bad weather and probably
weak from lack of food, and then to organize a large party of
mounted and armored warriors, take the Caddoans by surprise,
kill many of them, take the women and children captive, plunder
the village, and then set it afire. In the following May, these raiders
went to the trading fairs at Pecos, Taos, or Picurís and bartered
their captives to the Pueblos and Spaniards. In 1694 the Navahos
brought a number of captive Caddoan children to the trading fair,
but for some reason the Spaniards would not trade, and the Navahos in a fury beheaded all the children before the eyes of the
horrified spectators. This event led the King of Spain to order that
in the future royal funds should be available for the ransom of such
unfortunate captives. In effect, he ordered the Apache trade in
captives to be encouraged.

The Caddoans were now getting together for defense, it would seem, for in 1697 when the Navahos went on a raid in the east, they were badly defeated by the Pawnees. With their love of exaggeration, the Spaniards stated that Frenchmen aided the Pawnees, and that four thousand Navaho warriors were killed. In 1698 the Navahos tried again, succeeding in destroying three Pawnee rancherias and a fortified village, and in 1699 the Navahos came to a fair in New Mexico with their camp full of plunder from their latest Pawnee raid. The Spanish reports stated that besides large numbers of Pawnee women and children slaves, the Navahos brought to this fair French carbines and cannon, sword belts, jewels, waistcoats, shoes, and brass kettles.[19]

Despite the detailed nature of these Spanish reports concerning great Navaho raids on the Caddoan Indians, one suspects that the Navahos had nothing to do with these attacks. After all, at this period the Navahos were a small tribe, and they were fully occupied in raiding the Pueblo Indians in the district west of the upper Río Grande, particularly the Pueblos of Santa Clara and Jémez, while at the same time the Utes were keeping the Navahos busy by raiding them from the north. The Navahos were located west of the Río Grande in a position from which it seems unlikely that they should go into the buffalo plains and incredible that they should make extensive raids as far across the plains as the Caddoan lands. Moreover, the Spanish accounts state that the Caddoan captives were brought in and traded at Taos, Picurís, and Pecos, towns at which the Plains Apaches traded regularly; the Navahos, on the other hand, usually traded at Santa Clara or Jémez, close to their own lands, west of the upper Río Grande.

The Caddoan tribes, with populous villages strung along the eastern plains border from Kansas down into Texas, in the sixteenth century were in a secure position; but by 1685 they appear

[19] Thomas, *After Coronado*, 13–14, refers briefly to these "Navaho" raids; John B. Dunbar, in "The Pawnee Indians; Their History and Ethnology," in *Magazine of American History*, Vol. IV, No. 4 (April, 1880), also gives an account of the raids on Pawnees. The Spanish story that in 1697 the raiders brought quantities of French articles to trade in New Mexico is quite credible, for La Salle had formed a French colony on the Texas coast, and this colony had been destroyed by Indians about 1687, large quantities of French articles probably falling into the hands of the Texas Caddoan tribes.

to have been under heavy assault both by Apaches from the plains and by eastern tribes, who were now obtaining metal weapons and even some firearms from tribes that traded with the French, English, and Dutch. Dwelling in scattered communities in which each big grass lodge was usually separated from its nearest neighbor by an open space of considerable extent, the Caddoan villages were as a rule wide open to the assault of mounted enemies or those who came on foot, armed with guns. The easy victims of such attacks, Caddoans were known in New Mexico mainly as captives, while in the Mississippi Valley so many prisoners were of this Caddoan or Pawnee stock that *Pani* became a synonym for "slave." But by 1685, these southern Caddoans were obtaining some horses and metal weapons, and though they were still on the defensive, they were beginning to fight back strongly.

Regarding events in the plains north of the Arkansas River up to the year 1680 we have no clear evidence, but the glimpses that we obtain through archaeology hint that conditions in the plains of Kansas and Nebraska were similar to those farther to the south. In both regions the eastern border of the plains was occupied by horticultural, village-dwelling Caddoan tribes, and in Nebraska the primitive Pawnees of this stock had pushed far out into the plains of the Republican River drainage, where they dwelled and raised their crops of maize and vegetables during a long period of apparently peaceful times. Then they retired from their exposed position in the plains, and next we find the Pawnees on the Loup Fork of the Platte, where they have built villages in a less exposed position. Archaeologists date this withdrawal from Republican River about 1517, which seems too early a date if we accept W. D. Strong's view that an incursion of enemies forced the Pawnees to move. However, we must observe that the Pawnee villages on the Republican River were small, widely separated, and much exposed to attack. Apache hordes, although on foot and armed only with flint weapons, might have harassed the Pawnees and forced them to remove. W. R. Wedel's theory that great droughts drove the Pawnees from the Republican River lands does not seem to fit the situation. These primitive Pawnees prob-

23

ably obtained only a small portion of their food by growing crops. They were still, in the main, hunters, and if drought struck their little fields, they could still live comfortably by hunting and by gathering wild roots and fruits.[20] Here it may be noted that the Apaches and Navahos in the New Mexico region were causing serious trouble to the Pueblo tribes around the date 1500, and this makes it possible that the Apaches in western Nebraska were attacking the Pawnees on Republican River at the same period. After all, the Pueblos were much stronger and better placed for defense than were the tiny villages of the Pawnees in western Nebraska.

But the archaeological dating shows that the Nebraska Apaches, usually termed Padoucas, did not establish villages in the Republican River country until around the year 1650. Why did they wait nearly a century and a half after driving the Pawnees out before they established their own villages in the Republican River country? The answer may be that they were still roving hunters when they drove the Pawnees away, and that it took a century and a half for them to develop a desire to live in villages and imitate the Pawnees by growing crops and making pottery.

This is surmise, but it is based on some solid facts concerning conditions in a wide area and not on theorizing over the finds in a few ruined Indian villages.

[20] Of the two main archaeological authorities, W. Duncan Strong favored the theory that the Upper Republican Indians were forced out by enemies, while Waldo Wedel proposed the drought theory. Wedel has never made me feel the reasonableness of assuming that Indians who lived mainly by growing crops would leave a good climate and fertile lands in the southeast, move out into the arid plains, and continue to live mainly on crops. If they did not go into the plains to live mainly on buffalo meat, they had less sense than I should like to give them credit for. The small numbers of animal bones in the village ruins is not proof that the main source of food was crops. The usual practice of Plains Indians who grew crops was to plant at their villages, then go on a long buffalo hunt, come home to harvest, and then go on another extended hunt. They spent about nine months in the year away from their villages, and if few animal bones are found in village ruins, would that not be due to the custom the Indians had of cutting the meat into thin sheets, without bones, drying it, and bringing it back to their villages packed in rawhide cases? And why did the Pawnees of the upper Republican flee from drought into better lands in east-central Nebraska and then large groups of them move from these better lands into arid lands on the Missouri in Dakota? It is just not reasonable.

La Salle, in the Illinois country in 1680, heard of a tribe called Panas (perhaps Panis, that is, Pawnees or Arikaras) who had two villages on or near the Missouri, these Panas being on friendly terms with two tribes that lived south of them, the Gatakas (Prairie Apaches of later times) and the Manrahoats.[21] From the Gatakas the Panas were obtaining in barter some horses and turquoises, a clear indication that the Gatakas were trading with their kinsmen, the Apaches of the plains east and northeast of New Mexico. La Salle was also told of the Panimahas or Skidi Pawnees on Loup Fork in Nebraska, who were warring on the Padoucas, taking Padouca slaves, and evidently trading them to other tribes, as the Osages in Missouri had some Padouca slaves obtained from the Panimahas.[22] Here the Padoucas were undoubtedly the Apaches of the plains, and the Gatakas—whom we cannot reasonably locate farther to the south than the district of western Nebraska—were also Apaches. Indeed the Gatakas were always noted for their friendship with the Arikaras, and as this latter tribe was evidently on the Missouri in the extreme northeastern corner of Nebraska or across the river in southern South Dakota in La Salle's time, the Gatakas might have been the Apaches of the Nebraska Sand Hills country. La Salle was told that the Indians in the plains beyond the Missouri were fighting on horseback, armed with long lances; and here we have confirmation of a situation that we might expect from the course of events in the southern plains, namely, that the Apaches in the south were no sooner supplied with horses and metal weapons than they began to trade part of their supplies to their kinsmen north of the Arkansas River.

It was at this period that the Spanish writers in New Mexico began to concern themselves with Indian reports of the Kingdom

[21] An unidentified tribe. It may be noted that La Salle used the letter "m" for "w," as "Misconsin" for "Wisconsin." The tribe's name, therefore, might have been Wanrahoat. On a pure guess, they may have been the Otos, whose name was sometimes given as Watotato and similar forms. By tradition, the Otos had lived on the Missouri south of the Platte at about this date.

[22] La Salle in Pierre Margry, *Découvertes et établissements des français dans l'ouest et dans le sud de l'Amérique Septentrionale (1614-1754)*, II, 54, 201, 325.

of Taguayo, which was in the plains to the north or northeast of New Mexico and was, therefore, in the Apache country. Taguayo (an appellation evidently derived from the old name for the Apaches, *Tagui*) was described by the Indians as somewhat similar to Quivira and equally powerful and wealthy. Quivira was on the eastern borders of the plains, Taguayo in the western borders, and through these vast plains the Spanish writers depicted bands of Indians passing mysteriously back and forth, sometimes visiting in Quivira, again appearing in Taguayo. Pueblo captives and other Indians who had been slaves in Taguayo and had escaped to New Mexico brought occasional news of that country to the Spaniards, who with their love for wonders, accepted these fantastic tales and set them down in writing with appropriate embroidery, never getting down to earth long enough to attempt a plain report on this Apache land in the north. The supposed kingdom was probably only the plains occupied by wandering bands of Apaches in eastern Colorado, perhaps extending as far north as Nebraska.[23]

These vague Spanish reports are comparable with those made by the English and French traders in the Hudson Bay country at about this same period, 1680–1700, who set down tales of wonders obtained from Indians concerning lands to the southwest, where there were settlements of strange, bearded folk living in stone houses near a sea: a distorted description of the Spaniards in New Mexico. Curiously, it was through the Tinneh tribes, northern kinsmen of the Apaches, that these reports came to Hudson Bay. The Tinnehs at this period occupied most of the extreme northern reaches of the plains, from the Rockies east to near Hudson Bay, extending southward to the upper Saskatchewan. Here on the headwaters of the North Saskatchewan were the Sarsis, very closely related to the Apaches; and from both Apache and Kiowa tradition we know that in the eighteenth century the Sarsis at times came down through the plains to visit their kinsmen, the

---

[23] Thomas, *After Coronado*, 11–12. Escaped captives reported that Taguayo was in the plains about sixty leagues, say two hundred miles, northeast of the Utes, who at this date were known only as bands located in southern Colorado.

Gatakas or Prairie Apaches, near the Black Hills of Dakota. Some Sarsis married among the Gatakas and Kiowas, and even after 1900 there were families on the Kiowa reservation in Oklahoma who claimed descent from Sarsi ancestors. If there were Tinneh or Apache bands located in the plains between the Saskatchewan and the Black Hills in the period around 1670, we have no record of them, for there is neither historical nor archaeological information available for the plains regions of Dakota, Wyoming, and Montana. But we may assume some connecting link between the Apaches in the Nebraska and Dakota region with the Tinneh of the far north, for it was by means of news passing from camp to camp that the reports of the Spanish settlements in the south reached the white traders in the far north from 1680 down to the middle of the eighteenth century.

# 2. The Padouca Nation

THE PADOUCAS were a numerous and powerful nation of mounted Indians who held the plains from Nebraska to Texas during the seventeenth and eighteenth centuries and then disappeared. In some manner, after their power was broken and they were gone, they were identified as Comanche Indians, and from 1830 on every book that dealt with the plains tribes called the Padoucas Comanches. In the past forty years, however, new evidence has come to light that indicates the impossibility of the Comanches being the Padoucas and shows conclusively that this vanished plains nation was made up of various tribes of Apaches. Archaeology has now come to the aid of history and confirms this identification of the Padoucas as Apaches.

The new evidence not only shows who the Padoucas really were, but also suggests in what manner the name happened to be misapplied to the Comanches. In fact, the Apaches or Padoucas were in the plains for at least a century before the Comanches came out of the mountains, but once in the plains the Comanches defeated the Padoucas and drove them out, occupying most of their lands. It was after that event, after the disappearance of the Padoucas, that a misconception arose, and the Comanches, now living in the old Padouca country, were confused with the tribe they had driven out and were given the name of that tribe.

In the present volume this error in early plains history has been rectified and the Padoucas are recognized as Apaches. It is necessary to make this change, for it is no longer possible to write an authentic history of the early plains tribes leaving one of the most important groups incorrectly identified. The following pages set forth the principal facts concerning the Padoucas so that the reader may reach his own conclusions.

When La Salle came into the Illinois country in 1680, he heard of a mounted tribe in the buffalo plains called Padoucas, and he obtained a Padouca boy who was a captive among the Illinois Indians. By 1720 the French were well informed concerning the Padoucas, a great nation that extended down through the plains from near the Missouri River in Dakota to Texas. On their maps the French indicated that the Padoucas lived in settled villages, not in roving camps. On upper Red River on the Texas border a Frenchman (his report, printed by Margry, is unsigned and undated but is of the period 1720) mentioned a tribe in the southern plains which the Spaniards of New Mexico called Apaches but which were known to the French as Padoucas. Le Maire, a French missionary in Illinois, wrote a memoir in 1717 describing a nation of mounted Indians in the plains who were known as "Apaches or Padoucas."[1]

Nothing could be clearer than these assertions that the Padoucas were Apaches; and later, around the date 1770, when the French were in actual contact with both the Apaches and the Comanches on Red River on the Texas border, Gaignard and other Frenchmen identified the Padoucas as Apaches. These traders knew the Apaches and Comanches from daily contacts; they were trading with the Comanches and buying and selling Apache slaves, and they used the names Apache and Padouca as synonymous.[2]

The French map of Vermale (*ca.* 1717) has the high plains marked *Pais des Appaches ou Padoucas*, "Lands of the Apaches or Padoucas." The Gatakas or Prairie Apaches were called Pa-

[1] Le Maire, quoted by Baron Marc de Villiers, in *La Découverte du Missouri et l'histoire du Fort Orléans* (1673–1728), 66; Margry, *Découvertes et établissements*, VI, 236.
[2] Gaignard, in Herbert E. Bolton (ed.), *Athanase de Mézières and the Louisiana–Texas Frontier, 1768–80*, II, 87.

doucas as late as 1825, and as far back as La Salle's day they were trading horses and Spanish goods to tribes on or near the Missouri: a clear indication that they were trading with Apache bands that lived near the Spaniards in New Mexico. The "Account of Spanish Louisiana in 1785" terms the Gatakas Pados (an abbreviation of Padoucas) and also calls them Taguibaces, which comes from *Tagui*, an old name for the Apaches.

Thus, in both the southern and northern plains the Padoucas were identified as Apaches in the eighteenth century, when these Indians were still a great tribe. The French explorers and traders, coming from the Mississippi Valley westward, knew the Padoucas best and had a regular trade in Padouca slaves. The Spanish officials in New Mexico, Texas, and Old Mexico were evidently puzzled by the constant French references to a great nation in the plains called Padoucas that was unknown to the Spaniards, and for a long time the Spanish writers did not set down any opinion concerning the Padoucas. At last, in 1768, a Spanish map made by Alzate was published, showing Comanches as Padoucas but locating them in the mountains of southern Colorado. In 1770, Surville produced a map on which he copied the earlier mapmaker's location of the Comanches, with the wording, *Tierra de los Comanches o Padoucas*, "Land of the Comanches or Padoucas."

This Surville was recently brought forward as evidence that the Spanish officials in the eighteenth century recognized the Padoucas as Comanches. It would be more reasonable to put the map in evidence to exhibit how shockingly ignorant of the tribes to the east and north of Mexico Spanish officials were, as late as 1770. This map not only locates the Comanches incorrectly in the mountains; it places them in the San Luis Valley district, which was occupied by the Utes. The lands the Comanches held after the year 1735 were in the plains, and this map shows these plains crowded with Apache groups, Apaches that the Comanches had driven out before the year 1735. But the Surville map set a fashion in Europe, where, as Frank Secoy points out, later mapmakers adopted the Surville notion and set down the Padoucas as Co-

30

manches. Secoy adds that the French in Louisiana also shifted the name Padouca from the Apaches and applied it to the Comanches, but this is not correct. The French traders on Red River continued to term the Apaches Padoucas to the end of the eighteenth century, while farther north the Apaches of the Black Hills country in Dakota continued to be called Padoucas by those French traders who actually knew them.

The Caddoan Indian chiefs on the Arkansas River in eastern Oklahoma, speaking to the French explorer La Harpe in 1719, did not employ the name Apache, which was evidently not in common use among their people; but the chiefs described to La Harpe the Indian villages which they termed Padouca, in the plains of western Oklahoma or the Texas Panhandle and extending northward to or beyond the Arkansas. They located these Padouca villages in the same districts in which the Spaniards of New Mexico located Apache tribes and no other Indians. The Caddoan chiefs informed La Harpe that their people had formerly visited freely in New Mexico but that in later times the Padoucas had moved into the plains between them and the Spaniards, blocking their road. Now we know from Spanish documents that the last recorded visit of the Caddoans (Quiviras) to New Mexico was in 1606 and that at that time the Caddoans had to pass through the lands of a friendly Apache chief called Quima to reach Taos in New Mexico. This suggests that the Padoucas were a new and hostile Apache group that moved southward and occupied the Oklahoma plains after 1606. The Caddoans told La Harpe that their people now could not go farther west in the plains than the place of rock salt, for fear of the Padoucas, and that it was near the place of rock salt that their warriors often fought the Padoucas, whose villages were farther to the west. This place of rock salt, the Rock Saline, was on the Cimarron a little west of the 99th meridian, and the Padouca villages were to the west of the Rock Saline, in a district in which the Spaniards and Pueblo Indians of New Mexico placed Apache rancherias. It seems obvious that there was no space here in the plains in which to insert a large tribe of Comanches and that the evidence of the Caddoan chiefs in 1719, added to the Spanish and Pueblo Indian information, proves again that the Padoucas were Apaches.

In Nebraska we have Omaha and Ponca Indian traditions concerning early wars with the Padoucas who, down to almost the close of the eighteenth century, had a fort or some kind of village in the Sand Hills on upper Loup Fork, from which they frequently sent out mounted war parties, with the horses covered with rawhide armor, to attack the Omahas and Poncas at their villages on the Missouri in northern Nebraska. This Padouca war in Nebraska went on for years. The trader J. B. Truteau reported that the Padoucas were still living in western Nebraska in 1794, and in the following year another trader from St. Louis, James Mackay, made a map on which he located the Padouca village or fort in the Nebraska Sand Hills. Just when the Padoucas left Nebraska we do not know. Branches of Loup Fork continued to be called Padouca Fork until after 1800, and in 1813, Robert Stuart in his journal applied that name to the North Fork of Dismal River, the stream on which Padouca village ruins were first found by A. T. Hill.

Mr. Hill, curator of the Nebraska Historical Society Museum, knew the old reports concerning the Padouca settlements in the Sand Hills, and about twenty-five years ago he explored the Dismal River, a pleasant Sand Hills stream that has been badly treated by having such a name applied to it. It is a clear-flowing little river with considerable handsome scenery along its valley, which at some points is cut deeply, forming picturesque little canyons. Above the forks of the stream, Hill found patches of ground strewn with broken Indian pottery of a type hitherto unknown; flint arrowheads and stone implements were also scattered about, and the indications clearly pointed to an Indian village having been at this point in early times. All this was something new. It hinted strongly that these remains were those of the Padoucas, and the broken pottery was startling, as it strongly suggested that the Padoucas were a pottery-making tribe, something that had never been suspected before. Archaeologists, who avoid giving

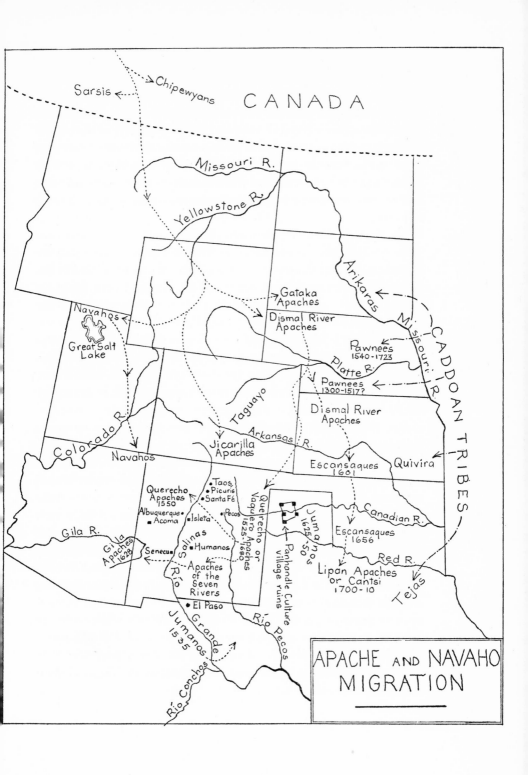

APACHE AND NAVAHO MIGRATION

Indian tribal names to any material they uncover, called the Padouca remains Mr. Hill had found "Dismal River."

Hill next led a party to the forks of the Platte to excavate the Indian remains in the Ash Hollow Cave. Here he found that the upper or most recent layer of Indian occupation was of the same type as the remains on Dismal River, and from growth rings in pieces of charcoal recovered from campfires in the cave a date of 1684–1704 was given to this Padouca or Dismal River deposit in the cave.[3]

In 1939 another archaeological party, led by Mr. Hill and George Metcalf, excavated an extensive village ruin of the Padouca or Dismal River type on a northern tributary of the Republican River in Chase County, Nebraska, and here again the broken pottery and stone work were of the now familiar Padouca make. This actual excavation of a village ruin disclosed interesting new facts. It was found that the huts had been of a type similar to Navaho hogans and that the Padoucas had cultivated maize and other crops. The entire village area was dotted with pits, some of which had deposits of burned stones in their bottoms—a clear indication that the Padoucas had made extensive use of the method of cooking food in pits with the aid of heated stones, which was in the main a custom of northern tribes. Pieces of charcoal obtained in this village ruin gave a tree-ring date of 1674–1706, and from another Padouca site not far off, in Dundy County, Nebraska, a charcoal date of 1667–1706 was obtained. In 1948 J. L. Champe excavated another Padouca village ruin, located three miles up Prairie Dog Creek, a southern tributary of Republican Fork. Called the White Cat Village by archaeologists, this ruin exhibited features very similar to those found by Hill and Metcalf in the Chase County ruins. Since 1949 other Padouca village sites have been located in Nebraska.

The ruins of these Dismal River or Padouca settlements are located in the districts in which the French placed the Padoucas in 1700–95. The ruined villages date to the period when the Padouca Nation was in the height of its power, and A. T. Hill and

[3] Champe, *Ash Hollow Cave*, 55, 86.

Painting on deerskin depicting Mexican Indians mounted on raw-hide-armored horses attacking an Apache *refugium* or stronghold. This skin was sent by Father Phillip Segesser from a mission in Sonora, Mexico, to his brother in Lucerne, Switzerland, in 1759.

This deerskin painting shows Pawnees with a captured priest. The man lying dead is evidently Villasur. This painting was sent by Father Segesser about 1750.

his assistant, George Metcalf, did not hesitate in identifying the ruins as Padouca. They also suggested that the culture disclosed was Apache. W. Duncan Strong, however, still clung to the old, accepted view, that the Padoucas were Comanches; but after an intensive search he failed to find any evidence that the Comanches had ever lived in fixed villages with huts, had ever cultivated crops or made pottery. Since the Indians of these ruined Padouca villages had done all these things, they obviously could not have been Comanches.[4] Finally, Waldo R. Wedel, authority on plains archaeology, in charting relations among Plains Indian cultures connected the Dismal River or Padouca culture with that of the Apaches, and that seems to be the final verdict of modern archaeology on this vexing problem. The Padoucas were Apaches.

The archaeological evidence in western Kansas confirms what was found in Nebraska. In Scott County, Kansas, there is a Padouca village ruin with the remains of some small Pueblo Indian buildings and Pueblo irrigation ditches nearby. Here there is another direct linking up of the Padoucas with the Apaches, for there can be no doubt that these village ruins mark the spot where a group of Pueblo Indians who fled from the Spaniards in New Mexico found refuge among the Apaches, as is set forth in seventeenth-century Spanish documents. Broken Pueblo pottery found in the ruins confirms this. It is late seventeenth- and early eighteenth-century ware. And here we may add that the Hill party found some Pueblo pottery bits among the Padouca pottery at the Chase and Dundy counties village ruins in Nebraska and also a few turquoise beads, which indicates some trade or other connection between the Nebraska Padoucas and New Mexico.

The fact that archaeology has demonstrated that the Nebraska and Kansas Padoucas were Apaches brings up the question of a possible link between these Padoucas and the Apaches who are proved by Spanish documents to have held the plains of eastern Colorado from before 1650 until driven out by the Comanches

[4] Since this was written, Marvin F. Kivett, director of the Nebraska Historical Society Museum, has excavated Padouca village ruins on the Middle Loup, east of Mullen, and he is of the opinion that in the future other Padouca settlements will be found on branches of Loup Fork.

after 1720. Etienne B. Renaud of Denver University, in only three short seasons of archaeological field work in the plains of eastern Colorado, discovered no less than 150 camp and village sites containing broken pottery, much of it of the Dismal River or Padouca type. These Renaud sites extend from south of the Arkansas River in the La Junta district north to the valley of the South Platte, where there are numerous sites of this type in the northeastern corner of the state. Other notable sites are in the ridge country east of Denver and in the Three Rivers district in Kit Carson County, where the branches of the Republican and Smoky Hill rivers head. Renaud carried his survey into western Nebraska, where he found more sites with pottery closely related to that in the Colorado plains; indeed, much of his Colorado pottery is apparently identical with the Dismal River or Padouca ware of Nebraska. Hill obtained samples of the Colorado plains pottery and stated that it is very similar to Nebraska Padouca ware.

A party from the University of Colorado found this Dismal River or Padouca pottery in sites in the rough country of Elbert County, Colorado, east of Denver. They found it in village ruins which they termed probably Apache. The ruins they investigated had small circular huts with floors about two feet below ground level, doorways to the east, and posts set along the walls, and it was surmised that the roofs had been covered with skins or perhaps bark.

Along the Apishapa River south of Fowler, Colorado, stone-center huts have been found and termed Apache by Colorado archaeologists. The stone circles have a diameter of as little as eight feet, and it may be that the stone structure was only the central portion of the huts. An outer part made of perishable material may have extended from the central stone circle to the rim of the hut, and the stone enclosure at the center was perhaps where the fire was built and the cooking done, and where the families gathered for meals.[5]

[5] Étienne Bernardeau Renaud, "Archaeological Survey of Western Nebraska," *Archaeological Survey Reports*; A. T. Hill and George Metcalf, "A Site of the

From this archaeological evidence we obtain clear confirmation that the Padoucas were Apaches and that in the late seventeenth and early eighteenth centuries the Apaches had a chain of little settlements or rancherias extending up through the plains from northern New Mexico and western Oklahoma into eastern Colorado, western Kansas, and western Nebraska. Considering that up to thirty years ago it was generally believed by historians and archaeologists that no tribe had ever dwelt in the high plains in fixed villages of huts, growing crops and making pottery, we have here a hitherto unknown chapter in plains history. By correcting the long-established error of identifying the Padoucas as Comanches and accepting their true identity as Plains Apaches, history and archaeology have made it possible to give to the Apaches the credit for being the first people, historically identified, who made a serious attempt to establish villages and begin the cultivation of the soil in the high plains.

There is still a blank area in the northern plains, extending from the Platte up through Wyoming and Montana, for which we have almost no information, from either history or archaeology. The fact that the Gataka Apaches near the Black Hills were exchanging visits with their Sarsi kinsmen on the Saskatchewan suggests that there was no strong enemy group in the Wyoming and Montana plains to prevent the Apaches of the Black Hills from making friendly visits as far north as the Saskatchewan. We find another clue to conditions in Wyoming at this early period in the fact that the Padoucas of western Nebraska were obtaining obsidian from deposits within the present Yellowstone Park of Wyoming, and that many of the stone tools and weapons found in Padouca

Dismal River Aspect in Chase County, Nebraska," *Nebraska History*, Vol. XXII (1941), 167; Colorado University archaeological investigations reported in the Pueblo *Star-Journal*. Some archaeologists and anthropologists have condemned the drawing of any conclusions from the Renaud surveys, stating that most of Renaud's work was surface gathering without excavation and that the pottery sherds he collected were of various periods and types. These critics ignore the historical evidence of Apache occupation of the Colorado plains; they brush aside the fact that a very large proportion of the pottery found is of identifiable Padouca or Apache types. They deny to any man (except archaeologists and anthropologists) the right to use his inborn ability to take a set of simple facts and draw deductions from them.

village ruins in Nebraska are made of flint, chert, jasper, sugar-quartzite, and other material brought from Wyoming, largely from the so-called Spanish Diggings, which are prehistoric Indian stone quarries north of the North Platte in eastern Wyoming. The quarries are near Willow Creek; and the whole countryside from Willow Creek east to Rawhide Butte is dotted with Stone Age camp sites littered with dropped stone from the quarries. It is clear that the Padoucas went to these quarries, but whether that tribe and their kinsmen actually lived in the Wyoming plains remains to be decided.

The exact application of the name Padouca is an unsolved problem. The name clearly originated among the Indians on the eastern borders of the plains, where it became known to the French, but the Spaniards of New Mexico never used the name. The most northerly Apaches, the Gatakas, who were near the Black Hills of Dakota even after 1800, were called Padoucas. They spoke of themselves as Lipans; but the main body of Lipans was on Red River and in West Texas before the year 1700, and although classified as Padoucas, they were more often given the Caddoan Indian designation of Cantsis. The Padoucas of Kansas, Nebraska, and Dakota we might assume were Lipans, as the Gataka Apaches of Dakota made that claim and denied that they were related to the Jicarillas of Colorado or the Faraon Apache group of the upper Canadian River.[6] However, in 1719 the Caddoan chiefs in speaking to La Harpe clearly included the Faraons under the name of Padouca, and the Apache settlement that these Caddoans termed the Grand Village of the Padoucas seems to have been the well-known Jicarilla group rancheria on the Arkansas River in Colorado, called *El Cuartelejo* by the Spaniards. Perhaps we might assume that the Caddoans and other eastern tribes knew all the

---

[6] DeBenneville Randolph Keim, *Sheridan's Troopers on the Border*, 189, gives the Gataka statement that they were Lipans and not related to the other Apache groups farther west. The account of Spanish Louisiana in 1785 states that the Gatakas of Dakota were obtaining Spanish goods from San Antonio in Texas. This hints that the Gatakas, who could have obtained Spanish goods from the Jicarillas in New Mexico, took a much longer road in order to trade with their Lipan kinsmen in Texas.

Apaches of the plains as Padoucas but that they sometimes gave other names, such as Cantsi, to particular Padouca groups.

The statement of the Gatakas that they were Lipans is supported by the fact that they called themselves Naichan, while the Lipans of Texas had the name Naizhan, which is clearly the same. The Faraon Apaches of the upper Canadian were called *Iyuta-jenne*, "Ute People," a name that was also applied to the Navahos, which suggests some connection in early times between these groups. This name is said to have originated in the intermarriage of some Apache or Navaho groups with the Utes before the year 1700. With the Faraons on the upper Canadian were the Apaches called Chipaynes, Limitas, and Trementinas, who had the native name of Sejine (*Se* plus *jenne*, meaning people: "Se People"). This Faraon-Chipayne-Limita group on the Canadian had rancherias and maize fields on both forks of that river and a famous rancheria known in Texas by the name *Pueblo del Norte*. When driven away by enemies after 1715, the Apaches of this group broke up; part joined the Mescaleros, while others seem to have gone to live with the Arizona Apaches.

The denial of the Gatakas that they were in any manner connected with the Jicarillas seems to refute the recent dictum of Harrington, that the Jicarillas were Lipans or, as he prefers to spell the name, Lipanans. This appears to be a twentieth-century judgment which is not supported by eighteenth-century evidence. Early in that century the Plains Apaches met overwhelming disaster, which not only broke up the old groups but even split families apart, sending some people in one direction and others in another. The new groups that later formed were made up of many fragments from various older groups, and even when these new groups were formed, it would have been very difficult to state that a particular group were Lipans or not Lipans. Today, after the passage of two and one-half centuries, how can we hope to unravel such an amazing tangle? Accepting the opinions of modern reservation Indians concerning just what the situation in their group was in 1700 does not help. Linguistic studies are a help; but they cannot work miracles.

We might trace the history of the Padoucas in a dim and general outline back to about the year 1600, by making use of archaeology and the Spanish references to old Apache groups, but it is not until the French traders and explorers begin to refer to this tribe under the name Padouca that we obtain specific information. Some Frenchmen were on the lower Missouri before 1700, but these first traders seem to have been illiterate men who brought back from their adventuresome expeditions nothing more substantial than tales of marvels and a little vague information concerning the location of the tribes they had seen or heard of. By 1714, however, an educated and intelligent man—Bourgmont—had gone up the Missouri to a point ninety leagues above the mouth of the Platte and had written clear reports on what he had observed. With reference to conditions in the plains his most interesting notations were that the Skidi Pawnees of Loup Fork in Nebraska were on friendly terms with the Padoucas, or perhaps with certain bands of that nation who were trading with the Skidis, and that the Pawnees (here he evidently meant the other group of Pawnees, who were not Skidis and who had a village on the south bank of the Platte) were mounted Indians.

The Skidis had been in Nebraska for a long period before 1700. They are evidently, in part at least, the people archaeologists term Upper Republican, who are supposed to have been in southwestern Nebraska as far back at least as the year 1300, and they may have been in touch with plains Apaches from as early as the year 1400. The Apaches probably drove the Pawnees from their old home on the Republican River to Loup Fork; indeed, the Apache or Padouca village ruins recently discovered on branches of the Republican indicate that the Apaches occupied the old Pawnee territory in southwestern Nebraska after driving the Pawnees out. The Skidi friendship with part of the Padoucas in 1714 is easily believable. These Padoucas had horses and Spanish goods to barter —articles much coveted by northern tribes like the Skidis. But the friendly relations with the Padoucas did not prevent the Skidis from warring on that tribe at times. As early as 1680, La Salle noted that the Skidis, or Panimahas as he called them, had Padouca captives and were bartering them as slaves to other tribes. The other Pawnees, those of the Platte, seem to have been more recent arrivals from the south, and they, too, were warring on the Padoucas; yet it was from the Skidis that Padouca slaves were being obtained in 1680.

The Skidi Pawnees at this period, 1680–1720, were the strong tribe of the Nebraska country. They had several handsome and populous villages on the Loup Fork, where they raised considerable crops of maize and vegetables. They went on two buffalo hunts each year, leaving their permanent villages deserted while they were following the herds, and they must have had quite a number of horses by 1717. Renaudière, who described these Nebraska Indians in 1723, gave the Pawnees of the Platte one village of 150 lodges and the Skidis of the Loup eight large villages. Estimating each of these nine villages as of approximately the size of the one Pawnee village of 150 lodges, these Caddoans of Nebraska must have had a population of 25,000 to 30,000.

A Spanish report, made in Texas in 1716, states that the French were trading up the Missouri as far as the Caynigua and the Pani tribes, who were white Indians.[7] The French traded cloth, guns, beads, and other articles. The Panis bordered with the Apaches, and being better warriors than that tribe, they took from them great numbers of captives whom they sold as slaves to the French.[8]

Does this document of 1716, which has not been regarded as important enough to be translated into English, contain our first reference to the Kiowas? It brackets the Cayniguas with the Panis,

[7] White Indians—*Indios Blancos.* This refers to the curious Caddoan Indian custom in the eighteenth century of dividing tribes into White and Black, with the Arkansas River as the dividing line. Thus the Pawnees north of that river were White Pawnees and the Padoucas, White Padoucas. South of the river were the Black Pawnees and Black Padoucas.

[8] Spanish documents of 1716 in John R. Swanton, "Source Material on the History and Ethnography of the Caddo Indians," Bureau of American Ethnology *Bulletin No. 132,* 269. Swanton guessed that the Cayniguas were the Cahinnios, a tribe in Louisiana, although the document clearly places the Cayniguas near the Pawnees in Nebraska or Dakota.

41

and we know that the Arikaras, often termed Panis in early times, were in contact with the Kiowas at an early date, in the region lying between the Missouri and the Black Hills.[9]

Up to 1700 the trade in slaves on the upper Mississippi was mainly for Panis or Pawnee captives, but as early as 1680 some Padouca slaves were being traded by the Skidi Pawnees of Nebraska. After 1700 the trade was mainly for Padouca women and children, and the Spanish statement of 1716 definitely termed the Padoucas Apaches and said that the Pawnees of Nebraska were trading great numbers of them to the French. In 1717, Bourgmont stated that one Padouca group lived eighty leagues up White River in South Dakota, which would put them inside the present Pine Ridge Sioux reservation, or perhaps farther south in the Nebraska Sand Hills. When, about 1720, the Ponca Indians moved up the Missouri to a point near the mouth of Bad River, east of the Black Hills, they were attacked and badly frightened by mounted Indians coming from the plains. The Poncas called the horses *kawa*, evidently an abbreviation of the Spanish word for horse, *caballo*, and we may conjecture that these attacks on the Poncas were made by the Gatakas or Prairie Apaches, possibly aided by their Kiowa allies.

The "Account of Spanish Louisiana in 1785" asserts that the Padoucas had some forts, or perhaps rancherias, on Bad River, the stream that enters the Missouri from the west near the present city of Pierre, South Dakota, and that these Indians visited their forts occasionally, probably meaning that they went to their rancherias seasonally, in spring and at harvest time, as all the Apache groups did. Truteau, in 1795, stated that the Padoucas were in the plains to the southwest of a point on the Missouri near the mouth of the Cheyenne River, and in the same year Mackay located the Padoucas in western Nebraska, on a branch of the Loup Fork. Late in the eighteenth century the Gatakas are said by Indian tradition to have held the land south of the Black Hills.

[9] Despite efforts to identify the Kiowas with the Quichuans of the Texas country early in the eighteenth century, I think the Kiowas were undoubtedly between the Missouri and the Black Hills until after 1750. The Quichuans were most probably the Keechi tribe on Red River.

Their allies were the Kiowas, and they had a trade in horses and Spanish goods, which Tabeau states they obtained from San Antonio in Texas.

Leaving the northern country and returning to Texas, we find that the old Jumano group of tribes in the upper Red River region was displaced after 1660, probably because of the movement southward of the Escansaque tribe, who may have been Lipan Apaches. When La Salle's French expedition landed on the Texas coast in 1686, the Jumanos were one of the first Indian groups encountered. They were now all mounted and were engaged in making trading and raiding expeditions into Mexico, bringing back horses and Spanish goods, which they traded to the Caddoan Indians in East Texas. The lands near the head of Red River were now held by a hostile tribe whom the Caddoans called Canoatinnos. Swanton has attempted to identify the Canoatinnos as Wichitas, while the *Handbook of American Indians North of Mexico* asserts that Canoatinno was simply the Caddoan Indian name for Red River.[10] But in 1686 the French found the Caddoans of East Texas carrying on a war with these Canoatinnos and eating the captives they took. It is a little difficult to believe that they were warring on and eating Red River or their own kinsmen the Wichitas; and from the location of this Canoatinno tribe it is a fair supposition that they were an Apache group of western Texas. After 1700 the French maps place Canoatinno villages near the head of the Colorado River with the Cantsi Apaches to the west of them, and Bienville (1699) speaks of these two tribes as neighbors. These Cantsis were apparently Lipans.

Thus the Red River and West Texas country, which in 1620–60 was held by the Jumanos, Aijados, and Cuitoas, with the Tejas to the east of them, had been cleared of these tribes by 1686, and their lands were now held by Apaches. Near the head of the Red River was a great Apache rancheria called Quiriroche. By 1686

[10] The modern Caddo Indians gave Swanton *Ka'n'tino*, "Red Swift River," as the old name for Colorado River or perhaps the Guadalupe, which are near each other in West Texas. As the old French maps place Canoatinno Indian villages in the Colorado River district, it is possible that the Apaches there were named for the river they lived on.

the Caddoans on the eastern borders of the southern plains had some horses and metal weapons and were striking back against the Apaches. La Salle's men found these Indians imitating the Spanish cavaliers, some of the warriors even wearing boots and spurs. They fought mounted, with long lances, both men and horses protected by rawhide armor. We may suppose that, when horses were few, these mounted and armored warriors formed a spearhead of attack to throw the unmounted enemy force into confusion and that the mounted men were followed by a large force of warriors on foot. Early in the seventeenth century the Caddoans must have been completely at the mercy of the Apaches when they made attacks on horseback, and the Spanish reports show that even as late as 1699 the Apaches were destroying entire Caddoan villages, killing all the men and older women and carrying off the young women and children to be sold in New Mexico as slaves. The Caddoans did not soon forget these terrible raids, and, when their turn came after 1690, they took a dreadful vengeance on the Apaches, slaughtering great numbers of them, eating part of the captives, and selling the rest as slaves.

These Apache mounted raids in the seventeenth century brought about profound changes in the southern plains. The primitive times of slow movements of small camps of foot Indians, of friendly relations with other tribes, made more interesting by occasional raids, were ended; and into the plains came stark war, the destruction of entire villages at a blow, and slavery on a commercial scale. The Jumanos and other primitive inhabitants of upper Red River fled; Quivira vanished—perhaps as much because of Siouan raids from the east as from any other cause; the Caddoan tribes abandoned many of their open and undefended villages to draw together in large groups on the Arkansas River in eastern Oklahoma, where many fragments of population from their older settlements were crowded together for mutual defense. By 1700 the French were trading guns to these victims of Apache aggression and the day of vengeance was at hand, for the Apaches were prevented by the strict Spanish prohibition against the trading of firearms to Indians from obtaining any weapons except

44

poor axes, large knives, and sabre blades for use as lanceheads. So fearful of firearms were the Apaches that two or three Caddoan Indians armed with French guns could throw a large Apache rancheria into panic by firing a few shots. By 1719, the Canoatinnos, under persistent attack, had vanished, and a group of fierce Caddoans and other Indians, known as the Wandering Nations, occupied the lands on Red River as far west as the Cross Timbers. They were warring on the Apaches they called Cantsis, and when La Harpe's lieutenant, Du Rivage, went up Red River to explore, he met a large force of the Wandering Nations returning from a successful raid on a Cantsi rancheria.

There can be little doubt that all the Apaches on upper Red River and on the Brazos and Colorado rivers in West Texas at this period, 1680–1720, were Lipans, although the Caddoan Indians and the French usually called them Padoucas, Cantsis, or Canoatinnos. If they were the Escansaques of Oñate (1601), they had moved southward in force from the Cimarron in northern Oklahoma down into West Texas in the course of a century. In fact, the Escansaques were on or close to Red River as early as 1650, as Spanish reports show. With the Lipans during this movement southward may have been the Natage Apaches, but the latter group apparently left the Lipans somewhere to the north of Red River and turned westward, occupying the lands in the Pecos country west of the Staked Plains. That was the country of the Apaches of the Seven Rivers, but this older group seems to have disappeared and the Natages to have taken their place. The close kinship of the Natages and the Lipans was set forth by Spanish military officers in a report dated 1774. They gave the native name of the Natages as Lipiyan and stated that this tribe was closely related to the Lipans, who in 1774 had moved farther westward and occupied lands south of the Natages.[11] The attempt to make out that the Natages were Mescalero Apaches was the work of modern ethnologists, who found a few Natages among the Mescaleros. In 1774 the Mescaleros were west of the Río Grande in the Bolson de Mapimí, and the Natages occupied all the lands

___

[11] Report of the Junta de Guerra at Monclova, 1774, quoted in Bolton, *Athanase de Mézières*, II, 163.

east of the Río Grande that in later years were held by the Mescaleros.[12]

The Faraon Apaches on the upper Canadian were a strong group in 1715. The Faraons themselves had rancherias on the South Canadian, and to the north on the North Canadian were the rancherias of the closely related Chipaynes and Limitas. It was against these Padoucas that the Pawnees, Wichitas, and other Caddoan Indians of eastern Oklahoma were directing their raids, taking large numbers of captives, eating some of them, and trading the others to the French as slaves. These Faraon rancherias had been established on the Canadian probably before 1690. The Picurís Pueblos who fled from the Spaniards of New Mexico in 1696 went eastward, met an Apache band in the plains, and were taken to the Faraon rancherias on the South Canadian. The runaway Pueblos were later taken northward, and in 1706 the Spanish expedition led by Ulibarri found them living in Apache rancherias in eastern Colorado. The Faraons and their kinsmen on the North Canadian were driven out by enemies sometime between the years 1720 and 1735. They fled southwestward and, as nearly as may be judged, reappeared beyond the Río Grande under the new name of Mescaleros. Whether we call them Faraons or Mescaleros, they were San Carlos–type Apaches, not related to the Lipans and Natages.[13]

From the account just given of these Apache groups we observe that, beginning perhaps as far back as 1640, the Apaches in the high plains, including the groups known as Padoucas, had one after the other decided to try their hands at growing crops. Group after group forgot its old contempt for tribes like the Pueblos and Caddoan Indians, who lived settled lives in villages and cultivated the soil. Each Apache group chose a favorable loca-

[12] Alfred Barnaby Thomas, in *Teodoro de Croix*, presents much interesting material on the Lipans, Natages, and Mescaleros in 1769–74.

[13] Escudero (1834) remarks that Sejene is the native name of the Mescaleros, but Orozco y Berra (1864) states that the native name of this group is Iyutajenne. As the close kinsmen of the Faraons (the Chipaynes and Limitas of the North Canadian) were definitely termed Sejenes by Hertado in 1715, the probability is that the Mescaleros were made up of a combination of Faraons (Iyutajennes) and the Chipayne-Limita group (Sejenes).

tion on a stream, usually a sheltered spot among hills, where they built a group of huts and dug small patches of ground for planting. They continued to live most of the year the old life of roving hunters in the buffalo plains, but they came to their rancherias in spring and remained for some weeks while planting was carried out, and in late summer they returned, to harvest their crops and feast for a season before setting off on their autumn and winter wanderings among the buffalo herds.[14]

That the Apaches of all the plains tribes should have been the only people in early historic times who thus attempted to alter their old way of life and live for a part of each year in settled villages is certainly remarkable, particularly when we consider that in early centuries the Spaniards and French and in later times the Americans regarded the Apaches as utterly untamable and fit only to live by rapine and murder. The Comanches and Kiowas, who had a much better reputation than the Apaches and were considered more intelligent than that tribe, scorned to live any life except the one of roving buffalo-hunters. In the northern plains the Cheyennes, Arapahoes and Crows, crossing the Missouri from eastward and coming into the plains, actually gave up old habits of living in villages of huts, growing crops, and making pottery to become roving hunters in the buffalo plains.[15]

[14] For descriptions of Apache crop-growing around 1720, see Thomas, *After Coronado*, 64, 81, 207, and map, 50. I am here speaking of the beginning of rancheria life among the Plains Apaches. The Querecho Apaches near Acoma in western New Mexico were reported as growing crops as far back as 1550. Oñate, about 1600, used the term "rancheria" to mean a moving camp. He stated that at first he was informed that the Apaches lived in rancherias, but that he now has learned that some of them dwell in pueblos, like the Pueblo Indians, and one Apache group had a pueblo with fifteen plazas. (Hammond and Rey, *Don Juan de Oñate*, 484). Fray Juan de Prada, writing in 1639, noted that when harassed by the Spaniards, the Pueblo Indians were inclined to flee to the roving Apache camps in the plains for refuge. Thus, about 1650, a group of Taos Pueblos fled to the Apaches on the Arkansas River in southeastern Colorado, and when Ulibarri visited that district in 1706, he saw houses these Taos people had built. The coming of this Taos group may have been the incentive that led the Apaches to start rancherias here on the Arkansas at El Cuartelejo. Escudero states that the Taos fugitives fortified themselves here and, of course, began planting crops (Thomas, *After Coronado*, 53). Hodge in a note in *The Memorial of Benavides* judged that the date of the Taos flight was 1639 (p. 284).

[15] The Cheyennes and Crows seem to have given up living in villages, planting

47

Although some Apaches of the old Querecho group had crossed west of the Río Grande and established little rancherias in mountainous districts in the Pueblo country of New Mexico as early as 1550, the main Apache impulse to form villages and cultivate the soil seems to have developed among the Jicarillas of eastern Colorado, after the year 1640. The Spanish documents refer to about a dozen Apache rancherias in eastern Colorado, and if we add the village ruins noted by Renaud in his archaeological survey, we have an impressive number of Apache settlements—enough to give some substance to the Spanish legend of the Apache Kingdom of Taguayo in the Colorado plains. Indeed, the Colorado Apaches seem to have been more advanced both in crop-growing and in the building of huts and the making of pottery than other Apache groups. They were trying to emulate the ways of the highly cultured Pueblos of New Mexico, and as they had considerable numbers of Pueblo captives living among them, their methods of hut-building, crop-growing, and pottery-making were improving slowly. In the Three Rivers district in eastern Colorado, on the headwaters of the Smoky Hill and Republican rivers, Renaud found broken pottery of Pueblo type, but locally made, evidently the product of Pueblo women who were captives among the Apaches.[16]

It is difficult at this late period to identify with certainty the Apache-Padouca groups of the plains of Colorado, Kansas, and Nebraska. The Gatakas of Dakota and northern Nebraska were Lipans, and the Jicarillas of Colorado were certainly of a different Apache group, closely related to the Navahos.[17] Ulibarri (1706) seems to be the first to use the name *Jicarilla*, which was a Spanish

---

crops, and making pottery as late as 1760, and by 1800 they were typical roving buffalo hunters. This sudden shift in culture is really startling.

[16] Besides Pueblo captives, the Apaches had at least two large groups of Pueblos living among them, Taos and Picurís folk, for a number of years, and this must have affected Apache ways of life strongly.

[17] In time of disaster, primitive folk turn to their closest kin for aid, and I think it significant that when the Jicarillas were driven from the plains, they fled to the Navahos for protection.

word referring to the small baskets or pottery bowls made by this Apache group, and at first the name was probably applied to only one band of the group. The native name of the Jicarillas was simply *Tinde*, meaning "people." The Mescaleros in the nineteenth century called them Kinya-Inde, which we have already suggested might be the same as Quinia-Inde, the Quinias evidently living in the plains between Taos and Quivira in 1606. The Pueblo Indians called the Jicarillas *Peshge*, "knife," referring to flint knives, and here we have a clue suggesting that the Jicarillas when first known in New Mexico were on the Arkansas River, the Napestle of the Spaniards. This name seems to come from the word *peshge*, meaning "flint knife," and all the tribes called the Arkansas River, Flint River, probably meaning Flint Knife River.[18]

The Apaches of this Jicarilla group were described by the Taos chiefs in 1715 as good people, friendly, keeping the peace they had pledged with the Pueblos and Spaniards, and not at all like the hostile and treacherous Faraons of the Canadian River.[19] This description of the Jicarillas was evidently correct, for it was not until after the Comanches and Utes drove them from their lands, broken and demoralized, that these Apaches took to thieving and making small raids in New Mexico.

In 1706, Ulibarri set out from Santa Fé with a force of Spaniards and Pueblo Indians to find the Picurís Pueblo families that had fled to the plains in 1696 and were now living among the Apaches in eastern Colorado. Marching eastward from Taos, Ulibarri came down into the valley of Río Colorado—the headwaters of the Canadian River—and there found the southern bands of Jicarillas.

[18] Napestle must be an Apache name for Arkansas River: Napetsli? Flint River? Could this be the true origin of the name Apache? I know all the explanations of the origin of that name, and they seem pretty far fetched. It seems at least possible that the name Apache came from the north and was an Apache name for their Arkansas River group: perhaps Flint Knife People or Flint River People. The Jicarillas had a band name Apatsiltlizhihi, which the *Handbook of American Indians* translates Black Apaches: *Apatsil*, "Apache"; *tlizhi*, "Black." Here the *Handbook* admits that *Apatsil* is the same word as *Apache* and is an Apache word.

[19] Thomas, *After Coronado*, 80.

Among them were the Conejeros or Rabbit band of Apaches,[20] with whom were the Río Colorado Apaches and a band called the Achos. No Apaches called Jicarilla were here, although these bands belonged to that group. Turning northward, the Spaniards found the Jicarillas in the Sierra Jicarilla and Sierra Blanca on the southern border of Colorado, and near them were the Apaches called *Fleches de Palo*, who are not mentioned in later reports, and the Carlana Apaches, named for their chief Carlana.

Continuing northward, Ulibarri came down into a deep and wide canyon where the Penxaye Apaches (not later mentioned) had a rancheria with patches of maize, beans, and pumpkins. This must have been on the upper Apishapa River, or a little to the north of the Cuchera district—the locality in which Renaud found curious remains indicating that the Indians had villages on the canyon floor, with caves up the canyon walls to hide in when attacked by surprise and lookouts on the high ground in which a watch could be kept for indications of the presence of enemy parties. It was a most sensible arrangement. Renaud found that the Indians had built stone walls across the fronts of some of the caves. In Arizona, late in the eighteenth century, the Spaniards came on just such an Apache hideout—a cave with a stone wall built across the front with maize, hides, and other supplies heaped up behind the wall.[21]

The Penxaye Apaches, who had these rancherias in the canyons in 1706, were under attack by the Comanches and Utes, and had been driven out of their lands before Valverde passed through in 1719. Valverde spoke of this district as the former home of the Carlana Apaches, and this suggests that the Penxayes and Carlanas belonged to an Apache group which was known after 1720 under the general name of Jicarillas.

From the excellent Ulibarri report and his story of the Picurís fugitives we learn that in 1696–1706 the Apaches, later known as Jicarillas, were roving in the lands east and north of the New

[20] In 1700 a Llanero Apache reported at Taos that the Conejeros, "on the most distant Apache borders," had been destroyed by white men.
[21] See Anza's report in Alfred Barnaby Thomas, *Forgotten Frontiers.*

50

Mandan earth-lodge village on the Missouri at the time of the bull dance. From a painting by George Catlin, 1832.

Caddoan grass-lodge village. From an illustration used in Marcy's *Exploration of the Red River of Louisiana in the Year 1852.*

An Apache camp scene.

A Navaho earth lodge.

Mexican settlements and that they had established rancherias at favorable spots, where they had huts and grew small crops; that they had among them captive Pueblo Indians in considerable numbers from whom they must have learned something about cropgrowing, irrigation, the building of houses, the making of pottery, and other arts. Here there was the germ of cultural advancement if these Apaches were left in peace. But they were not left so, and the rancherias which they had established in their quest for better living were proving to be death traps into which their new habits compelled them to venture at planting time and again at the time of harvest. The Apaches had made the fatal mistake of acquiring property—they had holdings at their rancherias, houses, horses, stored-up food, and other materials; they brought to these rancherias large supplies of dried meat and skins, the products of their hunting. And then often enough the fierce Utes came down on them, killing some and scattering the others, plundering and frequently burning the rancherias.

# 3. The Coming of the Utes
## and Comanches

THE INDIANS of the Shoshonean linguistic stock who are known to us today as Utes, Comanches, and Shoshonis or Snakes, occupied during prehistoric times the Great Basin and Plateau region lying west of the Rockies—a vast territory of desert and semidesert land, thinly occupied by seed-gathering and basket-making Indians who wandered about on foot, so preoccupied by the endless task of finding enough to eat that they apparently had little time or inclination for such social activities as the forming of permanent groups, the appointment of chiefs, and the organization of tribal ceremonies and dances. They were so very poor that they could not afford that universal Indian luxury of going to war and killing their neighbors.

In the opinion of Julian H. Steward, who has specialized on the Indians of the Basin-Plateau region, the Shoshoneans were comparatively recent arrivals who came into western and southwestern Nevada from the north in prehistoric times, the Paiutes of today remaining in Nevada and eastern Oregon, the Ute, Shoshoni, and Snake groups migrating on eastward and southward, some of them crossing the Rockies into the plains of Wyoming and Montana, where the Comanches split off from the Shoshonis and moved southward to their historic locations.[1]

When these first groups of Shoshonean people crossed the

[1] Julian H. Steward, "Native Cultures of the Intermontane (Great Basin) Area," *Smithsonian Miscellaneous Collections*, Vol. C, p. 454.

Rockies, moving toward the east and south, they emerged into plains that were already held by the Apaches. The date and circumstances of this coming of the Shoshoneans are unknown; but we may surmise from Spanish information that the Utes, the first Shoshoneans of this new migration to come out of the mountains, were enabled to do so by forming a friendship with some of the Apache and Navaho bands, even intermarrying with them; and this was apparently well on into the seventeenth century, as the Spanish documents do not refer to the Utes until after 1680.

It was in the Taos district in northeastern New Mexico that the Utes made their first appearance, and the Navahos and Apaches seem to have been the only wild Indians known to the Spaniards in that locality before the date indicated. The intermarriages of the Utes are said to have been with the Navahos, who lived in northern New Mexico and with the Jicarilla Apaches whose country lay in northeastern New Mexico and southeastern Colorado. To this we may add the conjecture that the Utes also married into the Faraon Apache group, which was known in the eighteenth century as the Iyutajenne or Ute People, and perhaps also into the mysterious A or Ae tribe that seems to have been in the plains of western Oklahoma in the eighteenth century near the Faraons, and may have been a group of mixed Ute-Apache blood.[2]

Looking into this matter of early Ute intermarriage with the Apaches, we may first observe that it would have been a reasonable thing for groups of Utes migrating down through the Colorado mountains and making contact with the Navahos in the lands west of the Río Grande to have sought the friendship of the Navahos and to have married into that tribe. The home country of the most southerly Ute group was usually located by Spanish authorities in the district near the New Mexico and Colorado boundary line, between the Río Grande and Río Chama, and they were located here as late as 1726. Their position was just east of the Navahos, east of the Continental Divide, west of the Río Grande

2 William Richard Harris, *The Catholic Church in Utah*, 107, 117, refers to this intermarriage of Utes and Apaches.

in the San Luis Valley with the Sangre de Cristo and Culebra ranges shutting them in on the east. But there were easy passes through these mountains, and, by going through them, the Utes would have found themselves among the Jicarilla Apaches in the Colorado plains. To the southeast, near and easily reached, lay the pueblos of Taos and Picurís; but it was nearly always at Taos that the Utes came to trade or raid. The Navahos, farther west, used the pueblo of Jémez as their trading place, and when at war they raided Santa Clara and Jémez pueblos. The Apaches to the north and east of New Mexico traded at Taos and Picurís. At the period 1630–70, the Spanish documents exhibit no knowledge of any wild tribe on the northern or eastern borders of New Mexico except Navahos and Apaches; but there were vague reports of unknown wild Indians coming down from the north to trade or raid and going home by the Río Chama trail, leading toward the northwest. These may have been the Utes.

From 1680 to 1692 there were no Spaniards in New Mexico, and the Pueblo Indians were fighting among themselves, with the Apaches and Navahos joining in. During this time, from 1680 on, the Utes are stated to have been raiding Taos. When the Spaniards reoccupied New Mexico in 1692, the Utes were alternately raiding Taos and making friendly trading visits there. Father Alonzo de Posadas stated that at this early period the Utes were as brave as the Apaches and that they never turned their backs on a foe.[3]

The Ute raids were so troublesome that in 1694 Governor Vargas invaded their country. The Utes surprised his camp at dawn and rushed it, armed with bows and war clubs. They wounded a number of Spaniards before the men could arm themselves.

The Spanish documents do not distinguish the first Utes that appeared in New Mexico from other Ute groups. These Indians are always termed simply Yutas; but when we examine on a modern map the district in which these first Utes are said to have dwelled we find the Ute name *Saguache* applied to a county and to a principal river immediately north of the upper Río Grande, and this name seems to be the same as *Chaguagua*, the apellation

[3] I have seen only brief quotations from Father Posadas.

of a Ute band that originally lived in northwestern Colorado near the Comanches of the Yamparika division, who were apparently the first Comanches to join the Utes in the country east of the Rockies. Moreover, the Spanish documents refer to a Ute band in southeastern Colorado after the year 1720 with a name similar to Chaguagua, and this name apparently was given to an eastern branch of Purgatoire River in Las Animas County, Colorado, which is still called Chucuaco Creek. Since after 1730 the Spaniards of New Mexico still referred to the first Ute band simply as Yutas and gave the name Chaguagua to the second band, we might conjecture that the situation about 1700 was that the Yutas or first band of Utes were near the southern border of Colorado between the Río Grande and Río Chama and that to the north of them were the Chaguaguas, later migrants from the lands west of the Rockies, who held the district north of the Río Grande. How they came there seems obvious. There is the Cochetopa Pass near the head of Saguache River, and through that pass or one farther north these Utes could come from their original lands west of the Rockies. Today there does not appear to be a trace among the Utes of such a group as the Saguaches or Chaguaguas. The latter name is given by Escalante and Domínguez as that of a Ute band in northwestern Colorado in 1776. This would make the Yamparika Comanches and the Saguache Utes still neighbors in northwestern Colorado in 1776. The best information obtainable from Colorado pioneers asserts that *Saguache* (also spelled "Sawatch") means "Blue Earth."

The Pueblo towns and Spanish settlements in New Mexico were a land of wonder to any wild Indians, who were attracted to this rich province as if drawn by a powerful magnet. They came in shyly to make their first friendly visits; but before long they acquired some metal weapons and perhaps horses, and then they began to raid. The first of the Utes, having crossed east of the Rockies and apparently met the Navahos and Apaches in friendly wise, even marrying into those tribes, began to visit at Taos, probably coming in to trade; but when the Pueblos revolted in 1680 and drove the Spaniards out, the Indians began fighting among themselves, and the Utes are stated to have raided Taos from 1680 on. From 1690 to 1700 the Utes, having grown in strength during the decade of the Pueblo revolt, turned on the Navahos and raided them persistently. It was about the year 1700 that the Utes brought the first group of their Comanche kinsmen into New Mexico, to visit Taos, and from that time the Comanches joined the Utes in their raiding operations. They raided the Navahos and Pueblos, then shifted their attention to the Apaches in the Colorado plains and began to raid them.

In making these attacks on the Apaches, the Utes, and probably the Comanches also, had to cross the mountains, going through passes near the head of the Huerfano River and probably through other passes farther to the north that brought them down into the plains near the present cities of Pueblo and Colorado Springs.

As in the case of the first Utes on the New Mexico border, we have no definite information concerning the coming of the first Comanches; but they, like the first Ute bands, apparently crossed the mountains into the park country, establishing themselves to the north of the Utes, who were in the San Luis Valley and in the Chama district.

Before the story of these Indians is continued, something must be said about the topography of the lands they occupied in Colorado, Utah, and Wyoming. Here are the vast ranges of the Rockies; to the east rises the Colorado Front Range, and east of these mountains are the high plains. The parks lie between the Rockies and Front Range, starting with the San Luis Valley in the south, where the Río Grande heads and where the first Ute group held the land. To the north of the San Luis is the Bayou Salada or South Park, where the Arkansas River and the South Platte head. Then come Middle Park, Estes Park, and North Park. Farther north lie the wide Laramie Plains, which are in truth a greatly extended example of the mountain parks farther south. In southern Wyoming the land is much more open than in Colorado; the Rockies subside, the Front Range dwindles to a succession of low hills, and the Bridger and South Pass give wide and easy access across the Continental Divide. Still farther north in the Wind River and Yellowstone country, the mountains rise into mighty barriers again, and the parks between the ranges are once more a principal feature of the country. West of the Rockies in early times the country was on the whole poorer: in many districts it was pure desert. Here there was little large game. If there were any buffalo herds at all, they were confined to the Green River country and to the district north of Great Salt Lake. Instead of hunting large game, the Indians here snared jack rabbits, caught salmon in the rivers, and eked out a bare living by gathering wild fruits and seeds and by digging roots.

The whole country west of the Rockies, in western Colorado and in Utah south of Great Salt Lake, was held by the Utes. Only a small fraction of this tribe had passed through the Rockies and come down on the New Mexican border. In 1776 the Utes informed Escalante and Domínguez, the two friars who were exploring these lands, that the Uinta Mountains were the northern frontier of their land, and to the north of these mountains lay the country of the Comanches. The Uinta Range extends from the northwestern corner of Colorado westward toward the southern end of Great Salt Lake. Green River, which is the upper course of the Colorado River of the West, takes a great bend to the east to get around the Uintas and, having passed the mountains, swings back toward the west and south. Here the Yampa River comes into Green River just south of the Uinta Range, its headwaters rising in the Rockies just to the west of the present Estes Park, with passes leading into Middle Park. Here on mountain slopes and in canyons along the Yampa River grew the yampa plant (*Atenia gairdneri*), the roots of which were dug by the Indians, forming a principal food for those bands that lived in the districts where yampa grew.[4]

It was evidently here on the Yampa River in northwestern Colo-

[4] Yampa is the Ute name for this plant or its tuber. Another tuber that was a principal food of the Indians of the Rockies and the basin-plateau was the camas, a kind of wild hyacinth, that grew in the great Camas Prairies and at other points in the Snake Indian country of Utah and Idaho. The Indians dried the tubers, put them into bark bags, and cached them in the ground for winter use.

rado that the Yamparika or Yampa Eater group of Comanches had their earliest known home, and from here they seem to have gone through the mountain passes into Middle or South Park, where they allied themselves with the Utes who were already established in the San Luis Valley to the south.

When Lieutenant W. P. Clark talked to the Comanches in 1881–83, it was mainly with the Yamparikas, and it was their tradition that he recorded. They stated that their original home was in the mountains to the north of the head of Arkansas River; there they lived with the Shoshonis or Snakes, and to the south of them "but still in the mountains" were the Kwahari Comanches or Antelope Eaters.[5] This seems to be the only Comanche tradition concerning their old homeland; the other Comanche bands had nothing to report or were not questioned.

The Surville map, dated 1770, was based on an earlier map of the 1727 period. It is so distorted as to latitude and longitude that it is almost impossible to state definitely where the Indian tribes it shows were located. But it sets the Comanches clearly in the mountains of southern Colorado, in a district that is known to have been Ute territory. This map location of the Comanches does not agree with our other information.

About 1720, the Spaniards of New Mexico set down in writing a report that the land of the Comanches was two hundred leagues (five hundred miles) to the northeast of Santa Fé and that the river called Casse was much frequented by this tribe. The distance indicated would place the Comanches near the North Platte in Wyoming.[6] It was less than ten years after this report that the Spanish map referred to above placed the Comanches in the mountains near or south of the Río Grande. Alfred B. Thomas, who has specialized in Spanish materials dealing with New Mexico and the plains region, has stated that, after the middle of the eighteenth century, the Yamparikas extended from the upper Arkansas River northward to the Platte and probably along the Platte,

[5] W. P. Clark, *The Indian Sign Language,* under heading "Comanche."
[6] Thomas, *After Coronado,* 232. Casse is clearly the Apache name for this river (Platte?) as the name was given by the Apaches.

with their allies, the Yupe or Yupine Comanches, extending in the same direction, partly in the mountains and probably as far north as Wyoming. To this we may add that in 1776 the friars Escalante and Domínguez were told by the Utes of western Colorado that the Uinta Range was the boundary between their lands and those of the Yamparika Comanches and that the Yamparikas were making mounted raids on certain Ute groups in the district south of Great Salt Lake. The Utes in their turn were sending parties northward, to steal horses from the Yamparikas. In 1779, Governor Anza of New Mexico marched against the Comanches. He went north into the San Luis Valley, where he found only friendly Utes, and that disproved the Spanish map of 1727, which locates the Comanches in this district. They were farther north. Anza surprised the Comanche camp of Chief Cuerno Verde in the plains, between the present cities of Pueblo and Colorado Springs, and this chief was probably a Yamparika.

It will be noted that the Comanche tradition and the early Spanish reports agree about the Yamparikas: they were in the mountains, sometimes in the plains to the east, extending from near the head of the Arkansas to the north, part of the group still in eastern Utah, north of the Uinta Mountains, as late as 1776. The Comanche tradition speaks of a second group, the Kwaharis or Antelope Eaters, who were south of the Yamparikas, "but still in the mountains." The Spanish documents also speak of a second group, extending northward in the same direction as the Yamparikas, partly in the mountains, to which Thomas adds that they probably extended into Wyoming. But the Spanish officials did not know the name *Kwahari,* and they called this second Comanche group Yupes, Yupines, Jupines, *Gente de Palo,* which means "People of the Timber" or "stick-people."[7]

Could these Yupes of the Spanish reports be the Kwaharis of Yamparika tradition? The Yamparikas told Lieutenant Clark that the original name of the Kwaharis was *Qua-he-huk-e,* "Back shade" because this group occupied the plains where there were no trees and shaded their faces by turning their backs to the sun;

[7] Thomas, *Forgotten Frontiers,* 323, quoting Spanish report of 1785.

59

but the probability is that the name refers to the type of wooden backrest or back shade that was made and carried by some of the Plains Indians as a regular part of their camp furniture. It is curious that both the Comanche story and the name the Spanish document gives to the Yupe group refer to timber, poles. The name Antelope Eaters, applied to the Kwaharis, indicates a location in the plains. The name Yupe might be the same as the name Yep-ee, which is placed in the Yellowstone Park region on the Lewis and Clark map of 1814, which included information obtained from fur traders who had been in the Yellowstone region after 1806. The entry on the map reads: "Yep-ee, a band of Snake Indians, 1,800 souls."

The Kotsoteka (Buffalo Eater) Comanche chief, Ecueracapa, whose lands were east of New Mexico, informed Governor Anza in July, 1785, that he was working to draw all the Comanches together for a council, but that the greater part of the Yamparikas were separated from the other Comanches by about one hundred leagues (250 miles), with the Yupes between the Yamparikas and the southern Kotsotekas. Here again the Yupes are put nearer to New Mexico than the Yamparikas and as late as 1785. Yet the information of the oldest Southern Cheyennes at the period 1910 was to the effect that the Kwaharis were northern Comanches, the last Comanche group to move south of the Arkansas River to live, and that these Kwaharis were the group nearest to the Kiowas when that tribe was still near the Black Hills of South Dakota. The southern Kiowas apparently began to raid southward from the Black Hills about 1725. They were known in New Mexico soon after that date. They made peace with the Comanches late in the eighteenth century, and they were so closely associated with the Kwahari Comanches that they were often termed Kwahari-Kiowas, as distinguished from the northern Kiowas or Cold Men. It has been stated by several writers that the Kwaharis moved south of the Arkansas River at an early date and occupied the Staked Plains; but such an assertion seems to lack any confirmation, and it is not until after 1850, or even 1867, that the Kwaharis can be definitely located in and near the Staked Plains.

All that we really know of the Kwaharis is that the Yamparika tradition placed them in the south, "but still in the mountains," that their name, Antelope Eaters, and their other name referring to their living in treeless country, both indicate that they were in the plains, living on antelope, early in the eighteenth century, and that they were, after 1780, a middle group between the Kotso-tekas south of the Arkansas and the Yamparikas of the north.

This new information, and particularly the facts disclosed in the Spanish documents published by Thomas, make it necessary to revise the older opinion, that all the Comanches were south of the Arkansas at a very early date and that the Kiowas came south from the Black Hills in the middle of the eighteenth century. It now appears that, as late as 1785 and probably for some time after that date, the two big Comanche divisions, the Yamparikas and Kwaharis, were still in the north, in the mountains and plains of Colorado and Wyoming, and that it was probably the appearance of new enemies, armed with British guns and raiding the Comanches and Snakes from the north and east, that induced the last Comanche groups to abandon Wyoming and Colorado and move south.

Before leaving the subject of the early Comanches, we should consider one more matter, the name *Comanche*. The origin of this name has been the subject of guesses for a century back. Usually an effort is made to show that the name is Spanish. De Benneville Randolph Keim, after talking to many Indian interpreters in western Indian Territory in 1868, set down in his book that *Comanche* is the Spanish word for "wild man." But in New Mexico the Spaniards always called wild men or wild Indians *gentiles*.[8] One of the few occasions on which they used a different term was when a group of Pueblo Indians revolted and ran off into the eastern plains to join the wild Apaches. The name *cimarron*, "wild, revolted," was applied to the runaways, and the name has

---

[8] The Spaniards applied the term "gentiles" (from the Latin *gentilis*, "of the same clan or race") to all peoples who were neither Jew nor Christian, beginning with their conquest of the Moslems. Changing the term *goyim*, used by the Jews to designate sects other than their own, to *gentiles*, they gave that name, at one time, to all American aboriginals.

stuck to a river in northern Oklahoma to this day. In a book published in 1952 we are told with no citation of authority that the name Comanche comes from two Spanish words, *camino* (road) and *ancho* (broad), evidently referring to the great Comanche Trail which that tribe used in making raids into Old Mexico; but that trail did not come into existence for about eighty years after the name Comanche was first recorded in New Mexico.

No one seems to have thought of going back to Taos in New Mexico and considering the situation under which the name Comanche was first recorded, in the year 1707. The Utes brought a group of Comanches to visit at Taos, and, when they introduced them, they probably used a Ute name for the new tribe. The Comanches called themselves Neum or Neuma; the Utes often added "ache" to tribal names (as in Saguache, Moache, Tabeguache), and if they did this with the Comanche name, it would have been something like "Neumache" or "Neumanche." The Spaniards were not very good at recording Indian names, and they might very well have altered the name to "Ceumanche" or "Comanche." Admittedly, this is another guess, but it is a guess based on conditions at the time the name Comanche was first recorded.

# 4. The Apache Debacle

WHEN THE UTES brought the first Comanches to visit at Taos in 1707, they probably treated them like country cousins whom they were bringing to town to be shown the sights. By this time the Utes had been familiar with the Pueblo towns of northern New Mexico for at least a generation; they had intermarried with the Navahos and Apaches, had joined them in trading and raiding expeditions into New Mexico, and now they were well acquainted with the situation on the Spanish border. They had taken part in the fighting during the years of anarchy when there were no Spaniards in the province, and in these intertribal wars they had equipped themselves with horses and weapons. They no longer needed the aid and support of the Navahos and Apaches but were ready to act by themselves, in their own interests, with some assistance from their Comanche cousins. In effect, the Utes about 1694–1700 were feeling strong and independent, and, like the wild people they were, they intended to forget old friendships which had been useful to them when they had first come down through the Colorado mountains, poor, all afoot, and in need of the friendship of the Navahos, Apaches, and Pueblo Indians. That first period when they had had to ask humbly for help was ended, and now they were ready to take what they desired by violent methods.

The Utes, aided by their new Comanche allies, were going to raid their old friends in northern New Mexico and southeastern

Colorado, and what a wonderful position they were in for accomplishing this! Their location in the San Luis Valley at the head of the Río Grande, extending southward into the Río Chama district in northern New Mexico, was an ideal position from which to launch their attacks, and their Comanche allies, to the north of them in the Colorado parks, were in a perfect location to aid them. To the south of the Utes, quite close and open to attack, lay Taos and Picurís; to the west the Navaho land was within easy reach; the Sangre de Cristo and Culebra ranges shut them off from the Apaches in the eastern plains, but there were passes through these mountains and passes farther north through which the Comanches could attack the Apaches from a different direction. In fact, the Utes and Comanches, holding central lines, were free to attack in any direction, with safe lines of retreat to their mountain-valley homes after they had accomplished their purposes. They had the further advantage of living in movable camps, and even if their enemies came to attack them, they would have difficulty in finding the camps. On the other hand, the Navahos and Colorado Apaches all had little settlements or rancherias, which were fixed targets for Ute and Comanche attacks.

The Apache group that was nearest to the Utes of the San Luis Valley and Chama district were the Penxaye and Carlana, also called Sierra Blanca Apaches, in the rough country south of the Arkansas River, east of the Sangre de Cristo Mountains, and west of Purgatoire River. These bands were related to the Jicarillas, and like them they were friendly people, on good terms with the Spaniards and Pueblo Indians of New Mexico. These Apaches and their country are hardly referred to in Spanish documents before 1706; indeed, their very names were unrecorded until Ulibarri with a small party of Spaniards and Indians marched through their country that year and made a detailed report concerning what he had seen. This Ulibarri report makes it apparent that the Utes and Comanches were raiding the Apaches in the rough foothill country between the present cities of Pueblo and Trinidad, but that they had not yet succeeded in driving the Apaches from this district. More interesting still is Ulibarri's information that the Apaches north of the Arkansas River in the plains of eastern Colorado did not mention the Utes and Co- manches. Their only enemies were the Pawnees and Jumanos with villages far to the east, on the Arkansas in northern Oklahoma, who were obtaining guns from French traders and were coming to attack the rancherias of these Plains Apaches.

At Taos, Ulibarri found the people worried by a report that the Utes and Comanches were planning a raid on that pueblo. In the district between Trinidad and Pueblo he found the Pen- xaye Apaches all in alarm and hurrying to collect their people in large groups to resist impending Ute raids. On his return journey from the Arkansas River, he was told by the Apaches that the Utes and Comanches in July, 1706, came and attacked a ran- cheria of Carlana or Sierra Blanca Apaches and a rancheria of Penxayes, killing a number of people. This was in the rough country between Trinidad and Pueblo.[1]

Thus the Apaches in eastern Colorado were just beginning to feel the force of Ute and Comanche attacks in 1706, but those to the south of the Arkansas River were already badly alarmed. By attempting to improve their condition by forming rancherias at which they had huts and fields of maize, kidney beans, pumpkins, and even watermelons, they had pinned themselves down at these rancherias during planting time in the spring and harvest time in July and August. At other seasons they were wandering among the buffalo herds in camps of skin tipis and were fairly safe from their enemies, but the Utes and Comanches knew that they would find these Apaches at their rancherias in spring and again in late summer. The purpose of the Utes and Comanches was always the same: to catch the Apaches off guard at their rancherias, to make a sudden assault, kill as many Apaches as they could, cap- ture some women and children for the slave trade in New Mexico, and plunder the rancheria and destroy the huts and crops. Thus with each succeeding attack the Utes and Comanches grew strong- er, the Apaches weaker and more alarmed. The attackers had an insatiable desire for more horses, and in every raid they swept off

[1] Ulibarri, in Thomas, *After Coronado*, 76.

all the Apache horses they could get at, leaving their victims without mounts, and thus without the means of making effective summer and winter buffalo hunts, from which they still derived their principal support; for the Apache crops were small and the people still had to live mainly on buffalo and other game.

The Ute war on the Navahos belongs to this period. The Navahos were continuing their raids into New Mexico strongly in 1706–12, but by 1716 they were so hard pressed by the Utes and Comanches that they ceased their hostilities in New Mexico and began to talk of turning Christian and seeking the protection of the Spaniards. Up to 1714, the Navahos followed their old practice of alternately going to Jémez Pueblo on friendly trading visits and then coming back to make a raid, but after 1714 they were eager to be on good terms with the Jémez people and with the Spaniards. The reason became obvious when in 1724 the Utes pressed a raid southward into the Jémez neighborhood. A Spanish witness who lived among Navahos in the period 1706–12 stated in later years that at this time the Navahos were very hostile, pushing their raids into New Mexico. He returned to live among them in 1722–31 and found them demoralized by Ute and Comanche attacks; they had ceased raiding in New Mexico and spoke anxiously of becoming Christians and obtaining the aid of the Spaniards against their Ute and Comanche foes.[2]

The Spaniards of New Mexico paid little heed to this growing danger from the Utes and Comanches until after 1715. Their attention was fixed on the hostile Faraon Apaches of the Canadian River, who were making savage raids into southern and eastern New Mexico and were regarded as the chief plague of the province. Thus the Spanish authorities ignored the operations of the Utes and Comanches in the north and made no effort to assist the friendly Apaches of eastern Colorado, who formed a protective screen for the New Mexican settlements and should have been assisted in their struggle to hold their lands.

[2] Thomas, *Plains Indians and New Mexico*, 8–9; Hodge notes in *The Memorial of Benavides*, 278; Rabal, translation of the MS, in W. W. Hill, "Some Navaho Culture Changes During Two Centuries," *Smithsonian Miscellaneous Collections*, Vol. C, pp. 397, 401.

As it was, the Ute and Comanche activities were ignored until 1716. That summer Governor Martínez took most of the Spanish forces on an expedition against the Moquis in Arizona, and while he was away, the Utes and Comanches drove a hard raid at Taos, also attacking the Tigua Pueblos and outlying Spanish settlements. On his return from the Moqui country, Martínez sent Captain Serna northward, and this officer was reported to have surprised the Utes "at Cerro de San Antonio, 30 leagues north of Santa Fé," killing a number of them and capturing their *chusma*, or "leader," and some women and children. The Governor and his brother sold the Ute captives as slaves in Nueva Vizcaya, Mexico, and pocketed the money. In attempting to make peace again with the Utes, he is said to have told them that the Ute prisoners died of smallpox. When the scandal came out, Martínez was removed and Valverde took his place as governor.[3]

In the following year, 1717, the Utes and Comanches made a heavy raid at Taos and in northern New Mexico; in 1718 they assaulted the Jicarilla Apache rancheria northeast of Taos, destroying a tower the Apaches had built for defense, killing sixty of them, destroying their maize fields, and so frightening the Jicarillas that they abandoned their rancheria and retired to a stronger position, where they built new huts.[4]

By this time these Ute and Comanche attacks had become so persistent and severe that even the inert Spanish officials were aroused, and, in 1719, Governor Valverde made an expedition northward with the avowed purpose of finding and punishing the raiders. Starting from Santa Fé on September 15 with a force of Spaniards and Indian allies, he took the usual route north to Taos and then struck northeast across the mountains to the valley which was known as La Jicarilla. Here the Apaches had their rancherias, and they were sitting on the flat roofs of their huts to watch Valverde's little force march in. The Carlana Apaches, who had been living in Colorado south of the Arkansas in 1706,

---

[3] Bancroft, *The History of Arizona and New Mexico*, 235.
[4] The attackers also carried off sixty-four Apache women and children to be sold at the slave market (Thomas, *After Coronado*, 115).

had been driven from their homelands by the Utes and Comanches and were now at La Jicarilla. Chief Carlana told Valverde that the Utes and Comanches had attacked his rancheria in the Sierra Blanca on the southern border of the present state of Colorado, twelve leagues north of La Jacarilla, forcing his people to flee. The Carlanas had then split, part of them coming south to La Jicarilla, the rest moving farther inland to join the band of an Apache chief named Falco. Even at La Jicarilla the Apaches were in a constant state of fear. The year before Valverde's coming the big Ute and Comanche attack had forced the Apaches to desert the old rancheria of La Jicarilla, and they had rebuilt in a location where they hoped to be better secured against enemy attacks. They had built terraced houses in the Pueblo style, but Chief Carlana and his band, recently driven by Utes and Comanches from their old home in Colorado, were living in a camp of twenty-seven skin tipis.[5]

Leaving La Jicarilla, Valverde marched northward, crossing the Sierra Blanca Mountains and coming down to the head of Purgatoire River, near the present Trinidad. Here Chief Carlana and his Apaches joined the expedition in the hope that the Spaniards were going to find and fight their Ute and Comanche foes. Going on northward by leisurely marches, Valverde found that the Apache bands Ulibarri had noted as located in this district between Trinidad and Pueblo in 1706 were now gone, driven out by Utes and Comanches. Just what route Valverde followed is a mystery. His day-by-day diary is mainly devoted to the finding of springs, ponds, and hills and the bestowing of saints' names on these minor features of the country; indeed, the commanding officer of the expedition was much more interested in celebrating saints' days and hunting deer than in seeking hostile Indians. Seven years later Valverde stated that on this expedition he marched two hundred leagues to the north and reached Río Casse, a stream frequented by the Comanches, and that he then turned eastward toward the Apache rancheria of El Cuartelejo. Casse is a stream mentioned elsewhere in the Spanish documents; some have sup-

[5] Valverde diary, *ibid.*, 111–14.

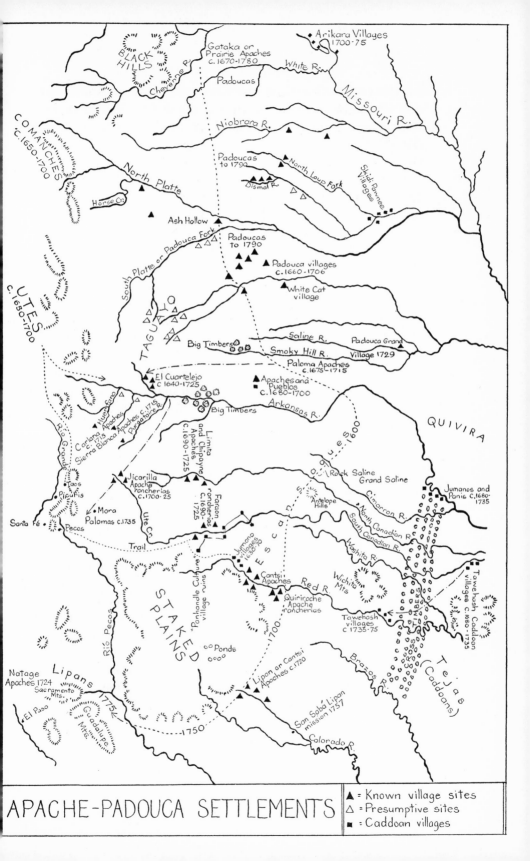

APACHE-PADOUCA SETTLEMENTS

▲ = Known village sites
△ = Presumptive sites
■ = Caddoan villages

posed that it was the Platte, but Valverde's diary makes it evident that he did not go farther north than the Arkansas in the Pueblo neighborhood. He does not mention Río Casse in his diary; he calls the river in this vicinity Chiopo, but refers to the Arkansas farther east as another river called Napestle by the Apaches. At any rate, it was in the vicinity of Pueblo that Valverde, or rather the Carlana Apaches who were with him, discovered a recently deserted Ute and Comanche camp of sixty tipis. The Spaniards and their Apache allies slowly followed the trail of these enemies eastward, evidently through the country north of the Arkansas, as it was buffalo plains with few trees and little water. As they advanced, they found that the trail was increasing in size, and the abandoned camps indicated that the Comanches (the diary now states that the foe being followed were Comanches) had collected two hundred lodges and had an immense number of horses with them. Chief Carlana and his Apaches were eager to find and attack the enemy, but Valverde dawdled, making short and cautious marches, interesting himself in naming all the creeks and springs for favorite saints. He now met all the Apaches from the big rancheria of El Cuartelejo, who were eager to join in making an attack on the Comanches. But Valverde held the usual Spanish council of war, and, as almost always happened, the council was unanimously of opinion that the best action that could be taken was to keep away from hostile Indians and to retreat. Valverde deserted his Apache allies and retreated.

The Valverde diary and the statements that he and some other Spaniards made concerning this march some years later disclose the important fact that the Apache groups of Penxayes and Carlanas that in Ulibarri's time, 1706, had held the lands in Colorado from near Trinidad up to Pueblo had been driven out by the Utes and Comanches before 1719; the Jicarillas and other bands that in 1706 had occupied rancherias in the Sierra Blanca Mountains near Trinidad had retreated to La Jicarilla, some fifteen leagues to the northeast of Taos, and, in 1719, Chief Carlana and his people were also at this spot, driven there only recently from their Colorado lands, as they had not yet built huts but were living in tipis. The old Apache lands in Colorado, south of the Arkansas, were now uninhabited, but roving camps of Comanches and Utes were passing through these lands. The Utes are still mentioned in 1718 in this district between Trinidad and Pueblo, but usually the Spaniards speak only of the Comanches, and it was evidently a big Comanche camp that Valverde followed from near Pueblo eastward to a point near the present town of Rocky Ford. Valverde stated in 1726 that he marched 200 leagues northward to the Comanche country in 1719, but his own diary indicates that from Santa Fé to the vicinity of Pueblo, his most northerly point, he marched about 105 leagues, or 250 miles. Martínez stated in 1720 that the Utes and Comanches lived in plains 100 leagues north of Santa Fé and 70 leagues north of Taos. An Apache Indian who came to Taos in April, 1727, stated that the Comanches were living at El Almagre or a little farther away. This would seem to place some Comanche camps near Pueblo, Colorado, and from the month—April—one would suppose that these Indians had wintered here.[6]

Putting together all this Spanish and Apache information, we find that between 1706 and 1718 the Utes and Comanches came through the passes in the Front Range from their homelands in the Colorado park country and drove the Apaches from their rancherias in the rough country east of the mountains and south of the Arkansas; they then moved into this district with their camps of skin tipis to hunt buffalo and to send out raiding parties eastward against the El Cuartelejo Apaches and southward to the valley of La Jicarilla, where the Apaches from southeastern Colorado had built new rancherias. By 1719 these Utes and Comanches, evidently having plenty of horses, could move freely and safely in the plains and send war parties on long-distance raids.

Just before he turned homeward from the Arkansas River, Valverde was joined by the Apaches from the El Cuartelejo ran-

[6] Valverde, *ibid.*, 232. Martínez statement, 171; Apache statements, 257. Thomas states that El Almagre was the Spanish name for the Colorado Front Range Mountains. However, this Apache was not referring to a long range of mountains, but to a particular spot where his people camped and where they probably dug red ochre for face paint.

cherias, which were on the north side of the Arkansas some distance below where he was encamped. Having harvested their crops and learning that Valverde was in the field, supposedly to find and fight their Comanche enemies, they had left their rancherias to join forces with him. These Indians were El Cuartelejo, Paloma, and Calchufine Apaches, about one thousand strong, including women and children, and they had a camp of about two hundred skin tipis which they put up on the Arkansas River bank near to the Spanish camp but across the river from it.

In this Apache camp there was a Paloma chief whose band dwelt "on the most remote borderlands of the Apaches," evidently in central Kansas. This chief had an unhealed gunshot wound in his abdomen, and, when questioned by the Spaniards, he stated that while his band were planting maize at their rancheria, probably in May, 1719, they were taken by surprise by "Pawnees and Jumanos" who were armed with French guns. The Apaches fled, leaving their rancheria in the enemy's hands. The chief, being badly wounded, escaped only because of the approach of darkness. The Palomas from this rancheria fled, at least part of them, to their kinsmen at El Cuartelejo. Greatly perturbed by the news that the French were so near to New Mexico, Valverde questioned the Apaches closely. They said that the French had built two pueblos as large as Taos among the Pawnees and Jumanos and that they also had built a fort there and were trading firearms to those tribes. Altering their tale, the Apaches said that it was not the Pawnees and Jumanos who had attacked the Palomas but the Canceres, the Kansa or Kaw tribe that had a village on the west bank of the Missouri some distance above the mouth of the Kansas River.

Alfred B. Thomas, in *After Coronado*, expresses the view that the rancheria of the Palomas was in Nebraska, near the forks of the Platte, but he must have been drawn to that conclusion by the fact that when the Spaniards set out in 1720 to reconnoiter the French establishments said to be among the Pawnees and Jumanos, they permitted Apache guides to lead them northward to the Platte to the Pawnees of Nebraska. Every word the Apaches said to Valverde in 1719 pointed to the Palomas' being in central Kansas, not far from the Pawnees and Jumanos, that is, the *Panis Noirs*, "Black Pawnees," whose villages were visited in that very year 1719 by the French trader Du Tisne, who found them on the Arkansas River in the northern borders of the present Oklahoma. To clinch the matter, the Apaches also spoke to Valverde of the Canceres or Kansa tribe on the Missouri in eastern Kansas. The Apaches embroidered their tale handsomely when they spoke to Valverde of the French towns as big as Taos and the French fort among the Pawnees and Jumanos. In 1719, Du Tisne and a few companions were the only Frenchmen among these Pawnees of the Arkansas River. Du Tisne came from the French settlement in Illinois, passing through the Osage Indian country, where the Osages stripped him of most of the guns he intended to trade to the Pawnees. At the Pawnee villages he traded two guns for horses. The Pawnees already had six guns, which they valued very highly. Du Tisne remained a few days, found the Pawnees most unfriendly, and then left to make his way back to Illinois. This was in the autumn of 1719, following the attack on the Paloma rancheria in the spring of that same year. It will thus be observed that the Pawnees and Jumanos who attacked the Palomas had only six guns and that the French towns and fort among these Pawnees were figments of Apache imagination. As for the Cancere or Kansa tribe on the Missouri in eastern Kansas, in 1719 they had no Frenchmen among them, unless some itinerant trader like Du Tisne happened to be at their village with a small pack of goods to barter for horses and Padouca slaves.

But Valverde was very much upset by what the Apaches had told him; and when he made his report to Mexico City, the officials there were almost in a panic, visioning French settlements and French forces, including regular troops in forts, established among the Pawnees, within striking distance of New Mexico. They wished Valverde to place a Spanish presidio with a force of twenty or twenty-five men at the Apache rancheria of El Cuartelejo, north of the Arkansas, to guard New Mexico against the French; they ordered him to send an expedition into the plains to reconnoiter the French positions among the Pawnees. Obviously this meant the Black Pawnees of the Arkansas River in northern Oklahoma. The Spanish officers in New Mexico opposed the plan for a small presidio at El Cuartelejo, isolated by over one hundred leagues of mountains and plains from its base at Santa Fé, and when it came to sending an expedition to the Pawnees, Governor Valverde decided that his own presence in New Mexico was indispensable. He therefore ordered his subordinate officer, Lieutenant Colonel Pedro de Villasur, to make the expedition, giving him all the force that could be spared in New Mexico, namely, forty-two soldiers, three Spanish settlers, and sixty well-equipped Pueblo Indian warriors.

Nothing could be clearer than that Colonel Villasur was expected to visit the Pawnees of the Arkansas River. The Spaniards of New Mexico had had news of these Pawnees, and of the alleged presence of many Frenchmen at the villages, from the Apaches ever since the year 1706. The other Pawnees, those of the Loup Fork and Platte in central Nebraska, appear to have been unknown in New Mexico at this period, as they are not once clearly referred to in Spanish documents. Yet Villasur permitted his Apache guides to take him northward into Nebraska; and neither Valverde nor any of the high officials who accused Villasur after he had met disaster was intelligent enough to observe that the ill-fated expedition had gone to the wrong Pawnee group.

From the Spanish documents, which include testimony of witnesses who were with Villasur, it is impossible to learn by what route the expedition reached the Pawnees on the Platte River. Villasur seems to have taken the route followed by Valverde in 1719, going from Taos to La Jicarilla, and there is a supposed incident of his rafting his command across the Arkansas in the vicinity of El Cuartelejo, near the present town of La Junta, Colorado. He is supposed to have rested his men and horses for some days at El Cuartelejo, where presumably he obtained Apache guides, including Paloma Apaches. These Apaches must have known that the Spaniards wished to go to the Pawnees of the

74

Arkansas River. Why they misled the expedition and took Villa-sur northeastward into Nebraska is a matter that was understood by the Apaches in 1720, but is a mystery today.

Leaving the rancheria of El Cuartelejo, Villasur and his men vanished into the plains. The testimony of the survivors who found their way back to New Mexico was confused regarding the distance traveled and the direction of the march; but when we find that the Oto Indians of Nebraska reported to the French that the Spaniards were traveling with a large camp of Apaches (the Otos called them Padoucas), it is not difficult to understand the vagueness of the Spanish witnesses concerning the direction and distance of the march. Traveling with an Indian camp meant starting eastward; the next day a swing to the north, on news brought in by scouts that buffalo herds were in that direction. Next would come a halt to hunt buffalo and stay in camp for some days to dry the meat. Then a move to the southeast, to visit a camp of kinsmen reported in that direction; and every day endless councils between the bewildered Spanish officers and the Apache chiefs. Marching in this manner, no one could keep an accurate account of distances and directions even in a daily journal, and the Villasur diary was lost. The survivors had to depend on memory in recounting the march.

It is from the French that our best information comes. Bois-briant, the French commandant in Illinois, reported that Villa-sur's fight with the Indians occurred about twenty-five leagues, perhaps sixty miles, from the Missouri, and on another page he locates the scene of battle at fifteen leagues from the Oto Indian village, which in 1720 was on the south bank of the Platte near the present town of Yutan, Nebraska. Fifteen leagues westward from this village would bring us close to the mouth of Loup Fork, on which stream the Skidi Pawnee villages were located. If we assume that the fight was south of the Platte, the distance would indicate that it was near or on the Big Blue River, a northern tributary of Kansas River. From the French account it would seem that when the news of Villasur's approach reached them, the Oto Indians were in a hunting camp in the marshes near the

75

present city of Lincoln, and if the distance of fifteen leagues is counted from this hunting camp, the location of the battle would be some distance west of the Big Blue. Just where the fight occurred has always been a mystery. The descriptions given in a fragment of the Villasur diary do seem to fit the geographical conditions between the Platte and Loup Fork, and the many islands in the larger river fits the Platte at this point.

It was between the two rivers that Villasur's scouts discovered a camp of Pawnees, and, after crossing both rivers, the Spaniards encamped opposite the Pawnees, whose camp seems to have been on the south bank of the Platte. Sending a Pawnee or Arikara Indian captive he had with him across the river, Villasur attempted to open negotiations with the Pawnees; but the Indians retained his messenger in their camp, and their attitude alarmed Villasur. He now called the council of war which was a Spanish commander's first thought when within sight of a hostile force. He then made the astonishing proposal to his subordinates that he should remain inactive in his camp while sending messengers to Santa Fé—a round trip of more than one thousand miles by horseback—to ask for instructions! His officers rejected this imbecile plan, and all voted for immediate retreat. Meanwhile, the Pawnees had evidently sent runners to inform their Oto allies of the appearance of the Spanish force. The Pawnees must have had few guns; but the Otos were well equipped with French firearms, and they now hastened to the scene.

The Spaniards withdrew under cover of darkness, recrossing one river and camping at a spot which must have been in the river bottomlands, as it was in an area of tall grass, which in this district grew only in the larger stream valleys. At dawn on August 12 the Spanish camp was thrown into sudden panic by a heavy discharge of musketry; flights of arrows followed, and then the Pawnee warriors charged into the camp, lances in their hands. The attackers were apparently all on foot; Villasur's men were in the main also afoot, for their horse herd had stampeded, rushing off with the horse guards in pursuit. The Apache allies seem to have fled at the first alarm, leaving Villasur and his Spaniards with a few faithful Pueblo Indians to withstand the Pawnee and Oto attack. Apparently all the men who remained in the camp, with the exception of the priest, were killed. Villasur fell with thirty-five of his forty-two Spaniards; of sixty Pueblos twelve or thirteen died; not an Apache was killed. The priest, Father Juan Mínguez, was captured and, according to one of the French accounts, taken all the way to the village of the Kansa tribe on the Missouri in Kansas and there killed. Small as these losses may seem to us today, this defeat was a terrible blow to the Spaniards of New Mexico. It was the worst defeat Spain ever suffered in battle against Plains Indians, and in the fight fell nearly all of the best and most experienced Spanish soldiers of New Mexico. With the men were lost all the best firearms and other military equipment in the province.

Of more importance to history than the exact spot at which this engagement was fought is the fact that the Spanish documents state that Villasur was accompanied and guided on this expedition by Apaches from La Jicarilla or the Colorado rancherias, while the French accounts made it equally clear that Villasur's Indian allies were Padoucas. The inference is obvious, that Padouca was a name the French and the Indians in eastern Nebraska, Kansas, and Oklahoma applied to the Apaches, including those of El Cuartelejo and La Jicarilla.

We have seen what the conditions were in the lands to the northeast of New Mexico at this period, with the Utes and Comanches waging war against the Apaches and clearing them out of the hill country east of the mountains and south of the Arkansas. Turning to the French documents, we find that at this time, about 1720, the Apaches were as hard pressed in the east, in Nebraska, Kansas, and Oklahoma, as they were by the Utes and Comanches in Colorado. Indeed, the Plains Apaches in the early eighteenth century were paying for the savage attacks they had made on all their neighbors when, in the seventeenth century they had obtained horses and thus the power to create terror among neighboring tribes that were still on foot and at the mercy of mounted raiders. Now, after the year 1700, the tribes in eastern

77

Oklahoma, Kansas, and Nebraska had horses, which they had obtained by raiding the Apaches or by trade, and they also had some firearms traded to them by the French. The Apaches, who were prevented by Spanish trade restrictions from obtaining guns, were terribly afraid of these new weapons; and a half-dozen men armed with guns and accompanied by a larger force equipped with bows and iron hatchets could throw a large Apache rancheria into a state of panic. Before 1700 the Panis—the Pawnees or Caddoan tribes on the eastern border of the plains, extending from Texas all the way up into Dakota—were the principal victims of Apache attack. They were also being raided by tribes to the east, on or near the Mississippi, and most of the Indian slaves that came into the hands of the French in the Mississippi Valley were Panis. But after 1700 the Panis obtained metal arms and horses; they began to raid the Padoucas with some success, and Padouca slaves began to replace Pani slaves in the Mississippi Valley. By 1716 the Pawnees of Nebraska were reported to be taking large numbers of Apache or Padouca slaves and selling them to the French for firearms; but this may have been an exaggerated account, for in 1724 the Nebraska Pawnee chiefs stated that they were willing to make peace with the Padoucas, because that tribe by making mounted attacks prevented their people from hunting buffalo successfully. The chiefs of the Kansa tribe in eastern Kansas had a similar view. These chiefs also wished to make peace so that they might obtain horses from the Padoucas, to enable their tribe to hunt buffalo more successfully. South of the Arkansas River the Panis and other Caddoans hated the Apaches with such bitterness that they killed and ate many of the captives that they took from that tribe, and French traders who came to buy Padouca slaves often found that the captives had been eaten.

The Indian slave trade was a lucrative business; but it was one that both the French officials on the Mississippi and the Spanish officials in New Mexico wished to keep as secret as possible. In New Mexico this disreputable trade was camouflaged as Christian charity—the ransoming of poor Indian captives from the wild Apaches and Comanches; the French traders and officials simply ignored the trade in slaves when making reports. It is amusing to find Bourgmont in 1717 reporting on each tribe in turn with the simple statement, "This nation's trade is in furs alone." He said that of every tribe along the Missouri, and at the time these tribes were the main suppliers of Padouca slaves. La Harpe in Oklahoma in 1719 was just as discreet in the matter of the slave trade, but he did record that the Caddoan chiefs gave him one small Padouca boy slave. Their excuse for not presenting him with more slaves was that they had eaten all their Padouca captives before they heard the news that La Harpe was coming to visit them.[7] This southern Caddoan custom of eating captives gave some of the French officials on the Mississippi the opportunity to follow the example of the New Mexican officers and to represent the trade in Padouca slaves as charity and a Christian duty. They saved the unfortunate Padouca women and children from the fate of being killed and eaten, and then sold them into slavery. Mainly interested in profits, the French traders were outraged over the Caddoan custom of eating women and children captives. One company of French traders had their business ruined because of this custom of the Black Pawnees, whose villages were on the Arkansas in eastern Oklahoma. The traders made the long journey to the villages in the summer of 1720 to trade for slaves and horses; but on their arrival they found that these Pawnees, who had recently destroyed a Padouca village, had already killed nearly all of the one hundred Padouca women and children captives.[8]

---

[7] Margry, *Découvertes et établissements*, VI, 289. The French officials, while pretending that there was no trade in Indian slaves, were worried about the possible loss of that trade. The Fox tribe of Wisconsin, enemies of the French, about 1724 were getting the trade in Padouca slaves into their own hands by offering better prices than the French traders would pay. Villiers, in his book on Bourgmont, states that he (Bourgmont) was given authority in Paris to stop the trade in Padouca slaves and even to confiscate the goods of traders engaged in the slave trade. The traders and officials in Louisiana were infuriated and attempted to sabotage Bourgmont's expedition.

[8] Boisbriant letter, 1720, *Nebraska History*, Vol VI (1923), 21. These captives were probably cooked and eaten; but the way Boisbriant put it, they were burned, a few each day. There is no evidence of Oklahoma Indians' torturing captives by burning at the stake. There is plenty of evidence of cannibalism.

These wholesale captures of Padoucas by the tribes on the Arkansas and Missouri are a clear indication of the demoralization of the Padoucas by the attacks of enemies armed with guns. Boisbriant reported in 1720 that the Oto and Kansa tribes had recently attacked the Padoucas, bringing home 250 slaves, and in the same year the rather small Black Pawnee group on the Arkansas took over 100 Padouca women and children, the fruit of a single raid. Such losses, from the point of view of primitive folk like the Plains Apaches of 1720, were really frightful. It must be borne in mind that in ordinary Indian warfare the loss of three or four men in a stiff fight was considered heavy, but in the type of surprise attack being made on the Apaches, entire villages were being destroyed in a few hours, and hundreds of people were being killed and captured.

This was the situation when Villasur and his Spaniards met disaster on or near the Platte in August, 1720. This affair aroused the French. The fact that a Spanish military expedition had found its way almost to the banks of the Missouri produced a shock in Paris, and plans were made to take advantage of the destruction of the Spanish force by advancing the sphere of French influence across the plains and to the New Mexican borders. To do this effectively it was considered necessary to make a French peace with the Padoucas.

Seeking the best man to execute this plan, the Paris officials chose Bourgmont, the veteran Missouri River trader, who had wound up his business affairs in America and gone back to France to spend his later years. By offering him great inducements, the officials persuaded him to leave his retirement; but when Bourgmont heard of the plan for peace with the Padoucas, he was unwilling to undertake the project. Becoming frank, he informed the officials that for a number of years past the French in Louisiana had been supplying arms to the tribes on and near the Missouri and Arkansas and had set these tribes to raiding the Padoucas, to obtain slaves to barter for more arms. With these slave raids continuing he could not hope to make peace with the Padoucas, and he refused to accept the position offered to him unless

80

he was given authority to stop the trade in Padouca slaves. Given some such power, he consented to return to Louisiana.

It required three years from the day Villasur met his fate in the Nebraska plains to get Bourgmont back to Louisiana. In the meantime opposition to the Paris plan had developed among the French officials and traders in the Mississippi Valley, and when Bourgmont came back with a bundle of official orders and requisitions, a concerted effort was made to block his plans and spoil his chances of success. Governor Bienville in New Orleans wrote to Commandant Boisbriant in Illinois, August 20, 1723, ordering him to cut the number of men and the supplies Bourgmont needed for his expedition. The plan of the opposition was to permit Bourgmont to go up the Missouri and establish a tiny fort, thus complying with orders from Paris, but to cripple him by lack of men and supplies so that he could not advance farther up the river. Bienville was thinking (like other Louisiana men) of the damage to trade that would ensue if peace was made with the Padoucas and the slave trade stopped; but he was of the opinion that even if, by a miracle, Bourgmont managed to make peace with the Padoucas, it would not last long enough to injure the French trade seriously. Boisbriant did not agree with these views. He stated that all the tribes near the Missouri and Arkansas hated the Padoucas intensely and would regard a French peace with that nation as an unfriendly act. Without openly approving of the trade in Padouca slaves, Boisbriant stated that the tribes allied to the French found it strange that Frenchmen were talking peace with the Padoucas and an end to the barter in Padouca slaves; and he feared that the result might be that all the trade on the Missouri would be thrown into the hands of the Sac and Fox tribes, who were bitter enemies of the French and were developing a strong trade in British goods, which they obtained from tribes farther to the east. On the lower Mississippi the same danger of British encroachment on French trade areas existed even more strongly. For many years past British traders from Carolina had been supplying guns to such tribes as the Chickasaws and urging these Indians to make raids and bring in Indian slaves, to barter

81

for more British guns and goods. Thus Pawnees from the Oklahoma region and Padoucas from the plains were being taken as slaves to Carolina and sent in slave ships to the West Indies. Both the English and the French colonists preferred Negro slaves. They shipped Indian slaves to the West Indies, sold them, and purchased Negro slaves with the money.[9]

Bourgmont obeyed his orders from Paris. He first established Fort Orléans on the lower Missouri and then led his expedition up the river to the Kansa Indian village which stood on the site of the present Doniphan, Kansas. Unlike the Spaniards, who did not know which group of Pawnees Villasur was to visit or how he was to reach them, Bourgmont was well aware that the particular Padouca group he wished to make peace with was on upper Kansas River and that it was through the Kansa tribe that he could best open negotiations with them. Indeed, as far back as 1719, Du Tisne had planned to visit these Padoucas of Kansas River, but he made the mistake of going to the Black Pawnees of the Arkansas, who were very unfriendly and refused to guide him or let him pass through their lands on his way up to Kansas River. Like Villasur, wandering about with his camp of Apache allies, Bourgmont started up Kansas River with the Kansa Indians, who were going on a buffalo hunt. Instead of making a steady ten leagues a day, as he should have made if traveling at an honest rate, Bourgmont and his Frenchmen had to humor their Indian allies and loiter along, one league one day, two and one-half the next, and one day only half a league, because it was hot and the Indian women were carrying heavy burdens. Then Bourgmont fell violently ill with a fever and had to turn back, but he sent a bold Canadian named Gaillard with some companions on with the Indians. Presently Gaillard left the Kansa tribe near the mouth of the Big Blue and, taking two Padouca slaves as guides, went on westward and reached the Padouca village August 25. Bourgmont, imagining that there might be some Spaniards in this Kansas Padouca village, had given Gaillard a polite letter in Spanish ad-

[9] Villiers, *La Découverte du Missouri*, 72–73. On the British trade in Indian slaves, see Secoy, *Changing Military Patterns*, 78–79.

dressed to the military commandant and a letter in Latin for the priest, but there were no Spaniards in the Padouca village. The Padoucas greeted Gaillard with great friendliness. He had brought home two of their captives, whom he now freed, and he easily induced some of the Padoucas to go with him to the Kansa hunting camp near the mouth of the Big Blue. Gathering a large peace party of Kansa chiefs and warriors, Gaillard returned to the Padouca village and there consummated a peace between the Padoucas and the Kansa Indians. The Kansa men gave French guns as peace gifts; the Padoucas gave horses and probably some Spanish articles.[10]

When he was taken ill and had to return to Fort Orléans, Bourgmont had left a great stock of trade goods in the lodge of the Kansa grand chief, with a guard of Frenchmen under the command of Sergeant Dubois. On the return of Gaillard with the news of peace between the Kansa and Padouca tribes, Dubois went down the Missouri to Fort Orléans; and on September 20, 1724, Bourgmont left the fort to go back to the Kansa village for a grand peace council in which the chiefs of all the tribes were to take part. Meanwhile, Gaillard had induced large groups of Padoucas to come to the Kansa village: the only instance on record of entire camps of Plains Apaches camping on the Missouri River. On October 2, Gaillard had eight camps of Padoucas, six hundred warriors and all their women and children, close to the Kansa village, and at night the fires of other Padouca camps that were moving in the same direction could be seen in the distance. In the Kansa village the chiefs of that tribe were entertaining chiefs of the Padoucas, with whom they had made peace, and the chiefs of the Missouri tribe and of the Iowas, Otos and Nebraska Pawnees were also present. The French were mainly interested in having the chiefs of the Pawnees, Otos, and Iowas make peace with the Padoucas, but these three tribes were unwilling to do so. In the council Bourgmont's men placed large piles of French goods on the floor in front of the Pawnee, Oto, and Iowa chiefs, and then Bourgmont asked them if this was not

[10] Bourgmont, in Margry, *Découvertes et établissements*, VI, 391ff.

83

enough to induce them to make peace with the Padoucas. They thought it over and decided to make peace, but they stated that they were only doing so because their people had a great need for horses, which they could obtain from the hated Padoucas by making peace with them.

The peace ceremonies completed, the Padouca camps melted away westward into the vast plains. But Bourgmont's task was not yet completed. He still had to visit the village of the Padouca grand chief to cement the new friendship and learn what he could concerning the Spanish borders and the best way for the French to advance toward New Mexico. On October 8, he set out with his Frenchmen and some Kansa Indians. On the eleventh he crossed what was apparently the Big Blue; fifteen leagues farther west he came into treeless buffalo plains and noted a number of springs. Fifteen or twenty leagues beyond he found a recently deserted Padouca camp on a little river. Just a short distance on he reached a salt river, evidently the Saline Fork near the present town of Salina, Kansas, where more deserted Padouca camps were noted. The Padouca grand chief now appeared with a large party of his men and conducted the French to his village, which was near at hand.

The grand village was probably so termed because the grand chief lived in it. It was evidently a permanent village or rancheria. There were one hundred "huts" with eight hundred warriors, fifteen hundred women and two thousand children present, but it is obvious that large numbers of Padoucas from other villages had crowded in to see the French. The numbers recorded would make forty-three Indians to a hut—an impossible number. Bourgmont reported that the Padoucas were not wanderers; they went on buffalo hunts in camps of skin tipis, but each band had a village of fifty to one hundred huts near which they had fields and planted little crops. In fact, they lived just as the Apaches in eastern Colorado did at this same period. They planted pumpkins and certainly maize, but not tobacco. Bourgmont stated that they had no maize, but they gave him a large bowl of cooked maize when he came to the village, and the probability is that they had eaten practically all of their crop by the time the French reached the village in October. The Padoucas and Apaches evidently did not grow maize extensively, and they ate most of their corn green. The Apaches of the upper Canadian, as stated in 1715, after harvesting their little crops, often came to New Mexico to trade for maize. Indians who grew any crops always started with maize, which was their favorite food. They added pumpkins, squashes, beans, and melons after they had learned to grow maize.

Bourgmont's Padoucas hunted buffalo on horseback in large bands, and they went to war in similar bands, men and horses protected by rawhide armor. They informed Bourgmont that they traded with the Spaniards for tobacco, knives, and bad axes, but were not permitted to obtain guns. They had quantities of *pierres bleues*, New Mexican turquoises, which were pierced like beads and made into necklaces. These blue stones, highly valued by tribes near the Missouri, were given to Bourgmont and some of the chiefs during the peace council at the Kansa village.[11]

Bourgmont stated that this Padouca nation was very numerous and that its territories extended for two hundred leagues: five hundred miles. The Padouca grand chief told him that he had under his control twelve villages with two thousand warriors. As we have seen, at the grand village when the French visited it, there were eight hundred warriors, fifteen hundred women and two thousand children; but, according to the chief's assertion, this was less than half of the people under his control. Whether his group was made up only of the Kansas Padoucas or included those in Nebraska, Oklahoma and Colorado, we will never know.

That these Kansas Padoucas were Apaches is obvious; yet in *American Antiquity* for April, 1949 (p. 290), another attempt is made to identify them as Comanches, on the grounds that a French map of the date 1720 sets down the White Padoucas, perhaps those of Kansas, as enemies of the Spaniards, that Bourgmont

11 *Ibid.*, 443ff. As to Padouca huts, they probably were not as large as Pawnee earth lodges, which housed an average of twenty persons each. Valverde in 1719 noted that the Apaches of El Cuartelejo, who were in moving tipi camps, had one thousand people in two hundred tipis, five to a tipi, about the same number the Sioux had to a tipi around the date 1860.

found plenty of horses among his Padoucas, while the Apaches of El Cuartelejo farther west in Colorado were seen in 1719 using dogs for transportation, and finally for the reason that in none of the several Padouca village ruins that have been excavated have any horse bones been found. This rather astonishing argument seems to be based partly on the fact that Valverde noted dog transportation among the Apaches on the upper Arkansas in 1719, a not unusual occurrence, as Indian camps even after 1860 could produce many examples of dogs used as transport animals. Whenever there was a shortage of horses, the Indian women naturally reverted to the old custom of using dogs to transport camp equipment. The Colorado Apaches were losing many horses to Comanche and Ute raiding parties in 1719, and that is a sufficient explanation for their use of dog transportation. For an archaeologist to argue that because no horse bones were found in the village ruins the Apaches of Kansas and Nebraska had no horses around 1700 is certainly surprising. Such a theory is clearly refuted by the Bourgmont report, which mentions the Padoucas of Kansas as a source of supply of horses for all the tribes near the Missouri. Frank Secoy was struck by this archaeological claim, and he made the neat retort that if the absence of horse bones in Padouca village ruins proves that these Indians had no horses, by the same argument the absence of human bones in the ruins indicates that no people ever lived in these villages.[12]

Taken by itself, the Bourgmont evidence explodes the legend that the Padoucas were Comanches. In Kansas, as elsewhere, the Padoucas were Apaches. Where the Comanches were and what they were doing while Bourgmont was making peace with the Kansas Padoucas is disclosed in the Spanish documents. Bourgmont left in October, 1724, but French traders remained at the Kansa village on the Missouri. They were now on friendly terms with the Padoucas as far to the west at least as the present town of Salina, and they probably went to the Padoucas regularly to trade. Moreover, the French purpose was to press on to the New

[12] Frank Secoy, "The Identity of the Paduca; an Ethnohistorical Analysis," *The American Anthropologist*, N.S., Vol. LIII (1951), 539.

Mexican frontier, and these traders must have had instructions to attempt with the aid of Kansas Padouca guides to penetrate farther toward the Spanish borders. And they did get as far as the Apache rancherias of El Cuartelejo, as the Spanish reports show.

Not a word was breathed by the Apaches to the Spanish authorities in New Mexico concerning the great peace councils with the French and their Indian allies. But why should the Apaches tell? They were coming regularly to New Mexico seeking Spanish aid against their Comanche and Ute enemies, and they were astute enough to keep quiet about their new alliance with the French enemies of the Spaniards. But the Spanish officials, though badly informed and slow witted, soon began to suspect that something was wrong, although not a hint of Bourgmont's doings in Kansas had reached them.

Governor Valverde had been removed, as a result of the Villasur disaster, for which he was held mainly responsible, and Bustamante was now governor of New Mexico. There were no indications of danger from the French when the new governor took over; but the Jicarilla Apaches were terribly alarmed over Ute and Comanche attacks on them. They needed Spanish aid, and they knew that the usual form of Spanish assistance to Indians was a mission with a presidio of soldiers to guard it. It was the protection of troops that the Jicarillas longed for, but to obtain the troops they had to become Christian neophytes, and now they began to talk earnestly of their longing for salvation. As for the Spanish officials and friars, they knew that a mission could not succeed among wild and wandering Indians.

Bustamante with a small Spanish force marched to La Jicarilla in November, 1723, and held councils with chiefs Carlana, Churlique, and others. They wanted a mission, and Bustamante told them that they must form a permanent pueblo and live like Christians. The chiefs expressed eagerness to be baptized and even more eagerness for Bustamante and his Spanish soldiers to join them in an expedition that several Apache rancherias were organizing against the Comanches. The Comanches had recently surprised an Apache rancheria, killing many men and carrying

87

off women and children, and the Apaches were afraid that other rancherias would be attacked. They wanted to strike back at the Comanches and urged Bustamante to join them, but he would not.

This was in November, 1723, with Bourgmont already preparing for peace with the Kansas Padoucas. That peace was made in October, 1724. In 1726 a band of Calchufine Apaches and Palomas, the latter certainly Kansas Padoucas, came to trade in New Mexico, and in their camp were Comanche captives who stated that when the Apaches came to attack the Comanche camps, they had white men, Frenchmen, with them. In April, 1727, a captive Comanche woman was questioned at Santa Fé, and she alarmed the Spanish officials by stating that when the Apaches came to the Comanche camp and carried her off, they had Frenchmen with them who wore red coats and caps with silver bands, and they had tents and many weapons. In fact, she depicted a force of uniformed French troops and shocked the Spanish officials by stating that this force was at El Cuartelejo. She asserted that most of the French were on the River Chinali, which was quite near to El Cuartelejo, and that the French had a walled house at an "inlet" on this river. As the head of Kansas River was quite near to El Cuartelejo and as the only French trading house known to us, west of the Missouri, at this date was among the Kansa Indians, we may conjecture that Chinali was the Apache name for Kansas River. An account somewhat more sensible than that given by the captive Comanche woman was obtained by the Spanish officials from a Pueblo Indian chief. In September, 1726, this chief with a party of his people went on a buffalo hunt into the Jicarilla Apache lands and there met some Jicarillas, who told him that there was a Frenchman at El Cuartelejo and that other Frenchmen had gone with a very large war party of Cuartelejo, Paloma, and Sierra Blanca (Carlana) Apaches with the purpose of driving the numerous and widely scattered Comanche bands out of the Apache plains. It was probably this war party that captured the Comanche woman referred to above.[13]

This advance of the French to El Cuartelejo in 1726 was a

13 Thomas, *After Coronado*, 257.

rational step after Bourgmont's peace with the Kansas Padoucas in October, 1724, and the attempted Apache offensive against the Comanches was the natural result of the gift of guns and ammunition to the Kansas Padoucas by Bourgmont and his Indian allies. Assuming again that the Paloma Apaches were Bourgmont's Padoucas, it was the most reasonable thing in the world for the French traders to employ some of these Palomas to take them westward to El Cuartelejo, a district with several rancherias of Apaches who were in close touch with the Spanish border and could aid the French in their effort to reach New Mexico. But something now went wrong with the French plans. Bourgmont had left the Missouri River country, and as the French officials and Indian traders were opposed to the peace with the Padoucas and the Indians in Kansas and Nebraska no doubt were eager to resume attacks on that tribe, the probability is that raids against the Padoucas were recommenced by 1726. Moreover, the French traders who penetrated to El Cuartelejo seem to have found out quickly that they could not depend on the Kansas Padoucas and Colorado Apaches. In 1725 and 1726 they joined these Apaches and Padoucas in making raids on the Comanches, but that tribe was clearly not much distressed, for in that year the Comanches chased a band of Paloma and Calchufine Apaches straight into the town of Santa Fé, and, for all we know, the Comanches also drove the Apaches out of their big rancheria at El Cuartelejo. In fact, El Cuartelejo had become an almost impossible home for the Apaches as far back as 1719, when Valverde reported that these Indians had left that place and dispersed the people among other Apache rancherias because El Cuartelejo was under heavy attack from the Utes.[14] Drawn back to El Cuartelejo by the hope of French aid against their enemies in 1725 and 1726, the Apaches were probably driven away again in the latter year, after their French allies had departed, for these French traders could not live permanently at El Cuartelejo. They came to trade, and, having traded and joined the Apaches in a raid on the Comanches, they went back to the Missouri. When the French returned to El

14 *Ibid.*, 132.

Cuartelejo in 1727, they apparently found the Apaches gone; they then made contact with the Comanches and seemingly made friends with that tribe and aided it in making attacks on the Apaches.[15]

Meanwhile the French officials were doing all they could to destroy the work Bourgmont had accomplished in 1723 and 1724. Men hostile to the peace with the Padoucas were now in control. In December, 1728, the council of the French colony took control away from Bourgmont's friends and gave a five-year monopoly of trade on the Missouri to two Canadians named Marain and Cutlas; and in April, 1729, Bourgmont's Fort Orléans on the Missouri was ordered abandoned on the excuse that it was a useless expense to keep the post up. The way was now open for resumption of the war on the Padoucas and heavy trade in captured Padouca horses and slaves. Meanwhile the French at El Cuartelejo had met the Comanches and found in them Indian allies far bolder and more enterprising than any Padoucas or Apaches.

The year 1727 can be fairly termed the date when final disaster overtook the Padoucas and Apaches of Kansas and Colorado. Abandoned by their new French allies and receiving no aid from the Spaniards, who talked endlessly and promised assistance, to be given only after the Apaches had all accepted baptism and settled down as meek Christians at missions, the Kansas and Colorado Apaches fled from their old lands and came crowding down on the New Mexican border. If the Spaniards would not help them, they seemed to hope that their ancient friends, the Pueblo Indians, might. Thus, some of the Jicarilla bands went to the pueblo of Taos, while the Palomas from Kansas and the Carlanas from southern Colorado moved down to Pecos on the eastern border of New Mexico and attempted to form new rancherias there.

We have few details concerning this disaster to the Padoucas and Apaches of Kansas and Colorado; but the Padoucas are not referred to as living in Kansas after the year 1724, and there is no mention of the Apaches' being on the Arkansas or at El Cuar-

15 Thomas, *Plains Indians and New Mexico*, 12–13.

telejo after 1726. As for the Padouca rancherias in southwestern Nebraska, all we know is that archaeologists report that the latest tree-ring dates obtained from wood and charcoal gathered in the rancheria ruins are 1704 and 1709. This suggests that the villages were abandoned not many years after the indicated dates; and if this is correct, the Padoucas of southwestern Nebraska were involved in the disaster that overtook their people in Kansas; but the Padoucas in northwestern Nebraska were not, for they were still holding out on upper branches of the Loup Fork as late as 1770 or even twenty years after that date. In South Dakota the Padoucas or Prairie Apaches held out near the Black Hills until the end of the eighteenth century.

In 1700 the Apaches and Padoucas had held undisputed sway in the high plains, all the way from Texas up into Dakota and along the whole length of this vast reach of plains these Indians had built permanent habitations and had started the growing of crops and the development of a higher culture. In the quarter-century following the year 1700, this incipient civilization had been attacked and destroyed by bold new tribes from the mountains: by the Utes and Comanches coming from the west and by the tribes along the eastern borders of the plains, who had now obtained firearms from the French.

It is difficult to avoid the impression that this disaster to the Apaches and Padoucas was the direct result of the mean and bigoted Spanish Indian policy that prevented free trade and particularly trade in weapons with friendly Indians and refused these people any real assistance until after they had given up their freedom and accepted the life of submissive slavery at Spanish missions. They were the most friendly of the Apaches and Padoucas to whom the Spaniards of New Mexico refused assistance in their time of need. The Jicarillas, El Cuartelejos, and Palomas gave abundant evidence of their wish to be on good terms with the Spaniards from 1700 to 1720. These Apaches and Padoucas had more horses than any of the tribes that were attacking them, and all they needed to hold their lands and to form a barrier of friendly tribes along the New Mexican border was a more liberal Spanish trade policy that would permit them to obtain proper weapons and particularly firearms. Speaking blandly at councils and giving voice to earnest wishes to aid these Indian allies, the Spanish officials only tightened the trade restrictions and sat and watched the disaster sweep the screen of friendly Apaches from their northeastern borders, to be quickly replaced by hostile Comanches, equipped by free French traders with better guns than any Spanish soldier in New Mexico was permitted to carry.

# 5. The Comanche Advance

THERE IS an almost complete lack of written reports on events in the southern plains during the decade following the flight of the Kansas and Colorado Apaches in 1727. Either the Spanish records of New Mexico for this period have been destroyed or the New Mexican officials failed to realize what the shift of control in the high plains from the Apaches to the Comanches and their allies really meant. At any rate, this decade appears to have been a season comparatively free from Indian attacks, so that the Spanish officials had the opportunity to amuse themselves in their favorite occupation of filling reams of paper with reports concerning missions. In 1733, after writing endless reports on the subject for twelve years, they finally established a mission for the Jicarilla Apaches near Taos and induced 130 survivors of that tribe to submit to Christian discipline. This was a victory for the faith, a matter closer to the heart of the average New Mexican official than the task of protecting the province from Indian raids. In the same year an Indian neophyte came to divine service at Albuquerque naked and with hair braided in the style of a pagan warrior. He did it on the advice of his grandfather, who had no use for Christian Indians and their meek ways, and the whole of New Mexico was thrown into excitement as a result of this shocking affair.[1]

We also have no information from the French documents con-

[1] Bancroft, *History of Arizona and New Mexico*, 242n.

cerning the Plains Indians from 1724 to 1735, but we know that a French company had a monopoly of trade on the Missouri and that the French established a little trading post called Fort Cavagnol at the village of the Kansa tribe in eastern Kansas and made it their headquarters. They were also trading regularly with the tribes on the Arkansas in Oklahoma, those known in Santa Fé as the Pawnees and Jumanos. The French had armed the Osages, who were making bloody raids on the Pawnees and Caddoan Indians in eastern Okahoma. John Law had established a colony on the Mississippi in 1721, and the need of the colonists for horses and Indian slaves bade fair to ruin the southern Pawnees and Caddoans; for the Osages and other tribes were persistently raiding the Oklahoma Indians, to obtain horses and slaves to trade to the French. By about 1735 part of the Pawnees and Caddoans were so distressed by the raids that they abandoned their villages on the Arkansas and lower Canadian and retired into Texas, south of Red River, but the Jumanos remained on the Arkansas in northern Oklahoma.

Jumano was the Spanish name for these Indians. The Jumanos had been first seen by the Spanish explorers on the Río Grande; in the seventeenth century they had moved eastward and seem to have had villages on upper Red River. Even at the early period, around 1685, this tribe was engaged in trading horses and Spanish goods to neighboring Indians. Forced to withdraw from Red River, probably because of mounted Apache attacks, the surviving Jumanos went eastward and joined the Caddoan Indians on the Arkansas. They are not mentioned clearly after 1740, and the probability is that what remained of the Jumanos became merged into the Wichita and Tawehash tribes of southern Pawnees. The French did not employ the name Jumano for any separate group, but La Harpe noted some Jumanos among the Tawehash on the Canadian River in 1719. The French, when they first referred to the Indians on the Arkansas in 1702, termed them *Panis Noirs*, "Black Pawnees," and a trade with these Indians was soon started. As early as 1706 the Apaches at El Cuartelejo were complaining

94

to the Spaniards of the attacks being made on them by Pawnees and Jumanos armed with French guns.

The importance of all this in plains history lies in the fact that the French, having penetrated to El Cuartelejo, met the Comanches there in 1727, then evidently introduced that tribe to the Pawnees and Jumanos, and that the Comanches began to trade with these Indians, probably exchanging horses and captives taken from the Apaches for French firearms and other goods.

It must have been during this decade between 1727 and 1737 that the Comanches, enriched with horses and plunder taken from the Apaches, began to supply their northern kinsmen, the Shoshonis or Snakes, with horses and metal weapons; for by the year 1740 the Snakes had become a power in the plains of Wyoming and Montana, where they were making savage mounted raids on neighboring tribes. Thus the disaster to the Padoucas and Apaches in Kansas and eastern Colorado was producing repercussions felt as far as the upper Missouri in Dakota and the Saskatchewan in western Canada. It was also having its effect in Texas; for the Apaches, pressed hard and robbed of their horses by the Comanches, were attempting to recoup themselves by stealing horses in Texas. The governor of that province reported that around the year 1730 the "Apaches, Yita, and Testasagonia" were making raids in the San Antonio district. Here the Yitas are joined with the Apaches; but most probably they were Indians of mixed Ute-Apache blood. By pure surmise, they may have been the Yutajennes, an Apache group of the upper Canadian River district. The Surville map (1770) put the Testasagonias in the plains near Apaches who are known to have been on the Canadian up to 1730.

The position of the Utes during this obscure period after 1727 is another puzzle. The Ute groups that were in contact with northern New Mexico in 1700 were regarded as more important than the Comanches, whom they first brought to Taos; and in the war against the Colorado Apaches the Utes clearly took the lead up to about 1719. It was evidently the Utes, mainly, who drove the Apaches out of the rough hill country south of the

95

Arkansas; but after 1719 the reports were more concerned with the Comanches, who were evidently on and north of the Arkansas. When the Apaches were driven from their rancherias north of that river, it was apparently the Comanches who did most of the fighting. The Utes are not mentioned. Yet, with the Apaches gone from the Colorado plains, one would expect the Utes to have taken a leading part in the events that followed. They apparently now had a strong hold on the district in eastern Colorado south of the Arkansas; they were in closer touch with New Mexico than the Comanches farther northward; yet the Utes played a minor part in later events, and they were presently attacked by their former protégés, the Comanches, who drove them from the plains back into the Colorado mountains. It might be conjectured that the good fortune of the Comanches in meeting the French at El Cuartelejo in 1727 and in being introduced to the Jumanos soon after that date, thus assuring themselves a supply of French firearms, may have caused jealousy among the Utes, jealousy that later ended in open war, in which the Utes, with few guns in their hands, got the worst of it.

One thing is certain, and that is that, after driving the Apaches from the Colorado plains, the Comanches and Utes did not let up on their defeated enemies. They followed the fleeing Apaches and Padoucas, driving them in on the New Mexican border and continuing to raid them. They probably then extended their attacks to the Apaches of the Canadian River—the Limitas and Chipaynes of the North Canadian and the Faraons of the South Canadian. At just what date the Canadian River Apaches were driven from their rancherias we do not know; but the Faraons were still located in this district on the Surville map dated 1770. This map shows the Limitas north of the Faraons, with the Ae tribe east of the Faraons, apparently southeast of El Cuartelejo and near the head of Río Guadalupe, which flows south and passes by San Antonio. Here also are the Testasagonias, who were reported joining the Apaches and Yitas in raiding near San Antonio about the year 1730. This map is so distorted that it is impossible to locate any of the tribes accurately, and it is clearly out of date. It locates these Apaches, supposedly about 1770, in positions they had been driven out of thirty to forty years before. The map shows the Apaches Natages on Río de Natages, clearly the Pecos, and west of the Río Grande it shows the Mescaleros, on the head of Río Gila east of the Gila Apaches.

When they fled from the Comanches in 1727, the Colorado Apaches and Kansas Padoucas mostly gathered in the valley of La Jicarilla northeast of Taos, where the Jicarillas and some other bands had already established rancherias. The chiefs appealed again to the Spanish officials for a mission, knowing full well that the only way in which they could obtain any Spanish aid against their enemies was by embracing Christianity. The officials in Santa Fé started the usual leisurely Spanish proceedings: holding solemn conferences on a matter that had been under discussion for the past ten years, writing reports to Mexico City, and waiting six months for replies that settled nothing. In the midst of this performance the Comanches came down on the Apaches at La Jicarilla, slaughtering a large number and forcing the survivors to flee. The fugitive Apaches broke up into small groups; part of them set off to seek safety among the Navahos, part went to Taos, and the rest fled southward through the plains and sought shelter near the pueblo of Pecos, to the southeast of Santa Fé.[2] The group that went to Pecos was made up of survivors of the bolder and more independent bands: the Carlanas and El Cuartelejos of Colorado and the Palomas of Kansas. They built new rancherias on Río Galinas near Pecos and went off into the plains eastward to support themselves by hunting buffalo, coming back to their rancherias in spring to plant and in late summer to harvest their crops. In alliance with the Pecos Indians, they had that ancient pueblo town to fall back upon in case of enemy assaults on them. In need of horses—they had probably lost a great many during the Comanche raids on them in Colorado—these Apaches made friends with the Faraons and obtained new supplies of horses from them.

The Comanches and Utes did not follow the fleeing Apaches southward. That is, they did not move south with all their camps

[2] Thomas, *Plains Indians and New Mexico*, 18.

and people and occupy new lands; they took possession of the old Apache hunting grounds in the Colorado plains, but they clearly sent war parties southward, to find the Apaches in their new locations, to kill the men, to carry off women and children, and to steal horses. With few written records to aid us, we have to piece together, as best we can, a picture of conditions after the year 1726. The Comanches and Utes did not even occupy the pleasant valley of La Jicarilla after driving the Apaches out, and the Apaches (after camping at Taos for a time, vainly begging for Spanish aid against their enemies) returned to La Jicarilla, where they led a precarious existence for a number of years, in constant danger from Comanche and Ute raiders. They must have ventured into the plains for buffalo meat and hides, for this was their means of life. Probably they did as the Apaches near Pecos, leaving the women and children at the rancherias while the men made a swift and cautious movement to the buffalo range to hunt, keeping constantly on the watch for enemy war parties, and then hastening back to the rancherias with their meat and skins.

Just where the Ute and Comanche camps were is unknown to us. About 1730 the Utes known in New Mexico were divided into four groups: Yutas or Utes, Chaguaguas, Moachis, and Payuchis.[3] As far as one may judge, the first two of these Ute groups were the only ones that were associated with the Comanches in the plains, and the first group, the Yutas, were still located in the San Luis Valley region as late as 1726, their evident practice being to make annual buffalo hunts in the plains south of the Arkansas and then retire to winter in their mountain valley. As for the Chaguaguas, the name seems to be a Spanish spelling of *Saguache*, which in Colorado is sometimes written as it is pronounced, "Sawatch," and from these clues one might conjecture that the Chaguaguas originally occupied a district in the present Saguache County, Colorado, north of the Ute group in the San Luis Valley and south of the Comanches, who were in the parks farther northward. An eastern head-branch of the Purgatoire River today

[3] *Ibid.*, 131.

98

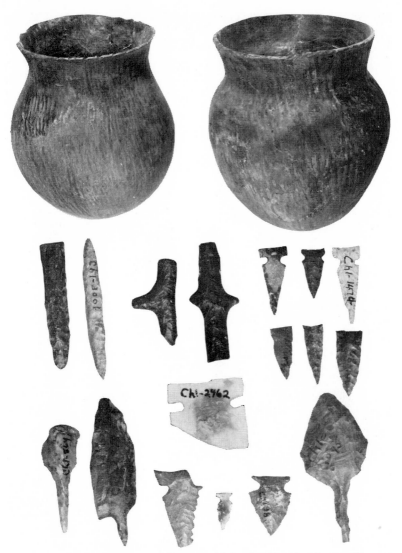

*Courtesy Nebraska Historical Society Museum*

Padouca pottery, arrowheads, and stone drills from the village ruins in western Nebraska.

Chief Ouray or Arrow and his wife about 1868 (Ute).

bears the name *Chaquaqua,* which is a hint that when the Apaches fled from the Colorado plains, the Chaguagua group of Utes occupied this district east of the present Trinidad and camped and hunted there. Indeed, all the clues we possess point to the probability that the Utes were primarily responsible for driving the Apaches out of the lands south of the Arkansas, while the Comanches operated mainly north of that river, and that the Arkansas was thus a kind of boundary between the Utes and Comanches.

Here we may mention the Ietans, that mysterious group that perhaps originated at the early period when the Utes and Apaches of southeastern Colorado were on friendly terms and intermarrying. The account of Spanish Louisiana, written at St. Louis in 1785, refers to the Ietans as Apaches and states that they were trading Indians, who supplied the tribes near the upper Missouri with horses and Spanish goods. This trade was an old one, in which the Gatakas or Prairie Apaches of Dakota had been engaged as far back as 1680, and the Ietans had apparently taken up the trade at a later date. Perhaps the Ietans were engaged in the intertribal trade before the Utes and Comanches started their attacks on the Colorado Apaches, and in some manner the trading Indians of the Ietan camp managed to hold out after the Apaches had been driven southward about 1727. Perhaps it was the mixture of Ute blood in their camp that enabled the Ietans to remain in Colorado after the Apaches had all fled.

The problem of the identity of the Ietans is further complicated by the fact that the Comanches were at times called Ietans. Lieutenant Zebulon M. Pike in 1806 used the name as that of all the Comanches, and the Pawnees of Nebraska termed the Comanches Laytanes while the Caddoan Indians of Red River on the Texas frontier called the Comanches Naytanes. These names are so similar to Ietan, allowing for the Pawnee and Caddoan pronunciation, that one is inclined to suspect a relationship between the Comanches and Ietans. One supposition is that originally this name might have been applied to the Utes in some such form as Iyuta and that the Pawnees and Caddoans, knowing that the Comanches were close kinsmen of the Utes, extended the designation to include people of both tribes. The camp of trading Indians, being partly of Ute blood, were also termed Ietans.[4]

In 1739 the Mallet brothers with a party of adventurous Canadian traders left the Missouri in eastern Nebraska and went to the Skidi Pawnee villages on the Loup Fork of the Platte. Here they probably obtained information about the route they were to take to reach New Mexico, for they went on up the Platte, then struck southward. They found the plains of eastern Colorado unoccupied; but perhaps this was a seasonal condition, the Indians having withdrawn toward the mountains after concluding their summer buffalo hunt. On the upper Arkansas, probably not far from the old Apache rancheria of El Cuartelejo, the Frenchmen contacted a camp of Ietans; but these Indians were unfriendly. They had in their camp at least one Arikara slave, taken from the tribe that lived on the Missouri in South Dakota, and this fact suggests that the Ietans were engaged in the business of passing back and forth between the New Mexican border and the Black Hills of Dakota, and that they had come south to obtain a supply of horses and Spanish goods, giving in barter northern Indian articles and slaves. They were camped near El Cuartelejo, in a district held by the Comanches and Utes, and they may have been on good terms with those tribes and trading with them. Yet these Ietans were hostile in their attitude toward the Mallet party of French traders, while the Comanches were on good terms with the French.

The Mallet brothers must have had excellent information, for they found their way from the Pawnees of Loup Fork in Nebraska to Santa Fé without difficulty. From the Arkansas River they went to La Jicarilla and thence to Taos and Santa Fé.[5] Strangest of all, the Spanish officials, who had strict orders to permit no intercourse with the French, received the nine Frenchmen of the

---

[4] It seems possible that the Ietans were identical with or related to the mysterious A or Ae tribe which was located south of the Arkansas in Oklahoma or Kansas on the Surville map. The Comanches were raiding the Aes in the middle of the eighteenth century, and after that the Aes disappeared.

[5] Mallet narrative, in Margry, *Découvertes et établissements*, VI.

Mallet party as friends, let them winter at Santa Fé, and actually permitted them to depart in the spring of 1740. Two of the nine remained in Santa Fé (Jean d'Alay and Louis Marie, as the Spanish records give the names). Heading eastward from Santa Fé, the Mallets struck the Canadian River; and here in the heart of the old Faraon and Limita Apache district, they saw only a few scattered groups of Padoucas, who were so frightened at the sight of strangers that they would not venture near the white men. Part of the Frenchmen now set off in a northerly direction to return to the Pawnees in Nebraska; the rest, led by the Mallet brothers, went on down the Canadian and down the Arkansas. They remained in Louisiana for a year and in 1741 returned to the Canadian River as guides for the French expedition that was intended to cross the plains to Santa Fé. When this expedition failed to accomplish anything, the Mallet brothers and some companions shouldered packs of trade goods and set out from near the mouth of the Canadian to cross the plains on foot. They were never heard of again, and as no Frenchmen reached New Mexico at that time (late in 1741 or early in 1742), they must have perished in the Oklahoma plains.

After Governor Bustamante left Santa Fé in 1731, his successors seem to have made no effort to deal with hostile Indians by sending expeditions against them. Bustamante's own pursuit of a Comanche band down the Arkansas was the last offensive effort of the Santa Fé garrison until 1746. On orders from the viceroy in Mexico City the New Mexican officials were testing a peace policy which meant, in effect, that if the Comanches and Utes made a raid, no reprisal was attempted, and when these Indians later came in peaceful guise to trade stolen horses and captives for Spanish articles at Taos, they were received as friends and urged to return at the time of next year's trading fair. This kind of peace, however, was not very satisfactory. The Utes had gone to war with the Navahos, and that tribe, hard beset, had developed a sudden longing for missions and baptism (also for a force of Spanish troops at the mission, who would aid them against their Ute foes). This plan for a Navaho mission went through the usual Spanish process of reports sent from Santa Fé to Mexico City and from Mexico City to Madrid, of instructions sent from Madrid and received in Santa Fé two years later. Meanwhile, the Utes had made such havoc in the Navaho country that the officials at Santa Fé had given up the plan for missions.

While the Utes were engaged in their war on the Navahos, the Comanches were occupying themselves in the plains; and here we may note the difference between these allied tribes, for the Utes in the main seem to have preferred to stay in and near the mountains, occupying themselves by raiding the Navahos and the Pueblo and Spanish settlements near the upper Río Grande, while the Comanches remained in the plains and pursued their war on the Apaches. By 1728 the Comanches must have had great numbers of horses and slaves taken from the Apaches; they were in need of trade; and as they seem to have met French traders only occasionally, they wished to trade regularly at Taos. But here they ran into Spanish trade restrictions. In 1726 the New Mexican officials issued a *bando* or prohibition against trade in firearms with wild Indians, Spanish offenders to be heavily fined and Pueblo Indians to receive one hundred lashes if caught trading arms to the gentiles. In 1737 a second *bando* forbade all trade with gentiles.

The trading fairs at Taos had probably existed before the Spaniards first came into New Mexico. The Plains Indians usually came with their camps and people to Taos in spring, from April to June, for only a little trading and a visit after their winter in the buffalo country. In spring the Taos people had little to trade, having used up most of their supplies of maize and vegetables during the winter. The big trading period was in autumn, and when the leaves began to turn, the Plains Indians flocked in with big camps, bringing dried meat and skins to exchange for maize and vegetables, Pueblo blankets, and painted pottery. After the Spanish occupation of New Mexico, European articles were added to the trading fairs, the Plains Indians being permitted to obtain knives, hatchets, sabre blades (to be made into lance points), tobacco, and other articles, but no firearms. The Spaniards always wanted Indian servants, and thus the trade in slaves was lively.

Horses also were in demand, and the Spaniards gave good prices to the Plains Indians, even for horses with Spanish brands. What if the animals had been stolen during raids on Spanish settlements? The brands were not local ones, and if the Spanish settlers in other districts were being raided by these Indians, that was no affair of the officials at Santa Fé and Taos. Whether the *bandos* forbidding trade were strictly enforced or not we do not know, but the Comanches appear to have obtained in some manner all the weapons and other supplies needed for prosecuting their war against the Apaches.

The few Jicarilla Apaches still left in northern New Mexico frequented the Taos fairs, but they were a broken people, with few horses and nothing but the baskets they made and other trifles to barter. The other Apaches from Kansas and Colorado—the Carlanas and their subordinate bands, the Sierra Blancas, El Cuartelejos, Palomas, and Calchufines—now had rancherias near Pecos on the eastern border of New Mexico. These bands were still free and still holding together, but their position was insecure. From the Spanish officials they received no support. Leaving their women and children at the rancherias, the men ventured into the plains to obtain buffalo meat and skins; and as they had lost most of their horses to the Comanches and Utes, they visited the Faraon Apaches of the South Canadian and obtained horses from them. But that only increased their difficulties; for the Faraons were regarded in New Mexico as the worst of miscreants, and since all the horses in the Faraons' possession were said to have been stolen in raids on Spanish settlers, the Apaches near Pecos were regarded as aiders and abettors of the hostile Faraons. And now the Comanches discovered these fugitive Apaches near Pecos and not only attacked them but extended the assault to the Pueblo Indians and Spanish settlers.

Up to this time the Comanches had made their raids from the north into the Taos district; but in 1744 they made their first big raid from the plains east of New Mexico, killing a number of Pueblo Indians at Pecos and driving their attack as far as Galisteo, only twenty miles south of Santa Fé. Continuing these attacks in

June, 1746, the Comanches again struck Pecos and Galisteo. The friendly Apaches near Pecos were evidently forced to flee, and Pecos itself was so severely shaken by the loss of men that the pueblo was almost defenseless. An incredible thing now happened. The submissive Spanish settlers, who were supposed to have no voice in public affairs, began to cry out for action against these hostile Indians, and presently the officials were forced to act.

They took eighteen months to get ready, holding councils at Santa Fé, sending messages to Mexico City, and months later obtaining a reply, which stated that the Governor of New Mexico must not make war on hostile Indians without special authority. The authorization finally arrived, and in October, 1748, Governor Rabal took the field with five hundred men, including Pueblo Indian allies. He did not march to Pecos, where the Comanches had been raiding, but went west of the Río Grande and north into the Chama River district, where he attacked a camp of Utes and Comanches, killing 107 of them, capturing two hundred Indians and one thousand horses. He then marched to Pecos and in January drove off a Comanche raiding party.

These events in New Mexico are obscure because of our lack of detailed contemporary information and the bitter factional quarrels that were going on among the Spaniards. The friars, a closely organized group with great influence in Mexico City and Madrid, were constantly trying to thwart the civil and military officers, whom they accused of causing Indian hostilities and of illegal trading to enrich themselves. They accused the governors of fabricating their reports of victories over the Comanches and Utes, and for this reason and others the historian H. H. Bancroft expressed doubts about the authenticity of these reports of military successes.

It does seem a little strange that Governor Rabal should have surprised the Utes and Comanches in the open near Abiquiu on Río Chama in October, 1748. That was the season when the Indians came into northern New Mexico on peaceful trading missions. Did the Governor attack such a camp and then report that it was one of hostile Indians? Without additional details we cannot judge. This district in the north had been ruined by Ute and Comanche raids; the pueblo of San Juan had lost half its population; Abiquiu, Ojo Caliente, Embuda, and Quesada had been completely abandoned. This was mainly the work of the Moachi and Chaguagua bands of Utes.

Some group in Santa Fé now got at the officials in Mexico City, and Governor Rabal's military career was cut short by an order from the higher officials for a junta or council of war, not to decide on further military operations but to deal with the question of whether hostile Indians should or should not be permitted to trade at Taos fairs. The military leaders voted to permit the Comanches to come in and trade, their opinion being (a quaint view for soldiers to hold) that if the Comanches were barred from trading, they would miss the Christian influences to which they were briefly exposed during visits at Taos, and thus, by barring these Indians, they would deprive them of their already slim chances of salvation.[6] No wonder the New Mexican settlements were being devastated by Indian raiders, with the leading military men at Santa Fé deciding war policy on theological premises. Quite obviously, no one expected the Comanches to accept baptism. They were too wild for that, but there was quite a trade at Taos in large silver crosses, which the Comanche men liked to wear on their breasts as war ornaments.

While the Spanish officials were busying themselves over the problem of exposing Comanche visitors to the beneficial effects of Christian contacts at Taos, the French were occupied in pushing their gun trade with this wild tribe. The Comanches now held all the old Apache lands along the New Mexican border; they were camping at the old Apache rancherias of La Jicarilla and El Cuartelejo, and while the Spaniards were still engaged with their scheme for drawing the Comanches to Taos for a little harmless trade, they were startled by news that thirty-three Frenchmen were camped with the Comanches at La Jicarilla, trading quantities of French muskets, and this within two days' march

[6] Bancroft, *History of Arizona and New Mexico*, 249; Thomas, *Plains Indians and New Mexico*, 17.

of Taos. There was also a report that the French were trading arms to the Comanches at El Cuartelejo. In 1749 the French arranged an alliance between the Comanches and the Caddoan tribes on Red River and in East Texas, tribes with whom the French had a regular trade. This French arrangement greatly broadened the field of Comanche activity, bands of Comanches going all the way down to Red River and to the Jumano villages on the Arkansas in eastern Oklahoma. To aid their new Caddoan allies, the Comanches joined in attacks on the Osages and the Kansa tribe of eastern Kansas. They also learned of the Spanish settlements in Texas, where they presently began to raid.[7]

Another important result of the coming of the French to the Comanche camps in 1748 was the breaking up of the old alliance between the Utes and Comanches. Just why the Comanches should have turned against the Utes we do not know; but Indian alliances rarely had deep roots, and the probability is that the Comanches, having been first introduced at Taos as protégés of the Utes, having obtained horses and other wealth with Ute aid, now found themselves in alliance with the French and in possession of French guns, which caused them to forget their indebtedness to the Utes. All they needed was an excuse for attacking that tribe, and it probably was not difficult to find one. The Utes, heavily engaged in their war on the Navahos, found that their bands frequenting the Colorado plains south of the Arkansas were under Comanche attack. The assault must have been sudden and sharp, for the trouble seems to have come in 1749, and the next year the Utes stopped raiding into northern New Mexico and startled the Spanish officials by begging for protection from the Comanches. Obtaining no aid from the Spanish, the Utes actually made an alliance with the broken bands of Apaches in northern New Mexico, with the Apaches they and the Comanches had driven out of the Colorado plains.

This Ute-Comanche war made abundant trouble for the New Mexican officials. Governor Velez Cachupin had to take special

[7] The arming of the Comanches by the French and Jumanos seems to date mainly after 1745.

precautions to prevent the Comanches and Utes, and the Apache allies of the latter tribe, from turning the peaceful Taos trading fair into a battleground. At this period every Comanche warrior who came to Taos had a new French musket, two pounds of powder, and a pouch filled with musket balls. The warriors were better armed than the Spanish soldiers, and they were ready to fight anyone. Naturally, the cautious Spanish officials favored the hostile Comanches. They were afraid of them, and they did not dare to take the side of the more friendly Utes and Apaches. In mid-August, 1752, the three principal Ute chiefs, Don Tomás of the Yutas, Chiquito of the Moachis, and Barrigon of the Chaguaguas, came to the pueblo of San Juan with one hundred lodges of their people, bringing large supplies of skins and other articles for trade, and the Spanish officials seem to have been afraid that permitting these Utes to trade might anger the Comanches.

The Comanche attacks on the Utes from 1749 on ended the chance of the latter tribe to become real Plains Indians. The Utes, as stated in later times, claimed the country in southeastern Colorado as far as the headwaters of the Cimarron, but by 1755 they were driven from these lands by the Comanches and forced back into the mountains.

Having dealt with the Utes, the Comanches devoted themselves to the exploitation of the lands in the plains south of the Arkansas, and it was probably at this time, around the year 1750, that they drove the last of the Padoucas or Apaches from the upper Canadian and advanced southward to Red River. The Faraon Apaches had held the South Canadian lands; the Apache bands called Limitas and Chipaynes had held the North Canadian, as late perhaps as 1735; but after 1740 the Comanches from the north and the Caddoan Indians of Red River, liberally equipped with French firearms, joined forces and drove these Apaches from the Canadian. Perhaps it was not until the French made an alliance between the Comanches and the Caddoan Indians in 1749 that the final blow fell. In Texas the Caddoan tribes on upper Red River were known as the Nations of the North, and a Spanish document of the late eighteenth century, quoted by Alfred B. Thomas, states that the Faraon Apaches at an earlier date had been forced to flee from their "old pueblos of El Norte" when they were attacked by the Nations of the North. In plain words, these Faraons and other Canadian River Apaches had been driven from their rancherias by the Caddoan tribes, probably aided by the Comanches.[8]

Indeed, as a result of the arming of the Comanches and the Caddoan tribes by the French in 1748–50, all the Apaches in the plains east of New Mexico were driven farther to the south and west, and a combined Comanche and Caddoan assault on the Lipan Apaches of West Texas was begun. The remnants of the Kansas and Colorado Apaches that had taken refuge near Pecos vanished from that district, evidently retreating down the Pecos River to a point east of Albuquerque; the Faraons also retired to the Pecos country, and in 1752 they were making raids from the Pecos on Albuquerque and joining the Natage Apaches, who were to the south of them, in raiding into the Mexican province of Nueva Vizcaya. The Sierra Blancas of the old Jicarilla group, first mentioned in southeastern Colorado, had fled first to La Jicarilla northeast of Taos, then to Pecos Pueblo east of Santa Fé, and then on southward to Pecos River east of Albuquerque. In 1777 these Sierra Blancas were west of the Río Grande, allied to the Gila Apaches, into which group they probably merged. Other Colorado and Kansas Apaches probably joined the Arizona Apaches after fleeing from one district to another to escape from the Comanches.

With the Kansas and Colorado Apaches dispersed in flight and the Faraons and other Apaches of the upper Canadian forced to remove to the Río Pecos, it was now the turn of the Lipans of Texas and their Natage or Lipiyan cousins to feel the power of the Comanche thrust southward. As late as 1730 the Apaches were the principal troublemakers in Texas, raiding the Spanish

[8] Thomas, *Teodoro de Croix*, 143. The flight of the Faraons from the Canadian may have been after 1750, for they were still there in 1749, as Governor Cachupin reported in that year that the Colorado and Kansas Apaches were still near Pecos and were going east into the plains, to trade with the Faraons for horses (Thomas, *Plains Indians and New Mexico*, 135).

settlers near San Antonio. There were still no signs of the Comanche approach. The Natages were the main Apache group in
the district west of the Staked Plains and east of the Río Grande
in the El Paso region; part of the fleeing Kansas and Colorado
Apaches had joined the Natages, and they were raiding in the
Albuquerque district and also beyond the Río Grande into Mexico. The Faraons from Canadian River joined the Mescaleros. As
for the original Mescaleros, they seem to make their first appearance on the Surville map of 1770, which shows Tierra de los
Apaches Mescaleros on the head of Gila River west of the Río
Grande. The modern Mescalero tribe appears to be a very mixed
group embracing descendants of the Faraons, Natages, Colorado
Apaches, and other groups that had fled from the plains in the
eighteenth century. Curiously, the first modern Mescalero band
bears the name *Natah* (Natage?) with the meaning given as "Mescal People."[9]

The Comanches must have possessed themselves of the old Faraon lands on the upper Canadian by 1749–50. Some Comanche
chiefs, giving information in New Mexico about that date, in-
sisted that none of their bands were living south of the Río
Napestle—the Arkansas, but this was clearly not true.[10] The Comanches probably still regarded the country north of the Arkansas as their homeland and returned there frequently, but they
must have moved south of the Arkansas before they made the
first raid at Pecos in 1744. They were established at La Jicarilla
northeast of Taos in 1748, and in 1749–52 they were again in the
plains east of New Mexico, probably on or near the Canadian.
This we know from reports of French traders and from the story
of the Cachupin expedition of 1751.

Velez Cachupin became governor of New Mexico in April,
1749, his instructions being to keep peace with the wild Plains
Indians, and one of the first acts of the new governor was to
notify the Comanches that they would be welcome at Taos. But

[9] Thomas, *Forgotten Frontiers*, 323; Hodge, *Handbook of American Indians*,
I, 846.
[10] Thomas, *Plains Indians and New Mexico*, 115. These chiefs stated that their
bands came south of the Arkansas only to raid and trade.

keeping peace with Comanches was not a simple matter of good will. These Indians saw nothing out of the way with their habit of raiding in New Mexico at certain seasons and then coming to Taos to trade their plunder for other articles which they needed.

Up to 1751 the Comanches were reported to have killed about five hundred Spaniards and Pueblo Indians; yet the Spanish authorities in Mexico City had no policy except that of appeasing these wild Indians by letting them trade at Taos. The Comanche chiefs who came to Taos to talk to Governor Cachupin were El Oso (the Bear), who was described as a little king whom all the Comanches obeyed, and his lieutenants, Nimircante and Guanacante. To which Comanche group they belonged is not stated. The chiefs were very friendly, but presently (in July, 1751) five hundred Comanches appeared at Pecos and attempted to make a raid. They had only six guns among them, as the Spanish report states, and ten soldiers and the Pecos Indian men held them off. Governor Cachupin now forgot the peace policy, and with a pick-up force of 164 Spaniards and Pueblo Indians he went to Galisteo and found the trail of the raiders, which first led southward through the sierras and canyons and then eastward into the plains, where the Indians divided into two groups. Following the trail of one party, Cachupin came on their camp at some springs and waterholes. He evidently took them by surprise, as the report states that the Indians fled into a *tulare* which the Spaniards and Pueblo allies set on fire, killing 101 Comanches and capturing all the survivors. The Cachupin report is vague as to the location of this fight, but it was evidently in the dry plains east of Pecos. The Comanche captives stated that the camp of five hundred was made up from two Comanche bands; that they had come from north of the Napestle (Arkansas River), leaving most of the women and children in their home camps. They were probably northern bands, for the Comanches who came to trade at Taos at this date all had new guns, obtained from the French either at La Jicarilla or in the plains to the east, but this war party of five hundred Comanches that Cachupin followed is said to have had only six guns.[11]

That there were Comanches in the plains east of New Mexico at this period was again shown by the story of some French traders who reached New Mexico in the spring of 1749. They stated that they had left the Jumano village on the Arkansas, in what is now northern Oklahoma, and had been guided across 150 leagues of plains to a Comanche camp. They found the Comanches preparing to attack the Ae tribe—a most interesting bit of news, as the Aes were either Apaches or Ietans, and from this report they were clearly in the plains south of the Arkansas in 1749 and near enough for the Comanches to raid them. These Frenchmen were evidently taken to New Mexico by some Comanches, for they came in at Taos, the usual Comanche trading place.[12]

The Spanish authorities in Madrid and Mexico City had forbidden any intercourse with foreigners in New Mexico, which meant that the French were not to be permitted to enter; yet, from 1720 on, the French had constantly striven to open a trade with Santa Fé. In 1739 the Mallet brothers and their party had entered New Mexico, and instead of being arrested, they had been permitted to live in freedom at Santa Fé all winter and to depart freely in the spring of 1740. In New Mexico there was much whispering that the Governor and other officials were shutting their eyes to French intrusions and secretly profiting from trade with the French. The welcome the Mallets had received suggests that there was something in these rumors; and, what with the high prices and bad quality of the Spanish goods New Mexicans had to purchase from the Spanish trade monopoly, we must suppose that both the people and the officials in New Mexico were eager to obtain good quality French articles at low prices. The French in Illinois and Louisiana must have learned from the Mallets what conditions were in New Mexico, and what they learned apparently encouraged them to make fresh efforts to take stocks of goods across the plains to Santa Fé.

In 1744 a French trader whose name is given in the Spanish documents as Santiago Velo reached Santa Fé from Illinois; in 1748

[11] *Ibid.*, 63–64; Bancroft, *History of Arizona and New Mexico*, 256.
[12] Thomas, *Plains Indians and New Mexico*, 19.

French traders were trading with the Comanches both at El Cuartelejo and La Jicarilla, close to Taos; in 1749 the party of Frenchmen from Louisiana, coming from the Jumano village to the Comanches in the plains, succeeded in reaching Santa Fé. In 1751, Jean Chapuis left Canada and went to Illinois, where he and his friends obtained a French permit to seek a trade route to New Mexico. Chapuis and his partners had a large stock of goods. They went up the Missouri in boats, stopping in December, 1751, at Fort Cavagnol, the French trading post among the Kansa Indians. They then went up the Platte and to the Skidi Pawnee villages. Here they traded for horses and obtained information concerning the country toward Santa Fé. Chapuis stated when questioned by the Spanish officials that eight members of the party refused to venture beyond the Pawnee villages and that he and one French companion crossed the plains alone; and the confiding officials at Santa Fé accepted this tale, although these two lone Frenchmen could not possibly have crossed the plains by themselves with the nine horses heavily loaded with goods with which they arrived at Pecos. They must have left their eight companions trading in some Comanche camp. At any rate, Chapuis did claim that the two of them had made this journey. They had met a camp of Comanches and had tarried with them for some time; they had found an Indian woman of the Ae tribe in the lands north of the Arkansas, and she had guided them to a camp of Apaches on Río Galinas, fifteen leagues from Pecos; the Apaches had then brought them to Pecos, where they arrived August 6, 1752.[13]

Chapuis and his companion were held, and their goods were seized. The ultimate fate of the Frenchmen seems to be unknown; but what is important in plains history is the fact that the Chapuis party left the Skidi Pawnees in Nebraska, contacted the Comanches, then met the Ae tribe, or at any rate one Ae woman, who guided them straight to a Carlana and Jicarilla camp near Pecos. Father Toledo of Pecos stated that this Ae woman had been a slave in New Mexico and had run away in the spring of

[13] *Ibid.*, Chapuis reports, 82, 90, 104–109.

1752 to rejoin her tribe. The muddled Spanish reports term her an Ae, an Apache, and a Canosso, which last may be a Spanish form of Canecy, a common name for the Apaches of the southern plains in the eighteenth century. It is difficult to believe that Jean Chapuis and his friend ran into this woman by accident in the plains near the Arkansas. The probability is that from the Comanche camp they passed on to an Ae camp and that the Aes took them to the Apache camp near Pecos, the Apaches then escorting them to that place. At any rate, we here have evidence that part of the Colorado Apaches, the Carlanas and Jicarillas, were still near Pecos in August, 1752, and that the mysterious Ae tribe was out in the plains toward the northeast, and evidently on good terms with these Apaches.

The result of these French activities, and particularly of the French effort to form an alliance of the Comanches with the Jumanos and southern Pawnees, apparently accelerated the movement of some Comanche bands into the lands south of the Arkansas. These Comanches were evidently on or near the Canadian in 1749; ten years later they were camping on Red River and trading at the fortified village of the Tawehash or southern Pawnees, in the western edge of the Upper Cross Timbers. It was these Pawnees, the "Nations of the North" as the Spaniards of Texas called them, who were credited by the Spaniards with the driving of the Faraon Apaches from their rancherias on the South Canadian. That must have happened about 1750, and now the Comanches were aiding the Tawehash and their Caddoan kinsmen in a crusade against the Lipan Apaches of western Texas. In 1751 the Comanche chiefs who came to Taos and talked with Governor Cachupin stated that their main camps were still north of the Arkansas and that they came into the southern plains only to make raids and to visit their allies, the Jumanos and the Pawnees of Red River.[14]

The Lipan Apaches had been in the upper Red River district perhaps as far back as 1670, and they apparently extended down to the upper valleys of the Colorado River and Brazos in Texas.

[14] Ibid., 115.

They lived in villages, probably similar to the Apache rancherias in the plains farther to the north. They were a numerous tribe, and with the advantage of having horses and some metal weapons they had driven several of the Caddoan tribes from their old lands and forced them to retire eastward by the close of the seventeenth century. Then the French from Louisiana began to trade firearms to the Caddoans, who had also acquired horses, by stealing them from the Apaches, and by 1720 the Lipan Apaches were having a hard struggle to hold their own. Still, as late as 1730, they were the dominant tribe on upper Red River and in northern Texas, and, with the aid of allies who occupied the plains between the Arkansas and Red River (the Apaches, Yitas and Testasagonia mentioned by the Spanish governor of Texas in 1730), they played a large part in the wrecking of the Spanish settlements and missions in Texas, forcing the Spaniards to abandon East Texas and concentrate their little settlements in the San Antonio district.

But now the strong Caddoan groups, the Tawehash and Tawakonis, were forced to withdraw from the Arkansas in eastern Oklahoma by Osage raiders, and retired to Red River, where the Tawehash built a fortified village in the western edge of the Upper Cross Timbers about 1735. The Tawakonis came to the same district, and then the Comanches came down through the plains and began to visit and trade at these Caddoan villages. Soon after this the Spaniards at San Antonio noted a falling off in Lipan attacks. The Lipans came in and pretended friendship; they began to ask for a mission; and when any wild Apaches did that it was a safe conclusion that some stronger tribe was attacking them so violently that they were seeking safety, even if they had to enter the sheep fold of a mission to obtain it.

The Spaniards went about it in their leisurely way. They discussed a mission on Río Guadalupe for the Lipans from 1750 to 1754, with the Lipans shouting for immediate help. Getting down to it in 1756, the Lipan mission was actually established in April, 1757, on Río San Sabá, a western branch of the Colorado River, near the present Menard, Texas. But the mission had hardly been

A Comanche (*left*) and a Paiute (*right*) in native dress.

Peso or Pacer, a Prairie Apache chief.

built when the friars discovered that the Lipans had no intention
of becoming Christian converts and settling down under the control of the church. These Indians intended to continue their old
custom of wandering in the plains, hunting buffalo and raiding,
and they wanted the mission solely as a safe place where they
could plant their small crops and run in to seek the protection of
the Spanish troops at the mission when hard pressed by enemies.
The mission once established, the Lipans went off to spend the
winter in the plains, leaving the friars to their own devices.

Up to this time there had been no mention of Comanches in
Texas, but in March, 1758, two thousand Comanches and Tawehash appeared at San Sabá and under pretense of friendship got
inside the mission. They apparently found a few Lipans and made
that the excuse for starting a fight, during which they killed two
friars and all the other Spaniards within reach and then destroyed
the mission buildings.[15]

Most of the Lipans were away when this attack on their mission
came. It is said that they knew what was coming and warned the
Spaniards, then fled into the western plains. They abandoned their
old haunts on the Colorado and Brazos, remaining farther westward; but in the summer of 1759 when Captain Parilla gathered
a Spanish force of Five hundred men at San Antonio with the
object of marching against the Tawehash and their Comanche
allies, the Lipans contributed a large force of their warriors to
the expedition. They guided Parilla to a Caddoan village near Red
River, which was taken by surprise, fifty-five Indians being killed;
but, on reaching the Tawehash town on Red River, in the present
Ringgold neighborhood, it was found that the village was fortified,
being surrounded by a deep ditch with palisades inside the ditch,
and six thousand Caddoans and Comanches had assembled inside
the fortifications. Captain Parilla attempted to storm the village,
but even with cannon he could not break in. The Lipans are said
to have fought bravely, but when they saw that the Spaniards were

[15] Lockwood, *The Apache Indians*, 16; Bancroft, *History of North Mexican
States and Texas*, I, 626. Bancroft states that one thousand Tawehash and Tawakonis were with the Comanches. See also Hodge, *Handbook of American Indians*, II, 705.

making no progress, they lost heart, and presently the whole of Parilla's little army was in retreat. He abandoned two of his bronze cannons, which were long exhibited by the Tawehash as trophies of victory.

The Caddoan and Comanche warriors followed Parilla almost the whole way back to San Antonio. They were armed with French guns and were full of fight, but Parilla got his men home safely.

The Spanish settlers in Texas were in despair. They wished to abandon the country, but the all-powerful friars refused to give up their dying missions and obtained an order from Mexico City for the settlers to remain where they were. A kind of temporary peace with the Comanches and Caddoan tribes was made about 1760, and in 1761 two Lipan missions, San Lorenzo and Cande-laría, were established, and four hundred Lipans were induced to come to them; but by 1767 even the friars admitted that the Lipan missions were dismal failures, and they were abandoned. The Comanches and Caddoans of Red River broke the peace and resumed raiding. The Lipans became hostile and also began to raid, and the little Texas colony at San Antonio was in a dreadful plight. The Comanche warriors, raiding beyond San Antonio, came to the shore of the sea. They had gone as far southward as they could, and seeking a new direction for their raids they turned westward, crossed the Río Grande and made their first raids into Mexico.

Thus, in just half a century, the Comanches, coming out of the Colorado mountains, had driven the Apaches from the plains, all the way from the Arkansas to the Texas coast. The supine Spanish officials had sat and watched while the Comanches stripped the barrier of Apache tribes away from the frontiers of New Mexico and Texas. Now those frontiers were wide open to Comanche attacks. Texas was already ruined; New Mexico was impoverished; but beyond the Río Grande lay the older, settled provinces of Mexico, where horses and other plunder offered an apparently inexhaustible field to Comanche raiding parties.

# 6. Rise of the Gens du Serpent

THE COMANCHES by 1750 had driven the Apaches from the plains, had fought a war with their former allies, the Utes, and had made themselves masters of the southern plains. How far to the north their power extended is a matter shrouded in mystery, our only information coming from the Spanish records of New Mexico which state vaguely that this tribe held districts in the north to about the latitude of the Platte River; but the Spaniards had rarely been more than a few miles north of the Arkansas River, and their knowledge of the northern country, obtained from scanty Indian information, was extremely vague. The Spanish officials knew of no tribes in the northern plains except the Comanches, but from the French and British traders of western Canada we obtain, after the year 1730, the information that the most important tribe in the plains of the present states of Montana and Wyoming was the Snake Nation, or *Gens du Serpent*, as the French termed these Indians.

The Snakes were very closely related by blood and language to the Comanches, and even today both these peoples retain a tradition that the Comanches were originally Snakes, who split off from that tribe long ago and wandered off southward. For this reason, the information that the Snakes controlled the northern plains from at least as early as 1730 is of great interest, for after 1800 the Snakes were not in the plains, but occupied the semidesert country west of the Rockies, and they were in the main a disorganized and unwarlike people, mostly afoot and utterly unlike the bold Horse Indians of the plains. Moreover, the basin-plateau country west of the mountains was always the homeland of the Snakes and their Shoshonean kindred, and, as few of the Snakes in the nineteenth century had the characteristics of the plains-dwelling tribes, some ethnologists have expressed strong doubts that any large number of Snakes ever held lands in the plains. But the evidence seems to be conclusive that the old Gens du Serpent or Snake Nation of the northern plains did hold most of the lands in Montana and Wyoming and that they were a numerous people.

In the seventeenth century the Snakes probably held the lands west of the Rockies that they still occupied after the year 1800: the country from Utah Lake, Great Salt Lake, and the Uinta Mountains northward to Snake River in Utah and Idaho, a vast area of semidesert lands, where in primitive times food was difficult to obtain, and the Indians (split up into small, loosely organized groups, all on foot) spent the whole of their lives wandering about, seeking for something to eat. There was little big game. Rabbit-snaring was a principal business of these poor Indians, and, whereas the Plains Indians made handsome garments of buffalo, antelope, and elk skins ornamented with dyed porcupine-quill embroidery and colored plumes, the Snakes west of the mountains —when they had any clothing at all—had beaver robes and robes made by cutting rabbit skins into narrow strips and weaving a furry fabric. They also made robes of woven strips of sage bark. They were too preoccupied with finding something to eat to care much about housing, and a common type of shelter was a mere roofless windbreak of sagebrush piled up to form a semicircle. The very names they gave to their groups indicate their absorption in the quest for food. The Snakes or Shoshonis were divided into Root Eaters, Rabbit Eaters, Squirrel Eaters, Salmon Eaters, Seed Eaters, Pine Nut Eaters, and one poor group was known as the Earth Eaters. The Mountain Sheep Eaters in the north were the only group named for any game animal that the proud Plains Indians would have condescended to hunt or eat.

Toward the end of each winter food ran out in most of the little Snake camps; the people starved, and early in the nineteenth century there was a story current among American beaver trappers in the mountains to the effect that every spring the Utes came north into the Snake country, knowing that the Snakes would be too weak from hunger even to attempt to run away, and, after killing as many Snake men as they desired, the raiders seized large numbers of women and children and carried them off, to be sold as slaves in New Mexico.[1] These poor Snakes were so immersed in food-gathering that they apparently did not organize themselves into real tribes. They had few social assemblies; dances and ceremonies, so dear to the hearts of the true Plains Indains, seem to have been little known among the Snakes west of the mountains. They had no chiefs, unless we care to consider the leading man in a group of several families a chief. They had neither the time nor the equipment needed for warfare on an organized scale, and in the early nineteenth century many of the Snakes were rated as too timid to engage in fighting.

That such Indians as these Snakes should have ventured across the mountains and out into the plains may seem improbable; but the Snakes were the same race as the Utes and Comanches, and we know that both those tribes had the hardihood to leave their home west of the Rockies and enter the plains at an early date. The picture of Snake timidity and disorganization was drawn after the year 1800, after these Indians had been terrorized over a long period of time by enemies armed with guns, and—theorizing aside—one piece of solid evidence concerning the Snakes at the period 1700–30 exhibits them as a warlike tribe, making long expeditions on foot to attack the Blackfeet.

In the winter of 1787, David Thompson of the Hudson's Bay Company was in a camp of Piegan Blackfeet on Bow River near the present Calgary, and here he met an aged Cree Indian of unusual intelligence who gave him a clear account of the history of the Piegans. He stated that in the years 1725–30 the Piegans

[1] Steward, "Basin-Plateau Aboriginal Sociopolitical Groups," Bureau of American Ethnology *Bulletin No. 120*, 8–9.

were near the Eagle Hills between the forks of the Saskatchewan, and to the south and southwest of them in the plains were the Snakes, Kutenais, and Flatheads. These three tribes were warring on the Piegans, the Snakes being particularly troublesome. At times the Snakes came and attacked the Piegan camps; at other times the two tribes met in the plains, all afoot, and fought in battle array, the warriors sheltering behind big shields. This was in primitive times, before the Snakes obtained horses and metal weapons.[2]

Here we have firsthand evidence from a Cree Indian, speaking of events that had occurred in his own lifetime—information that outweighs all the theorizing of modern ethnologists and historians. It proves that the Snakes were in the northern plains before 1730 and that, while still afoot, they were an aggressive tribe, sending war parties for ten days' journeys from their own lands, to raid enemy tribes. And the Cree account is supported by the Indian traditions collected by James A. Teit among the Flatheads and Kutenais and the Salishan tribes west of the Rockies in recent years.[3] By these traditions the Flatheads once lived in several big bands in the plains east of the Rockies in the district from the Three Forks of the Missouri north and east beyond the present Helena to the Little Belt Mountains and north to Sun River. To the north the plains were held by the Kutenais, from Sun River north beyond Teton River. The Snakes were in the plains to the south, southwest, and east of the Flatheads, occupying the lands of the present Yellowstone Park, upper Yellowstone River, the district around the present town of Billings, and the lands now included in the Crow and Northern Cheyenne reservations. In fact, the traditions picture the plains Snakes as living to the east of the Flathead lands near the Three Forks of the Missouri, the Snakes extending east of the Bighorn Range and north to the Sweet Grass Hills near the Canadian line. The Kutenais, living

2 John C. Ewers, *The Blackfeet: Raiders on the Northwestern Plains,* 15 (from David Thompson's *Narrative*); Secoy, *Changing Military Patterns,* 34-36, 38. The Pine Ridge Sioux used to call the Shoshonis "Big Shields."

3 "The Salishan Tribes of the Western Plateaus," Bureau of American Ethnology *Forty-fourth Annual Report.*

north of the Flatheads, extended eastward into the plains and were in touch with the Snakes near the Canadian border.

The Teit traditions are impressive; but when Teit and his Indian informants assume that the period the traditions refer to goes back to 1600, about which date they think horses were first obtained by these northern Plains Indians, it should be observed that the traditions are much too definite and clear-cut to go back that far. Besides, the information of the old Cree Indian and some other material indicate that horses were not introduced here in the north until after 1730, and part of the Teit traditions, one suspects, refers to a time later than the year 1800. The Teit material is important, but the dating too early.

Our other sources agree with the Teit material in locating large bodies of Snake Indians in the northern plains at an early date. From such materials we can even surmise the identity of the Snake group that was attacking the Piegans in 1730. They were evidently the Lemhi Shoshonis of later times, called *Tukuarika* or Mountain Sheep Eaters. At the period 1800–10 the Lemhis were still allied to the Kutenais and Flatheads, the three groups often going through the mountains to hunt buffalo together in the Three Forks district at the head of the Missouri. Lewis and Clark in 1805 met a camp of these Snakes just west of the Rockies at the head of Salmon River. These Indians had spent the winter hunting buffalo east of the mountains, and they informed Lewis and Clark that within the memory of living men their people had lived east of the mountains in the Montana plains, but that, being attacked by the Blackfeet, who were armed with guns, and by other enemies similarly equipped, they had been compelled to give up their old lands in the plains and retire west of the Rockies. But they still had the habit of going east of the mountains to winter in the buffalo plains, coming back across the mountains in early summer and joining other Snake groups to fish for salmon. For this reason they were often called Salmon Eaters. In 1805 they had some tipis of the Plains type and perhaps even a few firearms, but they were still using obsidian and flint to make arrowheads, knives, and other implements.

To the south of the Lemhis after the year 1800 were the Pohogue or Fort Hall Snakes of Snake River, and presumably the
Pohogues were included among the Snakes who had formerly
dwelled in the plains of the upper Yellowstone; for even after
1805 they were going at times into those plains to hunt, and they
were reported also to be going through passes that led to the
buffalo country at the Three Forks of the Missouri. *Pohogue* is
said to have been their name for themselves. It apparently refers
to sagebrush—People of the Sage—and part of this group, under
the name of *Pohoi*, "Wild Sage People,"[4] are known to have gone
south either late in the eighteenth or early in the nineteenth century to join the Comanches and become a part of that tribe. Indeed, what information we have concerning this Pohogue group
hints that they were with the Snakes in the Yellowstone region,
in touch with the Lemhi Snakes to the north and with the Comanches toward the south in the eighteenth century.

The third and last Snake group that may have occupied the
plains in the eighteenth century were the Kogohol, Kogohue,
or Wyoming Shoshonis of later times. The modern representatives
of this last group of plains Snakes are undoubtedly of very mixed
origin, but they have among them the descendants of the old Snake
tribe that claimed lands from near Great Salt Lake and the Uinta
Mountains eastward to Wind River Valley and the upper North
Platte. Indeed, they are descended from the Snakes who lived
in close contact with the Yamparika Comanches, and these Wyoming Shoshonis still have a tradition that the Comanches were
originally a part of their tribe. There seems to be no doubt of
the truth of this, for as late as 1776 part of the Yamparikas were
still in the lands north of the Uinta Mountains, and Spanish reports from New Mexico asserted that this group of Comanches

[4] Pohogue was the name of the Fort Hall Shoshonis for their own group.
Granville Stuart, *Forty Years on the Frontier*, said that Pohogwas (Sagebrush
River) was the Snake Indian name for upper Snake River, above the Clearwater;
but Philip Ashton Rollins, the editor of Robert Stuart's journal, states (p. 172)
that Peaogoie (seemingly the same as Pohogue) meant "Sage Hen River" and
was the Snake name for Green River. *Canna-ra-o-gwa*, "Poor River," referring
to poor soil and scanty grass in some places, was a name for Green River used
in the late nineteenth century.

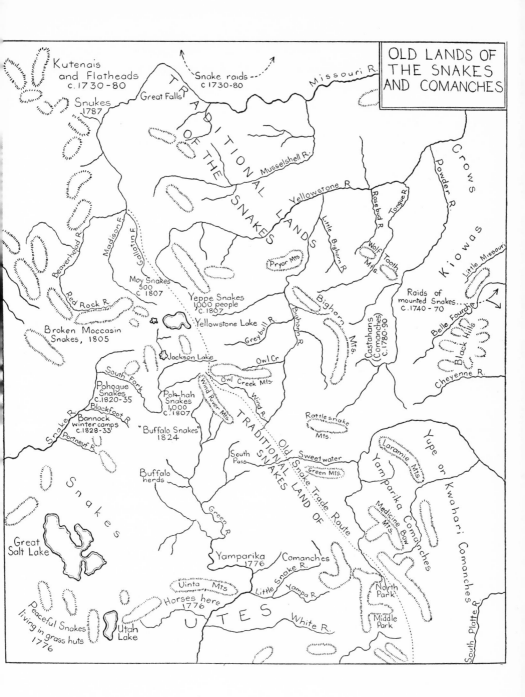

OLD LANDS OF
THE SNAKES
AND COMANCHES

Kutenais
and Flatheads
c.1730-80

Snake raids
c 1730-80

Missouri R.

Great Falls

Snakes
1787

TRADITIONAL

Musselshell R.

Crows

OF

Yellowstone R.

Powder R.

Rosebud R.

Tongue R.

Kiowas

Beaverhead R.

THE

Madison R.

Pryor Mts.

Little Bighorn R.

Wolf Tooth Mts.

Little Missouri

Gallatin F.

SNAKES

Red Rock R.

Moy Snakes
500
c.1807

Yeppe Snakes
1,000 people
c.1807

Yellowstone Lake

Greybull R.

Bighorn R.

Bighorn Mts.

Castahans
(Comanches)
c.1780-90

Belle Fourche

Black Hills

Raids of
mounted Snakes
c.1740-70

Broken Moccasin
Snakes, 1805

Cheyenne R.

Jackson Lake

Owl Cr

Owl Creek Mts.

South Fork

Pohogue
Snakes
c.1820-35

Poh-hah
Snakes
1,000
c.1807

Wind River Mts.

Wind R.

Rattlesnake
Mts.

Yupe or Kwahari Comanches

Blackfoot R.

Bannock
winter camps
c.1828-33

"Buffalo Snakes"
1824

TRADITIONAL

Sweetwater

Laramie Mts.

Yamparika Comanches

Portneuf R.

SNAKES

Buffalo
herds

South
Pass

LAND

Green Mts.

OF

Medicine Bow Mts.

Snake R.

S n a k e s

Great
Salt Lake

Buffalo
herds

Green R.

Old Snake Trade Route

Yamparika
1776

Comanches

Little Snake R.

Yampa R.

North
Park

Uinta Mts

Horses here
1776

U T E S

White R.

Middle
Park

South Platte R.

Peaceful Snakes
living in grass huts
1776

Utah
Lake

extended northward from the Arkansas River to a river which was almost certainly the North Platte.

To these groups of Snake Indians in the plains north of the Platte in the eighteenth century we must add the Bannocks, who were not Snakes but belonged to the Mono-Bannock group of Shoshoneans, speaking a tongue kin to that of the Snakes and Comanches. That the Bannocks were in the plains east of the Rockies in the eighteenth century seems to be well established. This is asserted by the Teit traditions, and it is hinted that Bannocks late in the eighteenth century were going with Flatheads and Snakes on trading expeditions to the Mandan villages on the Missouri in North Dakota, and even after 1800 the Bannocks at times crossed east of the Rockies to hunt in the upper Yellowstone. They may have been the tribe called the Broken Moccasins by Lewis and Clark, living in the mountainous country south of the Lemhi Snakes and north of the southern Snake group that in 1805 apparently lived on Green River. The most interesting point concerning the connection of the Bannocks with the plains lies in the fact that, unlike any of the Snake groups, they had the Plains Indian organization into bands, and of their five bands the names of three were identical with the names of three Comanche bands or tribes. It is really astonishing to find the Comanches of Texas called *Penatekas,* meaning "Honey Eaters," and a Bannock band in Idaho also called *Penatekas,* and the name translated "Honey Eaters."

This general statement of which Snake groups comprised the Snake Nation in the plains in the eighteenth century is inserted here to form a basis, perhaps not correct in all details, on which we may set up and arrange the rather scanty materials at our disposal concerning this tribe in early times. The plains and mountain park lands which are supposed to have been held by the Snakes in the eighteenth century are almost untouched by archaeology, but in recent years some important finds have been made that afford us a dim outline of probable conditions in Montana and Wyoming at the close of the prehistoric and opening of the historic periods.

In the Pictograph Cave near Billings, Montana, there are stratified deposits of Indian remains, the fourth or upper deposit containing broken Indian pottery and glass trade beads, indicating that it is late prehistoric verging on the historic. The third layer, one suspects, is Snake Indian in origin. It has no broken pottery or articles obtained from European traders. It contains grooved mauls, indicating a late prehistoric dating; arrows, complete with shafts, the stone points attached with some material resembling pitch and then bound with sinew; fragments of coiled baskets, stone mortars, stone knives, and hide scrapers. Arrowheads of the type found in this cave deposit have also been found in the upper or latest deposit at the bison traps near Billings and Livingston, Montana.

The Indians who left these remains were almost certainly either Snakes or Flatheads, and we here have a picture of a hunting people, who held communal hunts at bison traps, driving the animals over the cliffside and then shooting the crippled ones with arrows. They evidently had no pottery, a characteristic typical of the Snakes on both sides of the Rockies, and the finding of fragments of baskets suggests that even in the buffalo plains the Snakes kept up their old food-gathering practices, which they had brought from the lands west of the mountains, of filling their baskets with roots, seeds, and berries. In quite recent years a peculiar type of flat-bottomed pottery has been found at some points in the Yellowstone country, and it has been suggested by some archaeologists that this may be Snake pottery. This does not seem probable, for it is the general opinion of authorities that the Snakes did not make pottery. Nathaniel Wyeth was trading among the Snakes in the 1830's, and he asserted that the Snakes had no cooking pots.[5] They made watertight baskets and cooked food by dropping hot stones into the baskets to cause the water to boil. He saw one pot made of stone, but he observed that it was never put on the fire, and he thought it was used for pounding

[5] Henry R. Schoolcraft (ed.), *Historical and Statistical Information Respecting the History, Condition, and Prospects of the Indian Tribes of the United States*, I, 211.

125

seeds. W. D. Strong made an exhaustive search for evidence that the Comanches (practically the same people as the Snakes) were pottery makers in early times, but could find nothing to support that view.

A trail of broken pottery of the Mandan and Hidatsa type has been followed from the Missouri to the Rockies, going westward up the Yellowstone. This is probably Crow pottery, the Crows being an offshoot from the Hidatsas, having left that tribe on the Missouri in the eighteenth century and migrated westward. At Glendive on the lower Yellowstone there are the remains of a village with one earth lodge in it, the remainder of the dwellings evidently having been tipis. This was quite a sizable settlement, the inhabitants making pottery and, judging from the bone hoes, planting crops. Farther up the Yellowstone the same type of early culture is found in camps, but without indications of crop-growing. Curiously, in a number of these camps the broken pottery of probable Crow origin is mingled with the flat-bottomed pottery, which suggests a friendly relationship at an early period between the Crows and the makers of this flat-bottomed ware, who may possibly have been the Arapahoes or their cousins, the Atsenas. The latter tribe was trading and camping with the Crows about the date 1805.

No archaeological remains of Padouca type have been reported in western Wyoming or in Montana, and this suggests that the early Snake occupants of this region were free from molestation by the mounted Padoucas. As we know, the Padoucas were in the Black Hills region, in the Sand Hills of western Nebraska, and near the forks of the Platte. They were using the stone quarries in southeastern Wyoming and were obtaining obsidian from the deposits on the Yellowstone, perhaps in barter with the Indians of that district.

These faint clues uncovered in recent years through archaeology fit in well with the scanty information we have from other sources concerning the Snakes in the period before they obtained horses and metal weapons. They were basin-plateau Indians who had come across the mountains from the west in late prehistoric times, bringing with them their old food-gathering habits, to which they now added the plains practice of hunting buffalo and other big game, using the old Shoshonean communal hunting method, with the bison trap and the antelope surround methods which enabled Indians on foot to round up and kill large numbers of game animals with considerable ease. Archaeology has produced no evidence as yet that these Shoshonean Snake people occupied the plains, moving, camping, and living the year around among the buffalo herds. They seem to have done exactly what their Comanche and Ute kinsmen did in the lands south of the Platte, living in the mountain parks and going into the plains in early times only on hunting and war expeditions.

It was not until after 1650 that French traders and explorers came to the western end of Lake Superior. The English established a trading factory on Hudson Bay in 1668, and presently both the French and the English began to obtain from Indians vague reports of a tribe in the plains called Snakes[6] and bearded men in the west near a sea, who lived in stone houses and used metal implements—the distorted picture of the Spanish settlements in New Mexico mentioned earlier. Equipped with firearms by the French and English, the Crees and Assiniboins began to terrorize neighboring tribes. By 1690 they had pushed westward beyond Lake Winnipeg and up the Churchill River from Hudson Bay, and during this advance they seem to have driven the Blackfeet, Atsenas, and Arapahoes (tribes we will soon find warring on the Snakes) from their older homes, perhaps in the valley of Red River, forcing them to retire into the district west of Lake Winnipeg and south of the Saskatchewan. At this period there was a great mass of Tinneh Indians (kinsmen of the Apaches and Padoucas) in the country to the west and southwest of Hudson Bay,

[6] I am employing the name Snake deliberately. The fashion for terming this tribe Shoshoni is a late nineteenth-century affair. These Indians were invariably termed Snake in the eighteenth century and were so called by their closest kinsmen, the Comanches. Moreover, all the names applied to the Snakes by other tribes and quoted in the *Handbook of American Indians* seem to be of late origin, with the possible exception of the Crow name for the Snakes, Grass Lodge People, which may date back to 1750.

extending southward at least as far as the head of the Saskatchewan. The Sarsis, a people of this stock, lived on the Saskatchewan
and were in touch with the Apaches of the Black Hills of South
Dakota. Thus in 1690 there was a chain of Apache and Tinneh
tribes stretching unbroken from New Mexico to the vicinity of
Hudson Bay, and it was probably along this chain that the reports
of bearded men were relayed northward and eastward until they
reached both the English and French traders. It was along the
same chain that the first reports of the Snake Nation also came.

The French trader and explorer Verendrye was attempting,
after the year 1730, to find a route to the ocean in the west, and
when he came into the country at the upper end of Lake Superior,
he began to hear of the bearded men in the west. In 1735 he was
in Quebec, recounting these Indian reports and preparing to explore the unknown country to the southwest of Lake of the
Woods. In the spring of 1738 he left his small trading post on
Assiniboine River and went on foot with a party of Frenchmen
and Assiniboin Indians to the Mandan villages on the Missouri,
near the present city of Bismarck. He found that the Mandan villages were a trading center for Indians, who came in spring and
fall to trade for maize, dried vegetables, furs, and fine painted
eagle plumes. The Assiniboins from the north, who had a trade
with the French and also with the English on Hudson Bay, were
coming regularly to the Mandans to trade, giving guns, metal
hatchets, and knives in exchange for maize and other articles.
Here at the fortified Mandan towns Verendrye obtained reports
of mounted bands of men in armor passing through the plains.
His interpreter had run away; he could not understand clearly
what the Mandans said, and he got the impression that these horse-
men in the plains were white men. This is the one reference to
horses in the Verendrye report of 1738; he does not mention horses
among the Mandans, and the Assiniboins who were coming from
Assiniboine River to the Mandans to trade were making the long
journeys afoot, with their camp equipment packed on dogs and
carried by their women and girls.

Verendrye left two of his Frenchmen to winter at the Mandan

villages. They apparently remained for an entire year, for they reported to their leader in September, 1739. They stated that

Every year at the beginning of June there arrive at the great fort on the bank of the river of the Mandans [that is, at the largest fortified Mandan village on the Missouri] several savage tribes which use horses and carry on trade with them; that they bring dressed skins trimmed and ornamented with plumage and porcupine quills, painted in various colors, also white buffalo skins, and the Mandans give them in exchange maize and beans, of which they have an ample supply. Last spring two hundred lodges came; sometimes even more come; they are all of the same tribe but some are only allies; there was one tribe which said they came from the setting sun, where there are white men in towns and forts made of bricks and white stone. . . . They reported that to get to these whites the Indians had to detour to avoid the Snakes, a numerous people, the greater part of whom live in forts, while the rest wander about, occupying a large extent of territory.[7]

The mounted Indians referred to in this report as coming to trade in June each year at the Mandan villages were probably the People of the Horses of the later Verendrye reports. Bent on further explorations in this quarter, Verendrye sent his two sons and a party of Frenchmen to the Mandan villages in 1742, to join the People of the Horses and accompany them to their own country. The Frenchmen reached the Mandan villages May 19, 1742, to await the coming of the Plains Indians, who came to trade in June; but for some unknown reason they did not come, and on July 23 the Verendrye party set out with two Mandan guides to find the People of the Horses in their own country. Out in the plains west of the Mandan villages a camp of Indians called *Beaux Hommes* ("Handsome Men"—Crows?) was encountered, and the Mandan guides ran away, "fearing a nation who were their enemies."

It is impossible to follow the route of these wandering Frenchmen and their Indian guides. They evidently remained with the Beaux Hommes for a long time, roving with the camp; then on November 9 they set off toward the south-southwest with guides

[7] Beckles Willson, *The Great Company*, 366–68.

to seek the People of the Horses. On the second day they came to a camp of Indians called *Petits Renards*—the "Little Foxes," perhaps a Kiowa band.[8] Going in the same direction for two days more, they came on a very large camp of the same tribe, with which they evidently remained for some days. On November 15 they met the Pioya Indians, and we might surmise that Pioya is an error for Kioya or Kiowa. Continuing toward the southwest, on the nineteenth they reached another Pioya camp, and moving on, apparently accompanied by these Indians, they reached a camp of the People of the Horses.

They found this tribe in mourning, for the Gens du Serpent had raided and "destroyed" all the camps of the People of the Horses. Going onward, evidently with all the Indians, the Verendrye party sought to find the People of the Bow, the only tribe that did not fear the Gens du Serpent. The Bows were friends of a tribe that visited the sea, which evidently meant traded with the Spaniards of New Mexico, for the People of the Horses had spoken of some tribe that went on trading journeys by making a detour to avoid the Gens du Serpent. Going on toward the southwest, the French and Indians came to a very large camp of the *Gens de la Belle Rivière*, "Belle Rivière" being a name which the French traders in later times applied to the Belle Fourche or North Fork of Cheyenne River. On the twenty-first (December?), they found the Bow Indians.

These Indians now organized a great war party and set out to raid the Snakes. Advancing very slowly for at least twelve days, they came in contact with Snake camps, but immediately fell into a panic and fled back toward the Black Hills. Becoming separated from the other camps, the Verendrye men went off with the Bow Indians; and presently they encountered a camp of the *Gens de la Petite Cerise*—undoubtedly the Little Cherry band of Arikara Indians. Accompanying this group to their fortified village on the Missouri, the Frenchmen remained for some days. Here they took a lead plate with the arms of France stamped on it, and

[8] The Arikaras termed one Kiowa group "Fox Indians": *Tukiwaku* (*tu*, "a village," *kiwaku*, a kind of fox).

cutting the name Verendrye and the date on the back of the plate, they buried it nearby. This plate has been discovered near a group of ruined Arikara villages on the west bank of the Missouri north of Bad River, at the edge of the present town of Fort Pierre, South Dakota.

This Verendrye report is vague and far from satisfactory. It gives one the impression of a group of Frenchmen moving about, lost in a great smoke cloud through which dim shapes of Indian bands move, ghostlike. The quaint names given to the camps make it impossible to identify them accurately; but still we have in this report a most interesting picture of Indians—Kiowas, Arikaras, and others—in the Black Hills region, at the time after they obtained horses and when they were being raided and demoralized by the Gens du Serpent. The report states that in 1740 or 1741 the Snakes destroyed seventeen camps of the Indians near the Black Hills, evidently killing many men and carrying off women and children as slaves. About the location of the Snake camps we can only guess. They were probably west of the Black Hills, and one might suppose near the Bighorn Mountains. The report states that the war party that went to attack the Snakes in their own land advanced for "twelve or even twenty-eight days" before finding the Snake camps. In truth, the Frenchmen were wandering about with Indians who spent half their days in camp and, when they did march, went with extreme caution, five or six miles making up the day's journey. The total distance was probably not great, for when they saw the Snakes and fled, they got back to the starting point, presumably on the North Fork of the Cheyenne River, in two days and nights of panic flight.

The old Cree Indian, Saukamappee, who talked with David Thompson in the Piegan-Blackfoot camp in the winter of 1787–88, first spoke of the time before the Indians had horses, but when the Crees had guns. He was seventy-five or eighty years of age and stated that the time he was speaking of was when he was a boy of about sixteen. The date of his first fight with the Snakes, therefore, was between 1723 and 1728. At that time the Piegans were the advance group of the Blackfeet and, being farthest toward the southwest, they were much exposed to Snake attacks. The Snakes came in big war parties. They tried to locate small enemy camps and attack them by surprise at dawn, slaughtering the people; but the Piegans were too alert to be taken by surprise, and they usually kept together in big camps for mutual protection. At this time the Piegans sent word to a camp of Crees who were friends that they needed help, and Saukamappee's father led a party of about twenty Cree warriors, among whom his young son was included, to the Piegan camp. These Crees had a few guns, but they also carried lances, some with iron points, others with flint points. Each man had a bow of larchwood and a quiver of fifty arrows, ten arrows with iron points, the rest tipped with flint. The men had their knives hanging on cords on their breasts, and their hatchets tucked under their belts.

When the Crees reached the Piegan camp, they found a great gathering, for the Piegans had summoned aid from several camps. The reason for this gathering of forces was the discovery of a large camp of Snake Indians in the plains near Eagle Hills on the Saskatchewan. The Piegans set up "a great war tent" in their camp, and for several days there was feasting, speeches, and dances. The chiefs selected a war leader; then the force of some 350 warriors crossed the river on rafts and in canoes, carefully securing these as a means of retreat if they should be defeated. The Snake warriors came to meet them, both parties leaping, shouting, dancing, and singing. When quite close, the Snakes sat down in a line, covering themselves with their big shields; the Piegans and their allies did the same, but had fewer shields, many shields sheltering two warriors. The Snakes sat with shields touching each other, forming an unbroken wall. Their bows were shorter than those of their enemies and were of better wood and backed with buffalo sinew, which made them very flexible and strong. Their arrows were all headed with sharp, smooth, black stone (obsidian from the upper Yellowstone River) which splintered when they struck anything. When the fighting started, the Cree boy noticed that his party's iron-tipped arrows did not penetrate the Snake shields but stuck in them. These big war parties sat and fought in this manner until nightfall. Several men were wounded, but none badly, and not a scalp was taken. Such was the fighting before horses and guns were obtained in large numbers. In these early times, as this Cree Indian observed, the great mischief of war lay in the surprising of small camps of ten to twenty lodges by large enemy war parties, who killed the men in the camp and carried off the women and children. The big fights on foot, with the contending forces drawn up in lines, were mainly showing off. The warriors advanced in lines, leaping and shouting; they halted, danced, sang, and showed off their fine equipment in an attempt to insult each other. When they closed in, they sat down in two lines behind their shields and shot arrows which did little harm. Occasionally they charged in and attacked the enemy with clubs and lances, the defeated party taking to flight.

The Snakes, and probably their enemies, had leather armor, usually a sleeveless shirt of six-ply leather, and sometimes sand mixed with glue was spread between the plies of leather and held in place by quilting. When they obtained horses, these valuable animals were also protected with leather armor. In the southern plains the armor for both men and horses was made of tough, hard rawhide.

Between 1735 and 1740, according to this Cree information, the Snakes began to get some horses. The mounted Snakes charged in among the Piegans, striking them on the head with stone-headed war clubs that had very long wooden handles. In these fights the Piegans lost some of their best warriors; but the Snakes did not have many horses, and quite often they came to fight in the older manner, all on foot and hiding behind their big shields. At this time the Cree, Saukamappee, again went to aid the Piegans, accompanied by nine other Crees and Assiniboins, all with guns. They found a big gathering at the Piegan camp, and all the Indians feasted, made speeches, and danced. Then the war tent was put up and the expedition was organized. When they took the field, they met a Snake war party larger than their own; but the Snakes had no horses with them, and the fight was of the old type: two lines of warriors hiding behind shields and shooting arrows. But the Crees and Assiniboins with guns made a difference. Lying on the ground in the Piegan line, they fired at every Snake who exposed any part of his body, killing several men, wounding others; and presently some of the Snakes slipped away, leaving their shields standing to hide their retreat. The Piegans and their allies then charged and drove the enemy off, killing and scalping a number of them.

This Cree information fits in well with the facts set out in the Verendrye narrative of 1741–42; but the Verendryes were speaking of conditions near the Black Hills, far to the south of the Blackfoot country. In this more southerly region the Padoucas had introduced horses as far back as 1680, and thus when the Snakes obtained horses, evidently after 1730, they had to face enemy tribes near the Black Hills who had some horses and were accustomed to mounted fighting. Here in the Black Hills country, as in the lands up near the Saskatchewan, the main object of raiders was the usual surprise of small and isolated camps, the killing of men and the capture of women and children. The Verendrye narrative shows that this method was just as effective against Indians who had some horses as against those that were still afoot. For this reason the tribes that were subject to mounted Snake attacks tried to keep together in big camps as much as possible; and as late as 1722, Mathew Cocking, a Hudsons Bay Company trader, noted that the Blackfeet were nervous and constantly on the watch for parties of mounted Snakes. Even the Crees and Assiniboins, now well equipped with firearms, were afraid of the Snakes. The sight of a horse in the distance would alarm an entire camp.

From this information it is clear that the Snakes had few or no horses in the Montana plains as late as about 1730, but that by 1740 they were well mounted. The source of their supply of horses is obvious. In the Colorado plains the Comanches and Utes broke the power of the Apaches in 1726–27 and forced them to flee southward. The Comanches captured many horses and much plunder from the Apaches; and since they were closely related to the Snakes, indeed, identical with that tribe except for their name, we must suppose that they passed on some of the horses and metal weapons to their Snake kinsmen in the north. Nothing would have been easier, as our evidence shows that the Yamparika Comanches still extended north to the Platte and west to Green River and the Uinta Mountains as late as 1776; and here in the north they were probably in close daily contact with some groups of Snakes.

The Verendrye reports show that the tribes between the Missouri and the Black Hills had a number of horses in 1738–43; moreover, they had donkeys and mules, a certain proof that they were obtaining their livestock from the Spanish borders, for Indians did not raise donkeys and mules, and the report states definitely that they were trading with a tribe that traded with the Spaniards. In all probability this meant the Gataka Apaches and not the Ietans, as the latter group, one would suppose, were trading with the Snakes, giving horses and Spanish articles for slaves. The tribes near the Black Hills were friends of the Arikaras on the Missouri River, while the Ietans had Arikara slaves in their camp, far to the south on the New Mexican border when contacted by the Mallet brothers in 1739. The Beaux Hommes, living west of the Mandans and evidently near the Little Missouri, might have been the Crows. We should observe that Joseph La France, an Indian trader, noted the Beaux Hommes in the Lake Winnipeg country at about the date 1740. Their being west of the Mandans in 1742 is strong evidence that they were Crows. There seems to be no possibility of assuming that they were an Assiniboin group, which is about the only alternative. Verendrye's People of the Horses and People of the Bow are pure mystery. They might have been Kiowas or Gataka Apaches, two tribes that in 1742 must have been numerous, each with several camps.

We have little direct contemporary information concerning the Snakes after the Verendrye report. In the early 1750's St. Pierre and his French traders were in the Lake Winnipeg country and heard reports of the Gens du Serpent, a powerful mounted tribe that went on long trading expeditions, evidently to the New Mexican frontier. In 1754, Anthony Hendry, a Hudson's Bay Company trader, visited the Blackfeet and reported that they had many horses and that they fought mounted, with bows and lances, but had no guns.

Of the Snakes we hear no more at this period. Their kinsmen, the Comanches, at this date were armed with French guns and were finishing the work of driving the Apaches from the plains south of the Platte. In the far north it was the Swampy Cree tribe, dwelling near the shores of Hudson Bay, that first obtained guns in quantity from the English traders. Advancing up the Churchill and other rivers, these Crees drove the Tinneh and other tribes before them like flocks of frightened birds, meeting no real resistance until they encountered the brave Chipewyans—a strong tribe which was akin to the Apaches of the south—who faced the guns of the Swampy Crees and stopped their advance. But all of the other tribes fled in panic before the Cree guns. Little parties of ten or twelve Crees moved boldly through the lands of these alien tribes, hunting the frightened natives like game. These natives were in such terror that they hardly dared to hunt or fish; their gaze was constantly scanning the horizon, and if they saw strange smoke rising miles away, they broke camp and fled to some hiding place where they hoped that the Crees would not find them.

It was such attacks by enemies armed with guns that the Gens du Serpent had to fear. Like the Apaches in the south, their only trade was in New Mexico, where the Spaniards would not trade firearms to Indians, and they were as helpless against warriors armed with guns as the mounted Apaches and Padoucas of the south. Their first serious defeat, as we have seen, was when a small party of Crees with guns joined the Blackfeet and drove off the Snakes. This must have been about the year 1755; and with traders on the Saskatchewan supplying the tribes with firearms, the prospects for the Snakes were not bright. But the French and Indian war now came on; the British invaded Canada, and war ended the French trade on the Saskatchewan and Assiniboine rivers. It was not until after the British conquest of Canada that trade began to revive. Thus the Blackfeet and other northern enemies of the Snakes were without a supply of arms and ammunition until about the year 1770, and the Snakes must have continued to be the strongest tribe in the Montana and Wyoming plains until about that date. But by 1772 the English traders were in the Saskatchewan country once more, and the trade in firearms was brisk. Cocking, a Hudson's Bay Company man, visited the Blackfeet in this year and found them all mounted, well armed, and full of fight. He reported that they spent half their lives hunting buffalo, the other half in raiding the Snakes in the south, from whom they captured large numbers of horses and slaves.[9]

When the Snakes, still without horses, occupied the northern plains in the late seventeenth and early eighteenth century, they and their allies, the Flatheads and Kutenais (all three tribes coming from the lands west of the Rockies), seem to have had the splendid hunting grounds of Montana and Wyoming to themselves. We know of no other tribes that might have been in the mountain parks and plains at that early period. To the south and east were the mounted Padoucas, but that tribe does not appear to have occupied the plains farther westward than the Black Hills and the forks of the Platte. The Kiowas were apparently in the district immediately north of the Black Hills when the Verendrye party came into that country in 1742. How long they had been there we do not know. There is at present some doubt about the origin and migration of the Kiowas. It has been pointed out that there are some language connections between the Taos Pueblos of New Mexico and the Kiowas, and this has led some anthropologists to conjecture a northward migration of the Kiowas at an early date. These linguistic claims, however, are not impressive; the Kiowas themselves explain the presence of Pueblo words in their language by saying that their tribe formerly traded regu-

---

[9] The old Cree Indian told David Thompson in 1787 that as soon as the Blackfeet obtained some guns, they defeated their enemies, the Snakes, Kutenais, and Flatheads, and advanced rapidly from Red Deer River to the Rockies. Their enemies no longer came with big war parties to attack them; the Blackfeet had to seek the enemy camp, which they took by surprise, killing the men and capturing the women, children, and horses. This was the situation in the 1770's. Umfreville (in 1785–90) is the first to record that the Snakes were now well west of the Rockies, with the Blackfeet raiding them and carrying off large numbers of female captives.

larly at the Pueblo towns and naturally picked up some Pueblo words. James Mooney found Spanish documents that he stated gave proof that the Kiowas were known in New Mexico as early as 1732 and were raiding there in 1749. These dates seem too early for the Kiowas to have traded or raided in New Mexico. In 1751 a Kiowa woman was brought in to be sold as a slave by the Utes. She said that she had been captured by Comanches; the Utes had then raided the Comanches and taken her. This fits in with the situation the Verendryes had noted in 1742; but the Verendrye narrative termed the tribe that was raiding the Kiowas and their neighbors near the Black Hills the Gens du Serpent. This Kiowa woman was in all probability captured by Snakes near the Black Hills. Either the Utes or the Spanish officials turned the name Snake into Comanche, for they never used the name Snake in New Mexico.[10]

Kiem obtained the Kiowa migration tradition in 1868, twenty-five years earlier than Mooney. He was told that the old home of the Kiowas was in the mountains, where they had the Flatheads for neighbors. They left the mountains because of wars and migrated into the plains near the upper Yellowstone with their camp equipment hauled on sledges by dogs. The Comanches were angry with the Kiowas in 1868; and during a council at which the government officials were present the Yamparika Comanche chief Ten Bears scolded the Kiowas, reminding them of the fact that when they had first come into the plains, they were paupers, and that his tribe had taken pity on them and given them their first horses. Since the Kiowas came into the plains near the upper Yellowstone, they emerged into a district occupied by the Snake Nation; yet Ten Bears, like the Spaniards of New Mexico, did not make a distinction between his own tribe and the Snakes. They were all Comanches in his view.

Kiowa tradition asserts that the Crows gave them their first horses; but whether they obtained horses first from the Comanches or Crows, the event cannot have been very early, as the Indians

10 Thomas, *Plains Indians and New Mexico*, 17.
11 Keim, *Sheridan's Troopers on the Border*, 153.

north of the Platte evidently had few horses prior to 1730. The Kiowa migration southward seems to date after 1742, as they appear to have been north of the Black Hills until after 1750. That they were there when the Verendryes came in 1742 is conjecture; but it has the support of Indian traditions that appear to be reliable. The Cheyenne and Arapaho traditions place the Kiowas there, and the Cheyennes termed the Little Missouri Antelope Pit River, explaining that the Kiowas penned or pitted antelope herds there before 1760 and taught the Cheyennes and Arapahoes how to hunt in that manner.

In the Kiowa tradition of their life near the Black Hills, they speak mainly of their close association with the Gatakas and of their trading at the Arikara villages on the Missouri in South Dakota, where they went to exchange horses and Spanish articles from New Mexico for maize, vegetables, tobacco and other Arikara products. Some of the older Kiowas, born around the year 1820, told Mooney that it was when their grandfathers were young that the tribe lived near the Crows and Arikaras. All the Kiowa memories of that early time had to do with the Gatakas, Arikaras, Crows, and Sarsis, the latter being a tribe whose lands were in the wooded district at the head of the North Saskatchewan. Close kinsmen of the Gataka Apaches of the Black Hills country, Sarsis had the habit of coming down in bands through the plains to pay protracted visits, some marrying into the Kiowa and Gataka tribes. A number of prominent Kiowa families in the nineteenth century counted descent from Sarsi ancestors. That the Kiowas retained no memory of their early relations with the Snakes or Comanches in the northern plains may be due to the Indian's ability to forget unpleasant matters. From Verendrye's journal it may be assumed that in 1742–43 the Snakes were raiding the Kiowas and their neighbors vigorously, creating a kind of panic in their camps; and that was not the kind of memory that would remain for long in the Kiowa mind.

The Kiowa assertion that they found the Crows already in the country west of the Missouri when they migrated eastward from the mountains brings up the problem of the date and direction of

139

the Crow movement. The Crows and Hidatsas, then one tribe, came to the Missouri from the east or northeast, joining the Mandans on Heart River near the present city of Bismarck. The Hidatsas settled here, building a village, but the Crows moved out in the plains westward. Whether this was before or after Verendrye's visit to the Mandans in 1738 is unknown. Archaeologists have disclosed that the Crows lived on the lower Yellowstone, where they had a permanent settlement near the present Glendive. Here they apparently continued to plant corn and make pottery. Camp sites containing similar types of pottery have been found higher up the Yellowstone, clear to the Rockies. On the whole it seems very probable that the Beaux Hommes of the Verendrye journal, 1742, were the Crows and that at that date they had not occupied the country as far as the Yellowstone, or that at least their rear bands were in the country near the Little Missouri. Like the other tribes near the Missouri, the Crows were probably being attacked by the Gens du Serpent in 1742, and this would have discouraged a migration into the Yellowstone Valley.

The Arapahoes were apparently the last tribe to migrate into the lands north of the Black Hills at this period when the Snake Nation was at the height of its strength. To the Arapahoes we must link the Atsenas, for there can be no doubt that the two tribes were originally one. These two groups, the Hidatsa-Crow and Atsena-Arapaho, were apparently among the tribes that were attacked by the Assiniboins and Crees, who had obtained firearms, mainly from the English on Hudson Bay, late in the seventeenth century. In their old home the Hidatsas and Atsenas seem to have had some connection; they may have been neighboring groups, perhaps in the Red River of the North country. When attacked, they apparently fled into the country in the southern part of the present province of Manitoba, where there are many rapids and small falls in the streams. With or near them were the Blackfeet. All of this seems very conjectural; but there are clues, all pointing to some such conditions in what we may term late prehistoric times in the Red River and Manitoba country. At that early period French traders whose very names are unknown to us seem to have come among these Indians, and they gave identical names to both the Hidatsa-Crow and the Atsena group, calling both *Gros Ventres*, "Big Bellies." They made a connection between the groups even clearer by giving both a second name, Fall Indians, and in this latter name they included the Blackfeet, terming them Waterfall Indians.[12]

All these Indians when attacked by the Assiniboins and Crees, evidently late in the seventeenth century, left their old lands and fled toward the plains. The Hidatsas and Crows fled to the Mandan villages on the Missouri; the Atsenas and perhaps the Arapahoes as well went farther north to the Assiniboine River; the Blackfoot tribes were farthest north, near the Saskatchewan, and all these tribes presently found themselves in contact with the Gens du Serpent in the Montana and Wyoming plains.

We do not know when or by what route the Arapahoes reached the plains near the Black Hills, and, what is more, the Arapahoes themselves, even back in 1880, did not know. Their traditions were poorer than those of the Cheyennes. The Arapahoes had an idea that their tribe and the Atsenas and Cheyennes had lived with or near each other in early times, evidently in the Red River country, and they stated that all three groups moved together to the Missouri. W. P. Clark questioned the Arapahoes about the year 1880 and set down their tradition in his book, *The Indian Sign Language*. He stated that a "very reliable tradition" placed the Arapahoes in western Minnesota "several hundred years ago"; that from their old home this tribe moved out in the plains and met the Cheyennes (then living on the Sheyenne Fork of Red River of the North) and the tribes moved together to the Missouri and on to the Black Hills, where they separated. The Arapahoes then moved to the head of the Missouri, where the Blackfeet attacked them and drove them southward. The Arapahoes made

[12] It has always been said that before moving to the Missouri, the Hidatsas, Crows, and probably the Arapahoes lived in the northeast, evidently in the Red River country. An old Algonquin name for the Arapahoes was "Bison Path People," which suggests that they dwelled in early times on the edge of the buffalo range.

a raid on the Snakes and obtained their first horses. Another version states that the Atsenas were with the Arapahoes and Cheyennes but refused to cross the Missouri, moving off toward the northwest.

Thomas Fitzpatrick, the trader, who had known the Arapahoes back to about 1820, stated that the tribe was an offshoot from the Atsenas of the Blackfoot stock and had once lived on Assiniboine River, but, moving southward, they roamed the heads of the Platte and Arkansas. Colonel Henry Dodge met the Arapahoes on the upper Arkansas in 1835 and stated that they formerly lived on the Marias, a northern head branch of the Missouri, and that they migrated southward from that country "a long time ago." Dodge here speaks of the Atsenas as a separate tribe, making it clear that he did not confuse the Arapahoes with the Atsenas.[13]

Even if the Arapahoes did have a faint memory of being near the Cheyennes in the Red River country at an early date, it is probable that they left the Cheyennes there and moved with their own tribe, the Atsenas, toward the northwest. The Atsenas, then called Gros Ventres, were in the Assiniboine River or Saskatchewan country about the date 1752 and, as St. Pierre reported, were being attacked by Crees and Assiniboins armed with guns; but Alexander Mackenzie, writing about the year 1789, stated that the Atsenas were on the middle course of Assiniboine River and had permitted bands of Crees and Assiniboins to occupy the lower valley and headwaters of that stream, these tribes wishing to trap fur animals in the Atsena country. The implication is that the Assiniboins and Crees were on good terms with the Atsenas and were probably trading firearms to them. Mackenzie divided the Atsenas into two groups, one of which roved southward to the Missouri, and these are supposed by Mooney to have been the Arapahoes.[14] If this is correct, the Arapahoes were a part of the Atsena tribe as late as about 1790, extending south to or beyond

[13] Fitzpatrick in Schoolcraft, *Indian Tribes*, I, 295; Colonel Henry Dodge report, 1835.

[14] James Mooney, "The Cheyenne Indians," American Anthropological Association *Memoirs*, Vol. I (1905–1907), 372.

the Missouri, and their supposed migration westward to the Black Hills was a myth.

Living farther to the south than the Blackfeet, we would suppose that the Atsenas and Arapahoes were harder pressed by the mounted Snake war parties in early times than the Blackfeet were. There are hints that the Arapahoes later took a leading part in counterattacks against the Snakes. As early as 1790, possibly as far back as 1760, at least part of the Arapahoes had come as far south as the Black Hills, where they were allied to the Cheyennes, Kiowas, and Gatakas, aiding those tribes in fighting the Snakes. These Indians all traded at the Arikara villages on the Missouri, near the present Pierre, South Dakota. In 1795, Truteau noted that they were encamped far up Cheyenne River, afraid to come to the Arikara villages because of the hostile Sioux. It was evidently the presence of Sioux near the Arikara villages that induced the Arapahoes and Cheyennes to shift their trade to the Mandan villages higher up the Missouri. John Evans found them trading there in 1796. The name Arapaho was not in use until after the year 1805. Both Truteau and Evans applied forms of the name *Kananavich*, "Bison Path Indians," to this tribe. They were also termed Big Bead and Blue Bead Indians because of a type of large blue beads, highly valued by all the northern tribes, which they were known to have in quantity.[15]

The Cheyennes were the last of the old group of tribes on the Red River of the North to flee when attacked by enemies armed with guns. This was toward the middle of the eighteenth cen-

[15] Collot set down the Red Bead Indians in the Powder River country on his map of 1796, but as the Red Beads are not otherwise referred to, it may be that he meant the Blue Bead Indians, the Arapahoes. The blue beads that gave this name to the Arapahoes are supposed to have been New Mexican turquoises, which were widely traded among the Indians even in prehistoric times. In 1805, Larocque saw these beads among the Crows and Snakes, and he was probably in error when he stated that they were large blue glass beads obtained from the Spaniards. It may be noted that William Clark set down on his map, made about 1808–10, Blue Bead Mountain and Blue Bead River in the Bighorn district, with the annotation, "Here the Indians obtain clear and solid volcanic glass which they make into pipes." Perhaps they also made beads from this material. The Blue Bead Quarry here, in the Sunlight Basin near Cody, Wyoming, is said today to produce stone, not glass. The Indians worked this quarry and made pipes and other articles from the stone.

tury, and the Cheyennes moved westward to the Missouri and built two permanent villages on the west bank, below the present Fort Yates. But here they were followed by the Sioux armed with guns; and, after holding out for some time the Cheyennes decided that they would be less subject to Sioux annoyance if they took to roving. They therefore left their villages and little cultivated fields and went out near the Black Hills, where they met the Arapahoes and obtained horses. According to information obtained from the oldest Cheyennes forty years ago, this was about the date 1760. The Kiowas, or part of that tribe, were still north of the Black Hills in the Little Missouri district; but the Cheyennes in 1912 claimed that their tribe and the Arapahoes now drove the Kiowas farther south, toward the Platte. This we may well doubt, for in 1795 part of the Kiowas were with the Cheyennes and Arapahoes on upper Cheyenne River, apparently on good terms with them, and as late as 1820 both the Arapahoes and Cheyennes were usually on friendly terms with some of the Kiowas.

It has been necessary to put in here this account of the tribes in and near the northern plains area at the period 1700–70 for the reason that we have almost no direct information concerning the Snakes in the plains at this date, and it is mainly through our knowledge of neighboring tribes, their location, condition, and activities, that we may surmise the location and strength of the Snakes. We find from this material that the Snakes were in the plains before they obtained horses and, aided by the Flatheads and Kutenais, were engaged in raiding as far north as the Saskatchewan; later they raided in the Black Hills region, going almost to the Missouri. The raids in the Black Hills country were probably the work of Snakes who held the upper Yellowstone and Wind River valleys; the attacks on the Blackfeet and their neighbors in the north were obviously made by the Snakes who occupied the plains of Montana. Farther toward the south, on the head of the North Platte, on the Sweetwater and on Green River, was another group of Snakes, perhaps the ancestors of the modern Wyoming Shoshonis, and near them were the Yamparika Comanches, who were engaged in raiding both on Green River, west of the continental divide, where they were harassing the Utes, and on the Arkansas, where they were raiding into New Mexico. In all the references to the Snakes we have no evidence that they were living in the plains of Montana and Wyoming the year around. The probability is that they came into the plains to hunt buffalo and to send out raiding parties, and, having done this, they retired to the mountain parks, which were their real homeland, to winter. Thus, ethnologists may be right in stating that the Snakes or Shoshonis were never typical Plains Indians. Nevertheless, they dominated the northern plains for a time, and if they were not typical Plains Indians, they effectively kept any other tribes from coming into Montana and Wyoming and assuming that role during their time of power. Ethnologists have defined plains culture to suit themselves, and, having done so, they seem to wish to bar the Snakes or Shoshonis on the grounds that, after 1875, this tribe did not exhibit the plains traits necessary to be classed as Plains Indians. But, after all, have ethnologists demonstrated that their plains culture has any depth, any real age? For all we know it may be nothing more than an amalgam of traits brought into the plains by migrating tribes that did not enter the region until the dawn of modern times, after 1750.

# 7. Saskatchewan to Río Grande

THE IMPORTANCE of firearms in Plains Indian history in the eighteenth century cannot be too strongly emphasized. By their good fortune in making contact with French traders, first apparently on the upper Arkansas in eastern Colorado in 1726, the Comanches obtained guns and were enabled to create a panic among their Apache enemies, whom they drove from all their rancherias. Through the French traders the Comanches made an alliance with the Caddoan tribes in eastern Oklahoma and on Red River, thus assuring themselves of a fairly regular supply of guns and ammunition; and within twenty years they drove all the Apache and Padouca groups from the plains south of the Platte.

In the north the Snake cousins of the Comanches obtained the great advantage of having horses while most of their enemies were still on foot; and by the employment of mounted war parties, the Snakes were at first as successful in the north as the Comanches in the south. They were creating panic among their enemies, destroying entire camps and carrying off large numbers of women and children as slaves. Then—apparently about 1755—they had the misfortune to meet a small party of Crees armed with guns, who were with a camp of Blackfeet. The Snakes had come to raid the Blackfeet, but under the fire from the Cree guns it was the Snakes who broke and fled.

Like the Plains Apaches, the Snakes obtained only Spanish trade goods, which did not include firearms, and like the Apaches they

146

had a dread of these new weapons, against which bravery and fighting skill seemed to be of no avail. They now found that their enemies to the north, the Blackfeet and other tribes near the Saskatchewan, were obtaining guns in increasing numbers; even the Mandans on the upper Missouri were getting some guns in trade from the Assiniboins; and instead of the Snakes' sending out mounted war parties to harass these enemy tribes, they were facing the dreary prospect of being raided and driven from their own camps.

There seemed to be one hope for the Snakes. In the south their Comanche cousins were obtaining good supplies of guns and ammunition from the French in trade at the Caddoan villages, and from the Comanches the Snakes might acquire a supply of these new weapons and instruction in their use. But now the war in America between England and France broke out (1755), and even in the distant plains the repercussions of this struggle were felt; for the war practically killed the French trade with the southern plains tribes, as well as that on the Saskatchewan in the far north. The Comanches now not only had no surplus of firearms to trade to the Snakes, they probably had few guns for their own use and little ammunition. On the other hand, the tribes in the north that had been attacking the Snakes with guns were now cut off from fresh supplies of weapons and ammunition.

In 1759 the British captured Quebec; in 1763 the war ended. In Canada the British revived the old French-Indian trade, employing veteran French traders to assist them. By 1770 they were trading actively on the Saskatchewan and on the upper Mississippi. In the south the situation was different; for France had turned over her vast Louisiana territory to Spain to prevent its falling into British hands, and in 1769 the Spaniards moved in, establishing garrisons at New Orleans, at the mouth of the Arkansas, and at St. Louis. The new officials promptly clamped the usual Spanish restrictions on trade with Indians. The trade in firearms was barred; but French traders slipped across the Mississippi into the British zone in Illinois, obtained stocks of guns and ammunition, and smuggled the weapons to tribes in the Spanish territories. Thus the Osage tribe of Missouri was rearmed about 1770 and at once resumed raiding the Caddoan tribes, forcing some of them to flee from Oklahoma and seek safer locations in Texas and on upper Red River. Taking possession of the hunting lands of these fugitive tribes, the Osages came in contact with the Comanches in the plains; and, as the Comanches were probably still without a new supply of guns, the outlook for the immediate future was for them far from bright.

But at this juncture the Spaniards appointed a Frenchman, Athanaze de Mézières, as agent for the Texas and Red River Indians, and De Mézières, under the pretense of arranging a peace with all the tribes, employed a number of experienced French traders in reviving the gun trade on upper Red River. Thus by 1772 the Comanches, coming to trade at the Caddoan villages on Red River, were again obtaining guns and ammunition in quantity. In the north, however, it was the enemies of the Snakes who obtained guns from the British traders, and the Snakes, with only bad knives and hatchets from New Mexico, were in a precarious position. In 1772 they were being raided persistently by the Blackfoot tribes and probably also by the Assiniboins and the Atsenas of Assiniboine River. To make the situation worse for the Snakes, new enemy tribes—the Arapahoes and Cheyennes—had established themselves in the Black Hills, from which location they were probably raiding the Snake camps.

It was during this period, around 1760–70, that the Kiowas, as asserted in tradition, began a war against the Comanches; but here in the northern plains the names Comanche and Snake were practically synonymous, and injury to one group meant injury to the other. Here again we must resort to conjecture and the piecing together of small bits of information. In 1742 the Kiowas and their Gataka and Padouca allies near the Black Hills were on the defensive and were being heavily raided by the Gens du Serpent. By 1760 they were evidently in a much better position and were raiding the Snakes or, to use the name in the Kiowa tradition, the Kwahari group of Comanches, whose home is vaguely stated to have been to the south and west of the Black Hills. The Ietans were now probably allies of the Kiowas and Padoucas, bringing horses and Spanish articles up to the Black Hills to trade to those tribes. In 1760 the Ietans were for a season on upper Red River on the northern Texas border, and it appears that their trade was with the Texas Spaniards, not with those in New Mexico.[1]

The Arikaras at this period lived in a group of strong villages, some of them fortified, on the Missouri near the present Pierre, South Dakota, and there can be no doubt that they were allies of the Indians out near the Black Hills, who paid regular visits to the Arikara towns to trade horses and other articles for corn, vegetables, native tobacco, and other Arikara products. We may therefore assume that the Snakes were being attacked by this group: the Kiowas, Gatakas, Ietans, and Arikaras; but since these tribes were still without firearms, the Snakes probably were not greatly affected by their raids.

Concerning the Crows and Arapahoes at this early time we have almost no information. Tabeau wrote, about the year 1804, that before the smallpox epidemic of 1781 the Crows were very numerous and were the heroes of the northern plains. In 1742 they were evidently near the Little Missouri, north of the Black Hills; twenty-five years later they were on the Yellowstone, where camp sites with pottery attributed to their tribe have been found. This suggests a Crow advance into lands the Snakes held; but the Crows apparently were not allied to the tribes near the Black Hills, for their only known allies were the related Hidatsa and Mandan tribes on the Missouri in North Dakota. Indeed, the Crows were probably fighting the Snake groups that held the upper Yellowstone lands and the district near the Three Forks of the Missouri, while the Kiowas and other Indians near the Black

---

[1] An old French trader told John Sibley, about the year 1814, that in 1760 he was trading on upper Red River with Hietans, Apaches, and Canceys (*American State Papers*, I, 729). It is true that the Comanches were often termed Ietans, but apparently not until about the year 1800. Besides, Tabeau tells us (*Tabeau's Narrative of Loisel's Expedition to the Upper Missouri*) that as late as 1790 the Ietans traded at San Antonio and then brought horses and Spanish goods to the Black Hills of Dakota to trade with the tribes there, and this Ietan trade is confirmed in A. P. Nasatir (ed.), "Account of Spanish Louisiana in 1785," *Missouri Historical Review*, Vol. XXIV (1930).

Hills were raiding Snakes (or Comanches) farther south, those in the Wind River country and near the upper North Platte.

It is possible that the Arapahoes and Atsenas joined the Crows in warring on and clearing the Snakes out of the lands in the Bighorn and upper Yellowstone districts. The Arapahoes and Atsenas are Algonquian tribes and, as we have seen, in prehistoric Crow camp sites along the Yellowstone broken pottery of evident Crow origin is mingled with another type, possibly of Algonquian origin. Glass beads and European gunflints were found in some of these camp sites, indicating their late date, and in one camp an Indian pictograph was uncovered which shows men in a canoe armed with flintlocks guns.[2] The Crows are known to have been on the Bighorn by about 1795, and here the Mountain Crows apparently left the River Crows and advanced toward the southwest into the Wind River country. By 1800 the Arapahoes were in the same district, extending south to the upper North Platte and frequenting Green River. This fact hints that the Mountain Crows and Arapahoes formed an alliance and drove the Snakes out of the Wind River country and lands near the North Platte; but by 1800 the Arapahoes were on rather friendly terms with part of the Snakes and were frequenting the Snake country on Green River, west of the continental divide, where they were apparently trading with the Snakes.

Teit quotes Salish traditions that the Crows advanced up the Yellowstone, occupying former Snake territory, while the Blackfeet moved southward, pushing the Kutenais and Salish-Tunaxe tribe from the plains east of the mountains in northern Montana. These traditions state that about the year 1800 the Kutenais and part of the Pend d'Oreille tribe formed an alliance which the Flatheads and evidently part of the Snakes also joined, and that this alliance stopped the advance of the Blackfeet southward and of the Crows westward. This was after 1800, after British and American traders supplied the Kutenais, Flatheads, and Snakes with guns.

[2] James Bennett Griffin, *Archeology of Eastern United States*, 132–35.

Excellent Cheyenne traditions state that when their tribe left their fixed villages on the Missouri, below the present Fort Yates, and moved out near the Black Hills, they found the Arapahoes already there and formed a close alliance with them. This was supposed to have happened about 1760 or perhaps a few years later. The Cheyennes were near Bear Butte in the northeastern edge of the Black Hills; the Arapahoes were near them; the Crows were off to the north, in the Little Missouri district; the Kiowas and their Gataka or Padouca allies are said to have been to the southwest of the Black Hills. Some Cheyennes claimed that their tribe and the Arapahoes attacked the Kiowas and Gatakas and drove them down to the upper Platte; but this is represented by the Kiowas as an advance their tribe made, following the retreating Kwahari Comanches southward. One thing is certain: at the period 1790–1800 the Kiowas and Gatakas were on good terms with the Cheyennes and Arapahoes, frequently joining them in making trading trips to the Arikara villages on the Missouri, or camping with them near the Black Hills. But it does appear to be a fact that at the period 1780–90 the Cheyennes alone were left near the Black Hills; for the Sioux came west of the Missouri at this time and advanced to the Black Hills, and the Sioux records (the winter counts) contain no references to the Arapahoes, Kiowas, or Gatakas.

One Arapaho tradition asserts that, after living with the Cheyennes for a time near the Black Hills, they moved to the headwaters of the Missouri; but there they were attacked by the Blackfeet and other tribes and turned southward, skirting the eastern edge of the mountains. This seems to fit in with Fitzpatrick's statement that the Arapahoes had lived on the Marias, a northern tributary of the upper Missouri, close to the Blackfoot range. The Collot map, dated 1796, does not show the Arapahoes, unless they are the Red Bead Indians near the Crows. In later years the Arapahoes were sometimes termed Big Bead and Blue Bead Indians, but never Red Bead. Collot may have been in error here. He seems to have made his map from information obtained from French traders at St. Louis. His map is almost identical with the Spanish manuscript map Lewis and Clark obtained in 1804; indeed, Collot may have copied that map with certain alterations.

In following the Kiowa movement, we come into actual touch once more with the Snake-Comanche groups of the north. The Kiowa story, as set down by Mooney, relates that they left the Black Hills and followed the retreating Kwahari or Antelope Eater group of Comanches southward, skirting the eastern edge of the mountains. This is supposed to have been at a date as early as 1760; but the Kiowas were still near the Black Hills long after that date. It seems obvious that we here have to deal with different Kiowa groups. No one has ever attempted to divide this tribe and describe its movements in separate groups; but when we do this, it becomes apparent at once that the southern Kiowas, the main body of the tribe, followed the Kwahari Comanches southward, warring on them and later making peace and becoming their allies. For this reason the southern Kiowas were sometimes termed the Kwahari-Kiowas from their close association with the Kwahari Comanches. The northern Kiowas or Cold Men, also called the Upper Band, remained near the Black Hills with the Gataka-Apaches until driven south by the Cheyennes and Sioux, probably after 1795, for in that year the Kiowas and Gatakas were with the Cheyennes on Cheyenne River near the Black Hills, as reported by Truteau.

James Mooney seems to have believed that the Kiowa war on the Comanches was of early date and that the retreat of the Comanches before the Kiowa advance southward was also early; but what evidence we have outside the Kiowa traditions collected by Mooney contradicts such a view. The Verendrye report of 1742 seems to exhibit the Kiowas as on the defensive and greatly alarmed over the Snake attacks on them. The tribes near the Black Hills, including the Kiowas, do not seem to have become strong enough to assault the Snakes and Comanches with much effect until after 1780, and after that date these tribes and the Snakes and Comanches were probably only exchanging long-distance raids and not injuring each other greatly. There is no evidence that the Kwahari Comanches were driven south by the Kiowas. For all we know, these Comanches moved southward with the expectation of improving their position, and the Kiowas merely followed in their track. It appears that the Kwahari Comanches were the group known in New Mexico as Yupes, and as late as 1785 the best Spanish information placed most of this group of Comanches far in the north, as far up probably as the North Platte.

This difficulty in locating the Comanche and Snake groups in the north has led some ethnologists to express doubts that there ever were any large bodies of Snakes in the Wyoming and Montana parklands and plains. A study of the modern Snakes or Shoshonis may easily produce such an attitude of doubt, for the present-day Shoshonis have preserved almost no memory of their early history. The Snakes and Comanches evidently withdrew from Wyoming and Montana in the closing years of the eighteenth century; but immediately after the Lewis and Clark expedition (1804–1806) American fur companies entered the Wyoming and Montana field, and their traders and trappers met and talked with Indians who could remember the course of events back to 1750. Washington Irving, when he was preparing his fine books on the western fur trade, talked with many leading fur company men; he examined their old letters and journals, and what he has to state concerning the Snakes is immensely more important than any ethnological study of the Shoshonis of today can be.

In his book *Astoria*, Irving states that the Snakes were a powerful tribe of the northern plains but that they were attacked, broken, and scattered by the Blackfeet, who were armed with guns. The Snakes retreated into the Rockies and the lands to the west of the mountains, part of them becoming frightened skulkers, whose timidity and poverty caused the fur traders and trappers to term them contemptuously Root Diggers and Seed Shuckers; but those Snakes who managed to retain their horses were of a superior type and were termed Shoshonis by the Americans. This group kept their organization into bands and continued to venture into the plains for buffalo, often going with camps of Flatheads for mutual protection; but these journeys into the plains were rendered so hazardous by lurking bands of Blackfeet and other enemies armed with guns that only the most adventurous of the Snakes undertook such expeditions. One American fur trader informed Irving that he once witnessed the incredible sight of five hundred Snake and Flathead warriors standing guard on a hill while fifty of their men were hunting buffalo in the plain below, all the Indians watching anxiously for signs of Blackfeet and ready to rush together for defense if the enemy appeared. It was a common experience after the year 1800 for camps of Snakes and Flatheads who ventured into the Montana plains for a good buffalo hunt to be attacked by Blackfeet, who killed a large number of the hunters in a surprise attack, capturing horses, camp equipment, dried meat, and buffalo skins and driving the Snakes and Flatheads back into the Rockies in wild flight.

This was the state of affairs after the Snakes and their allies had been vindictively harassed by the Blackfeet, Atsenas, and other tribes over a period of twenty or thirty years. As to the condition of the Snakes at an earlier date, Washington Irving asserted that they had once been a powerful nation, holding vast lands east of the Rockies, their lands centering particularly near the Three Forks of the Missouri; that they had long wars with the Blackfeet; that finally that tribe had obtained firearms from the Hudson's Bay Company traders, the Piegans (the Blackfoot tribe nearest the Snakes) being particularly well equipped with guns. The Snakes, trading in New Mexico, were broken and scattered, the survivors retreating into and beyond the Rockies, as a result of the Spanish ban on the firearm trade.[3]

Zenas Leonard, trapping beaver in Montana and Wyoming in 1832, wrote in his journal what he had heard from trappers and traders who had been in that country for the past twenty-five years. He wrote that the Snakes had once held "a glorious hunting ground" east of the Rockies, but that the Blackfeet, equipped with firearms, were in a position to defeat any Indians who were without guns; that the Blackfeet almost exterminated the Flatheads and broke and scattered the great Snake Nation, pursuing

[3] Washington Irving, *Astoria*, 335–36.

the survivors through the mountains, until, like the Flatheads, the Snakes were almost destroyed.[4]

Alexander Ross, who was trading with Indians in the Snake country west of the Rockies about 1818, wrote that for almost a century back the Snakes had been compelled to defend themselves against tribes that had obtained firearms from traders, the Snakes having only bows; that the Snakes had been broken by the Blackfeet, particularly by the Piegans, who had now followed them into the Rockies and were continuing to harass them.

When Colonel H. B. Carrington was in command of Fort Phil Kearny in the Bighorn country in 1866, he heard these stories of the former Snake power in the plains, probably obtaining his information from Jim Bridger, who had known the Snakes and Crows since about 1820. Carrington added to the information given by Washington Irving and Zenas Leonard the fact that the Snake lands east of the mountains had extended down to the Yellowstone and its southern branches; in fact, the Snakes had formerly held the lands south of the Yellowstone that were known before 1850 as the Crow country, embracing lands on both sides of the Bighorn Mountains, extending east to the Rosebud or Powder River and south to the head of the Powder. He asserted that the Crows had driven the Snakes from these lands at an early date.[5]

The recently collected Teit traditions of the Flatheads and Kutenais confirm the older statements about the lands held by the Snakes and add the information that this tribe extended north to the Sweet Grass Hills near the Canadian border. The Teit traditions give the lands at the Three Forks of the Missouri to the Flatheads, as far back, perhaps, as 1600; but our other information indicates clearly that the Three Forks country and the lands northward at least as far as the Great Falls of the Missouri were held originally by the Lemhi group of Snakes.

Since both the Yamparika Comanches and the modern Wyom-

---

[4] Zenas Leonard, *Narrative of the Adventures of Zenas Leonard* (ed. by Milo M. Quaife).

[5] Margaret Carrington, *Ab-sa-ra-ka: Home of the Crows.*

ing Shoshonis are known to have been on the North Platte, which was their territory in the eighteenth century, we have in these quotations from the older writers a picture of a Snake Nation holding the mountain parks and plains from the Three Forks of the Missouri down to the North Platte, where the Snakes linked up with their Comanche cousins. This Snake Nation had vanished from the plains before 1800. Both Tabeau, who was trading on the Missouri in South Dakota about 1802–1805, and Lewis and Clark, who came up the Missouri in 1804, heard from the Missouri River Indians stories of a great Snake Nation in the plains, and Lewis and Clark attempted to exhibit the Snakes as still in the plains; but it is obvious that the Snakes were already gone and that the information given on the Missouri after 1800 was out of date. It was an Indian account of a nation in the plains that was no longer there.

The quotations given above refer mainly to the Blackfoot attacks on the Snakes. To this we must add that the tribes in the Black Hills district and the village Indians on the Missouri were nearly all raiding the Snakes after the period 1760, and the Crows —a very strong tribe before the smallpox of 1780–81 decimated them—were also raiding the Snakes.

Confined on the north and east by enemy tribes that were raiding them, the Snakes could find a kind of refuge in the lands to the west of the mountains, in Idaho and Utah: lands occupied by tribes that were their kinsmen or friends; but these tribes were, in the main, too poor and unwarlike to aid them. The Snakes had only one recourse: to keep in touch with their powerful Comanche cousins in the south and with the Spaniards of New Mexico, for from the south was their only possible source of assistance, in the form of horses and Spanish trade articles.

Early writers have informed us about how the Snakes conducted their trading journeys to the south. Lewis and Clark found the Lemhi Shoshonis or Snakes engaged in crossing the Rockies from the Three Forks of the Missouri to the upper Salmon River in Idaho in the summer of 1805, and these Indians gave information that they had formerly lived east of the mountains in the

156

Three Forks district, but had been driven out by enemies. They still crossed the mountains to hunt buffalo, and they gave Lewis and Clark a description of the trails taken by parties of their people going south to trade for horses and Spanish articles. They stated that the best route was from the Three Forks to the Yellow-stone, and thence it was a ten-day journey to the Spanish settlements, or to a trading center at which Spanish articles and horses were obtainable. Now, the Indians Jacob Fowler and his party were camped with on the upper Arkansas near the present Pueblo, Colorado, in 1821 stated that from their camp it was six days' easy travel to the Spanish settlements near Taos and three days' hard travel north to the Platte, probably meaning the South Platte near Denver. It would be another two hundred miles or six days from the South Platte to the North Platte near Casper, Wyoming, and about eight days from Casper to the Yellowstone. Therefore, when these Lemhi Snakes said in 1805 that it was a ten days' journey from the Yellowstone to their trading place in the south, they probably meant to an Indian trading fair in the old Comanche district on the North Platte. This trade route was still in use in later years. In 1811, the Astorian party met a camp of Snakes and Bannocks near the head of the Bighorn River, who stated that they were going south to trade, and as late as 1826, the British trader, Peter Skene Ogden, reported that a big camp of Snakes in the Yellowstone country that spring sent out a party of one thousand persons to go south on a trading expedition.[6]

It will be noted that this trade trail was not through the plains, but went southward through the mountain parks. The trading trail west of the Rockies, described by the Lemhis to Lewis and Clark in 1805, ran from upper Salmon River in Idaho southward for twenty days' travel to the country of the southern Snakes, who were friends of the Lemhis and had Spanish goods and horses for trade. The trouble with this route west of the mountains, as stated by the Lemhis, was that it was much longer than the one

---

[6] Ogden, quoted by Agnes Laut, in *Conquest of the Greater Northwest*, II, 277. Ogden reported that this big camp of Snakes went on the long journey southward to trade dried buffalo meat for Spanish articles and to steal horses.

via the Yellowstone and it ran at one point through mountains occupied by a fierce tribe called Broken Moccasins, who attacked parties of mounted Snakes traveling through their mountains, took their horses, and killed and ate the animals. The Broken Moccasins were evidently a Snake group; their eating of horses suggests that they were a meat-eating group that had formerly lived on buffalo in the plains, and, having been driven into the mountains, they were satisfying their longing for meat by killing and eating horses that came into their hands.[7]

While the Snakes in the north were faced by the dreary prospect of being raided with ever increasing violence by vindictive Indian enemies armed with guns, the Comanches in the south were enriching themselves by raiding where they pleased into Spanish territory. Still living mainly in the lands north of the Arkansas in eastern Colorado, the Comanches were going as far south as Texas, to raid the Spanish settlers and to trade with their Caddoan allies on upper Red River. With the Spanish border left wide open to attack because the viceroy in Mexico was saving every peso to send to the royal court in Spain and had no money for frontier defense, the Comanches had a heyday. It mattered little whether they were at open war with the Spaniards or in a condition of pretended peace, going confidently to Taos to trade and to exchange friendly visits with the Spanish officials, then driving a raid into the Spanish settlements, sweeping off horses, carrying away women and children as slaves. Governor Cachupin made a peace with the Comanches at Taos in 1752; then he was succeeded by a new governor, and the Comanches resumed raiding. They ruined most of the settlements in northern New Mexico, depopulating the land. Governor Portillo (1761–62) now retaliated by ordering that the Comanches should not be permitted to trade at Taos, and when a Comanche camp that had not been warned of this change came to Taos in December, 1761, on a friendly trading visit, they were attacked and driven off,

[7] The Broken Moccasins evidently lived in the Snake River district in eastern Idaho, possibly in the Pahsimaroi or Lost River Mountains. This was a lonely, desolate region in early times. Can Pahsimaroi mean Broken Moccasin? In Snake or Comanche *pahsi* or *pisi* meant "moccasin," *manpat*, "broken, worn out, rotten."

apparently leaving a number of women and children prisoners in Spanish hands. Fearing Comanche vengeance, the officials in Mexico City removed the Governor and ordered Cachupin, the peacemaker, back to New Mexico. He released the Comanche captives, sending messages of good will to the tribe; some chiefs came to Taos, and Cachupin promised them perfect freedom of trade. One suspects that this trade was more important to the leading Spaniards of New Mexico than to the Comanches. The New Mexicans were very poor; they had little money; and when the annual caravan set out for Old Mexico to lay in a year's supply of Spanish goods, the main portion of what was taken south to barter consisted of stolen Spanish horses and Spanish captives, brought in by Comanches and traded at Taos. When Cachupin talked to the Comanche chiefs about the resuming of trade at Taos, he must have been shocked by the news that they had few horses and Spanish captives to barter, since they had been taking them to the Jumano villages on the Arkansas in eastern Oklahoma and trading them for French goods, including guns and ammunition.[8]

Peace was wonderful. In 1760 the Comanches had made a raid near Taos, killing many people and carrying off fifty captives. They had traded these captives at the Jumano villages, probably for the very guns that they now exhibited proudly at Taos, and the Spanish governor was charmed to meet them. They were his brothers. The good friars were happy; peace had come again, and the Comanches could now be mollified by exposure to Christian influence at Taos.

Meanwhile, the French came to the Jumano villages and traded seventeen horseloads of guns and ammunition. The Jumanos then went into the plains, found a Comanche camp, and bartered the arms and ammunition, probably for stolen horses and captives.

In 1767, Colonel P. F. Mendinueta was appointed governor and military commandant in New Mexico. He tried to continue the peace policy toward the Comanches, despite the fact that these Indians were raiding New Mexico vigorously both from the north

---

[8] Bancroft, *History of Arizona and New Mexico*, 257; Thomas, *Plains Indians and New Mexico*, 25, 14-15.

and east. Still, the Comanches liked the kind of peace they had with the Spaniards and wished to continue trading at the Taos fairs. The French traders were far away, and their trading visits were not very regular. At Taos the fair was an old-established institution, and even if the Spaniards did not permit a trade in weapons, there were many articles the Indians desired that could be obtained at Taos.

Thus, in May, 1769, a Comanche band came to Taos, riding in with white flags flying. The Spaniards and the Taos Indians welcomed them, and trading was started; but while this was going on, a war party of one hundred Comanches appeared suddenly at Ojo Caliente not far off and attempted to make a surprise attack. The Spaniards for once were on guard and drove off the raiders. But when word of this affair reached Taos, a fight broke out between the Comanches who had come to trade and the Spaniards and Taos people. The Comanches fled into the plains.

Governor Mendinueta now laid aside the peace policy. He raised a force of five hundred men and marched northward, to punish the Comanches. He was far on his way, approaching the Arkansas River, when the Comanches discovered the Ute and Apache guides who were with the Spanish force and skipped nimbly out of reach. Sadly the Governor marched homeward, having accomplished nothing; but he had hardly disbanded his little army when the Comanches came down from the north and resumed raiding. They were probably led by their great war chief Green Horn. This man, who was either a Yamparika or a Yupe Comanche, wore in battle a green headdress—a leather cap with buffalo horns attached to it and painted green.[9] He was a bold and skillful raider, a thorn in the flesh of the New Mexican people.

In 1771, Mendinueta returned to the peace policy. A treaty was made with the Comanches, but no peace resulted, and in 1772 the Governor reported a desperate situation. The Comanches were

[9] The German scientist, Ferdinand Roemer, observed a number of green war bonnets in a Penateka Comanche camp in West Texas in 1847. They were caps of buffalo skin with buffalo horns attached to them and were colored green. Chief Green Horn may have taken his name from a headdress of this type.

striking into New Mexico as they had before; Apaches, Navahos, and Utes were raiding, and settlements were dwindling away under Indian attack. There was a lack of arms and horses for pursuing Indian raiders and no arms to provide to settlers, who were anxious to protect themselves. The Governor wished to abandon all outlying settlements and concentrate the population in large communities that might protect themselves; but how could that be, with a government whose policy was to forbid the supplying of weapons to its own citizens? In 1776, Colonel Antonio de Bonilla reported that the Plains Indians were now equipped with firearms and that the only way to deal with them was to concentrate a real striking force of Spanish troops in New Mexico and start a serious offensive against these savages. At this time it seemed probable that Indian hostilities would destroy all the northern provinces, and the Spanish government became so disturbed that it placed these provinces under military rule—military rule, but no troops. The royal court in Madrid refused funds; there was no money for sending regiments to New Mexico.

By 1772, Comanche camps were in the plains east of New Mexico and were raiding Pecos heavily. They soon extended their attacks to the Albuquerque district, but their main blows still came from the north. In July, 1774, one thousand Comanches came down through the Chama district and drove a raid as far as Santa Clara and San Juan. They killed seven men and wounded six; but they carried off captives and three hundred horses, wantonly killing cattle and destroying property. This raid almost reached into Santa Fé, and the weak Spanish military force was helpless to stop it. In August, one hundred Comanches made a small raid in the Pecos district, and Governor Mendinueta with a force of militia followed the Indian trail some seventy leagues eastward, coming on a great Comanche camp on an arroyo. He claimed that he surprised the Comanches, killing many of them. Amazing as it may seem, in spite of Comanche raids, the Spaniards still permitted them to come to Taos and trade their stolen horses and Spanish captives. The most shameful part of it was that the Comanches were even trading some new guns, obtained from

French traders on upper Red River, to the people at Taos, who were prevented by Spanish trade restrictions from purchasing guns in Mexico.

In September, 1774, Mendinueta claimed another victory. He sent a force of some 600 men, including Indian allies, eastward into the plains, under the command of Carlos Fernández. Getting on the trail of a Comanche camp of eighty lodges, Fernández took them by surprise. Part of the warriors mounted and fled; the rest of the people took refuge in marshy ground near a pond, digging a trench and fighting for two hours, until only 150 Comanches remained alive, most of them being wounded. Fernández claimed that he killed or captured nearly 400 Comanches and took 1,000 horses. This reported victory, like others the Spanish officials recorded at this period, lies under the suspicion of being grossly exaggerated. Twitchell in his New Mexican history pointed out that the Comanche camp totaled only sixty lodges, probably around 300 to 400 Indians, so that Fernández killed or captured more Comanches than were in the camp, even after part of them had escaped on horses at the beginning of the fight. However this may have been, the officials in Mexico condemned Mendinueta for fighting at all. They stated that he should keep peace with the Comanches, purchasing Spanish captives that this tribe brought to Taos. This was certainly a unique policy of frontier defense—to permit the enemy to raid at will and then to buy back the captive women and children these Indians brought to Taos.[10]

In 1779, Colonel Anza, a regular army officer who had been appointed governor of New Mexico, did strike a real blow against the Comanches. For many years the northern Comanche chief, Green Horn, had been regarded as the greatest menace to the province. He raided persistently, always coming down from his camp in the north. Instead of attempting to block these raids or pursue the Indians after they had made a raid, Anza adopted the sound strategy of coming down on the Indians from the rear and taking them by surprise in their own camp. He marched north-

[10] Twitchell, quoted in Rupert Norval Richardson, *The Comanche Barrier*, 57–58; Thomas, *Plains Indians and New Mexico*, 172–74.

ward by way of the San Luis Valley, picking up a force of Ute allies, who were bitter enemies of the Comanches and knew all the Comanche camping places. Crossing the mountains, Anza came out into the plains near the present Colorado Springs and took Green Horn's camp by surprise, capturing the camp and many women and children. Luck was with Anza. After he had crossed south of the Arkansas River, near the present Pueblo, he ran into Green Horn and a large war party, returning to their camp from a successful raid in New Mexico; and in the ensuing fight Green Horn and his principal lieutenants were killed. This affair must have shocked the Comanches. They had been attacked in their own country, their women and children had been captured, their great chief and his headmen killed, and an estimated one thousand tipis had been burned in the captured camp. Anza, if aided with arms, men, and horses, might have made things very interesting for the Comanches; but the officials in Mexico were wedded to the idea of making peace with Indians who did not desire peace. In his campaign against Green Horn, Anza had only eighty-five Spanish soldiers; the rest of his force of about six hundred men was made up of Indian allies. He needed reinforcements badly, but he did not get them.

The Spanish officials in New Mexico continued to accept the Comanche statements that their land was north of the Arkansas and that they went south of that river only to raid and trade; but it is obvious that some bands were living south of the Arkansas even as early as 1759, when they aided the Caddoan Indians on Red River against the Texas Spaniards. They must have occupied the Canadian River plains before 1760; ten years later large Comanche groups were on Red River on the northern border of Texas. It was fine country for their camps during the winter, as the climate was mild and grass in favored spots stayed green all winter. Here on Red River the Tawehash tribe of Caddoans had their fortified village and their fields. Their village was a trading center, and the Comanches visited it regularly to trade for maize and vegetables. Here, after 1770, they got in touch again with French traders and began to obtain guns, ammunition, and other

French supplies in quantity. The Comanches were now on Red River in force. Gaignard, a French trader, stated in his journal for 1773–74 that four thousand Comanche warriors assembled at the Tawehash village to greet him. He called the Comanches Naytanes, but he mentioned the Yamparikas particularly; indeed, this band was reported on Red River several times about 1770–75, although the Spaniards of New Mexico continued to report that the Yamparikas lived in the north from the Arkansas up toward the Platte.[11] The Comanches, obtaining new guns from the French on Red River, began to raid vigorously into Texas. They attacked the Spanish settlers near San Antonio, pushed on to the Río Grande and began to raid into Old Mexico, into the provinces of Santandar and Coahuila. This was in 1779. Up to this date the Lipan Apaches had still held their lands in West Texas; but now the Comanches made a terrific attack on them, driving them across the Río Grande. It was evidently in pursuit of the fleeing Lipans that the Comanches crossed the Río Grande, but once across they began to raid the Spanish settlements.[12]

Both in New Mexico and in Texas the Spanish military leaders were pleading for reinforcements, so that they might take the field in force against the hostile Indians; but both in Mexico City and in Madrid the officials opposed such a policy. The King of Spain had humanitarian scruples, and he ordered that a soft policy should be pursued in dealing with the wild tribes. Fate now took a hand in the game. The Comanches were raiding vigorously in New Mexico and Texas in 1780, when smallpox broke out among the Spanish settlers in Texas. The epidemic spread among the Texas Indians, killing great numbers of them; it then reached the tribes on Red River, the Comanches included, and next spread into New Mexico, where it killed over five thousand Pueblo Indians and compelled the friars to abandon seven missions, as there were not enough Indians left in these districts to maintain them. Spreading from tribe to tribe, smallpox reached the Snakes and the Indians on the Upper Missouri. Assiniboins who were visiting

[11] Gaignard, quoted in Bolton, *Athanase de Mézières*, II, 90–95.
[12] Thomas, *Teodoro de Croix*, 45–46.

164

on the Missouri took the disease home with them, and an entire camp of Assiniboins on the Red River of the North died. The Crees were struck, and their losses were so dreadful that the spirit of the survivors was broken and the Crees, who had been a bold and warlike race, sank into a kind of lethargy and lost their reputation as warriors. A Blackfoot war party made a raid on a Snake camp, where they contracted smallpox and took it home with them, and so many Blackfeet died that for a time they ceased to make raids on the Snakes. The Crows were a strong tribe before the smallpox epidemic of 1780–81; they had one thousand lodges; but after that year they had less than half that number, and by 1805 they had only three hundred lodges left.

Just what effect this terrible epidemic had on the Comanches and Snakes is unrecorded; but the losses of both tribes must have been very severe, and it would be reasonable to assume that the survivors for the time being lost spirit and wanted peace and quiet until they could recover from the blow. H. H. Bancroft found a record written by Pino which stated that in 1783 the Comanches made peace in New Mexico. They made peace, both in New Mexico and in Texas, and this time the Comanches, not the Spanish officials, sought it.[13] But only one "congregation" of Comanches—the Kotsotekas or Buffalo Eaters, who occupied the plains east of New Mexico and north of Texas—made this offer of peace. What their purpose was we do not know, but it is obvious that they wished to be on friendly terms with the Spaniards in New Mexico and Texas and to trade in both these provinces. Their losses in the smallpox epidemic may have had something to do with their wish for peace; and, again, their old trade with the French on Red River may have dried up, leaving them with no resources except the meager trade the Spaniards offered at San Antonio and Taos. Evidently, these Kotsoteka Comanches had another purpose. They were now living in the plains of the Canadian River and farther south, and they found it inconvenient to go all the way to Taos to trade. Taos suited the northern Co-

---

[13] Bancroft, *History of Arizona and New Mexico*, 267–68; Thomas, *Forgotten Frontiers*, 316.

manches, who were still on or north of the Arkansas, but the Kotsotekas desired to have a trading center for their own benefit at the ancient pueblo of Pecos.

Governor Anza of New Mexico wanted peace, but not with a single Comanche group, leaving the others free to continue their raids on Spanish settlements. He suspected, quite correctly, that the Yamparika and Yupe Comanches were not interested in this peace. But the Kotsotekas desired it enough to betray their own tribesmen, warning the Spanish authorities in August,1785, that the Yamparikas and Yupes were planning a raid into northern New Mexico. In September, they informed the Spaniards of another raid being planned by the northern bands, and they even offered to help the Spaniards against their kinsmen by blocking the routes of the raiding parties into New Mexico.[14]

Governor Anza now urged the chiefs to hold a council at which all Comanche congregations should be represented, and to select a chief to head the tribe, with authority to speak for and control all its groups. To this the Kotsotekas agreed; but the Yamparikas and Yupes, who had come to Taos to trade, seem to have been much more interested in going on their autumn buffalo hunt than in holding peace councils. They did their trading at Taos and hastened off into the plains to hunt. However, the Comanches did meet in council after the hunting season ended. The meeting was at a place called *Casa de Palo*, "House of Sticks or Timber," on the Arkansas, near the present Pueblo;[15] all three congregations of Comanches were present: Kotsotekas, Yamparikas, and Yupes, and the chiefs selected Ecueracapa (Leather Jacket, called *Cota de Malla*, "Coat-of-Mail," by the Spaniards),[16] to speak for the

14 Thomas, *Forgotten Frontiers,* 72.

15 As the Yupe Comanches were termed in New Mexico *Gente de Palo,* "People of the Sticks" or "Timber," presumably there was a connection between these Comanches and the place called *Casa de Palo* on the Arkansas near the present Pueblo, particularly as the Yupes are known to have frequented that district.

16 Thomas states that Ecueracapa (Coat of Mail) and the Comanche chief Iron Jacket of the period 1850 were both Kotsoteka chiefs. Their names were the same, but we have no information about whether they were of the same family.

tribe, and the Spaniards at once gave him the handsome title of commissioner general of the Comanche Nation. He certainly was eager to help the Spanish officials. White Bull, a Yamparika or Yupe chief who was shouting against peace, was assassinated by the peace-seekers. His family and followers were driven out of the Comanche camp and, while camping by themselves, were taken by surprise and killed by a Pawnee war party.

The Spanish officials wrote reams of reports on this peace with the Comanches; but what it boiled down to was that the Kotsotekas obtained the right to trade at Pecos and that a peace was also agreed to in Texas. Ecueracapa organized a grand Comanche war party to carry out a clause of the agreement that had to do with the killing of Apaches; but the total bag was six Apaches killed, two women and eighty-five "riding animals" captured: a rather thin return for all the time and the 641 pesos, 6 reals Anza had spent to induce the Comanches to help fight the Apaches.

There was a falling off in Comanche raids in New Mexico after this peace was made; but that seems to have been due to a shift of Comanche population, the northern bands moving southward, and also to the fact that New Mexico had been raided until the people in general were too poor to make raiding them profitable. The traders at Taos and Pecos had the only articles in New Mexico the Comanches desired. In Texas the trade at San Antonio was about all that interested the Indians. Their main business now was raiding into untouched territory in Old Mexico, where horses and other plunder, including captives, to be traded at Taos, Pecos, and San Antonio were to be had in abundance. And this was the bitter fruit of nearly a century of Spanish official policy in dealing with the Comanches. It had started with a few small Comanche raids in northern New Mexico about the year 1705. The Comanches had now ruined New Mexico and Texas and were busily engaged in ruining the northern provinces of Old Mexico.

Even at the date of this Comanche peace in 1785–86, the Spanish officials continued to believe the Comanche reports that only the Kotsotekas were camping south of the Arkansas, that the Yupes were mostly north of that river and that the Yamparikas were farthest away, about one hundred leagues north of the Kotsotekas. Alfred B. Thomas accepted this Spanish view and set it down on his map, which shows the Yamparikas still in the Uinta Mountains and Green River district in eastern Utah, extending east and south across the Platte and down toward the Arkansas, with the Yupes extending from a point perhaps north of the North Platte down through Colorado to the Arkansas River. This does not fit in with the known fact that large bodies of Comanches were on Red River, allied to the Tawehash and other Caddoan Indians, even prior to 1758, the year that about one thousand Comanche warriors helped the Caddoans destroy the Lipan mission on the San Sabá, and the fact that from 1770 on, large camps of Comanches were apparently wintering on Red River near the Tawehash village. When the French trader Gaignard referred to four thousand Comanches gathered on Red River about 1772, he mentioned the Yamparikas as a leading group in the camp. The Yupes were evidently also on Red River; for when Anza was making peace in 1786, a Yupe Chief, Chamanada, wished to go to Texas, and Anza gave him a letter to the Texas governor, to be delivered at the Tawehash village on Red River. Here is evidence that the Yupes had some bands that frequented Red River and felt more at home on the Texas border than in New Mexico.

There were shifts and changes in Comanche groups at this period, 1770–90, that cannot be explained from the Spanish documents, and the Comanches of the present day are without any real memory of their tribe's past, as was plainly illustrated in the recent study of the tribe by Wallace and Hoebel. The truth concerning the Comanche drift southward probably is that the bands moved haphazardly, mingling for a few seasons and then separating, and that groups of all the Comanche divisions reached Red River on the Texas border at an early date. The Spanish officials of Texas at the period 1770–85 termed one Comanche group the Kotsotekas or Orientals—the Buffalo Eaters or Eastern Comanches. The western Comanches of this period were evidently the Yamparikas. Comanche tradition in 1881 was to the effect

168

that when the Yamparikas first went south, they found the Pena-tekas living there in Mexican territory. The Penatekas are not mentioned at all in the Spanish documents; but we have one bit of evidence that seems to prove that this Comanche tribe was on Red River at least as far back as 1785. In 1881, Lieutenant W. P. Clark was collecting material for his book on the Indian sign language, and, coming among the Comanches, he talked with an old Snake Indian named Straight Feather. This man said that he was seventy and that his father was a Snake and his mother was half Penateka and half Pawnee—that is, Red River Pawnee or Tawehash. Straight Feather was born about 1811, and if we as-sume that his mother was about twenty-five at the time of his birth, she was born about the year 1785 on Red River, her father a Penateka Comanche, her mother a Tawehash Pawnee. This is the only solid evidence we have that places the Penatekas on Red River at such an early date, and it hints that the Penatekas were in close association with the Tawehash. They were, therefore, part of the Comanches who were at the Tawehash village in 1786 and were then engaged in peace negotiations with the Spanish governor of Texas.

The Spanish peace with the Comanches on the Texas border in 1786 was arranged by the same methods as the one in New Mexico. The chiefs were bribed with presents and a promise of trade—a strange kind of peace that left the Comanches free to raid into Mexico and then bring the Spanish captives they had taken to San Antonio and barter them back to the Spaniards. An added inducement to keep this peace, in Texas, was annual gifts to the chiefs—tobacco, colored cloth, Spanish clothing, knives, glass beads, and vermilion face paint. It was the Orientales who got these peace benefits, the Spanish officials expending five thousand pesos a year for gifts to chiefs. In one matter the Spaniards were adamant: no guns were given or sold to Comanches. This pre-tense of peace was kept up by the Spanish officials at San An-tonio until 1809. The Comanches are said to have been relatively friendly during the twenty-five years after 1786, the peace bring-ing some relief; this meant simply that the Comanches raided into

Texas when they chose, then went to San Antonio, got peace gifts, swaggered through the streets of the little town, and forced the obsequious Spanish soldiers to care for their horses and perform other menial services. The warriors took anything they fancied from the frightened townsmen; the chiefs collected their peace gifts, and the band rode off, often rounding up a herd of horses from some Spanish ranch near the town and carrying the animals away as an additional peace perquisite.

In New Mexico, Governor Anza made a valiant attempt to reclaim the wild Comanches, to induce them to settle down and live by growing crops. The Spanish officials claimed that the Comanche chiefs asked for aid in doing this, and the Gente de Palo or Yupe chiefs are said to have made the request. This was certainly an ambitious and optimistic project. Anza sent workmen up to the Arkansas to a point near Pueblo (probably on the stream still called San Carlos or St. Charles), and here the workmen constructed a group of houses in the New Mexican style: a real pueblo or little town for the Yupes to live in. It was called *El Pueblo de San Carlos de los Jupes*, and it cost seven hundred pesos for labor and material, much of which had to be taken across mountains from Taos up to the Arkansas. Some Spaniards stayed at this pueblo to teach the Yupes how to plant crops. All seemed to be well; and then a woman (seemingly the favorite wife or concubine of the Yupe chief) died at the pueblo, and the Comanches got the notion that this place was bad medicine. They moved away, put a taboo on the place, and would not return to it.[17]

[17] Richardson, *The Comanche Barrier*, 65. The Yupes fled from their pueblo in July, 1788.

# 8. The End of Old Times

THE GREAT smallpox epidemic of 1780–81 may be taken as the event that presaged the dawning of modern times in the plains. New tribes were pushing into the northern plains, shaking the hold of the older inhabitants: the remaining Apache groups and the Snakes; the trade in firearms had been revived on an extensive scale, and as soon as the tribes recovered from the shock of the smallpox epidemic, they began to war more vigorously on the Apaches and Snakes.

The last two Apache or Padouca groups in the north after 1780 were in western Nebraska and western South Dakota. Those in South Dakota were the Gatakas; the identity of the Nebraska Padoucas is unknown, but one suspects that they were very closely related to the Gatakas and probably joined that group toward the end of the eighteenth century. How these northern groups of Padoucas managed to hold their lands after their tribesmen farther to the south in Kansas, Colorado, and Oklahoma were forced out by the Comanches after the year 1726 is quite easily explained. In the first place, the northern Padoucas were far off the line of the Comanche advance, which left the mountains in southeastern Colorado and struck eastward and then south toward Texas. Even the Kansas Padoucas do not appear to have been driven out by direct Comanche attack. They probably withdrew because the Comanches had cut them off from their trading bases in New Mexico and because they were under attack by all the tribes near the Missouri River, tribes that now had firearms with which they could create panic in the Padouca villages. The French trade in firearms did not extend up the Missouri farther than eastern Kansas, the result being that the Padoucas in Nebraska and South Dakota did not have to fear attacks by enemies armed with guns. Moreover, they had been here in the north for a very long time and had gained the friendship and alliance of such neighboring tribes as the village-dwelling Arikaras on the Missouri and the Kiowas in the Black Hills. Continuing their old practice of trading, the Padoucas in some manner managed to make expeditions to the south, where they obtained large numbers of horses and some Spanish articles, which they traded to the Arikaras and other friendly tribes. The Ietans were mixed up in this intertribal trade; indeed, the account of Spanish Louisiana in 1785 terms the Indians who traded horses to the tribes near the upper Missouri the Laytanes or Apaches—Ietans or Apaches, and it terms the Padoucas of South Dakota the Pados or Taguibaces (Pado being the French abbreviation of Padouca, and Taguibaces coming from Tagui, an old name for the Apaches). In this Spanish document, written at St. Louis from French trader information, both the Dakota Padoucas and the Ietans are termed Apaches. Bourgmont in 1717 placed the Dakota Padoucas eighty leagues up White River, which would locate them near the present Pine Ridge Sioux reservation. Truteau in 1795 termed the Padoucas "a great nation," seven days' march or eighty leagues southwest of the Arikara villages on a branch of the Platte. His Arikara villages were on the Missouri just below Cheyenne River, his Padoucas on a branch of Loup Fork. Perrin du Lac, in 1802, on information from French traders, made a distinction (as "The Account of Spanish Louisiana in 1785" does) between the Ietans and Padoucas. He called the Ietans Baldheads and stated that they wandered between the Platte and Arkansas, going as far as the foot of the mountains of New Mexico; the Padoucas were a great nation on the Platte, ten days' ride from the Arikara villages.

When the Omahas and Poncas moved down the Missouri into northeastern Nebraska, about 1730 apparently, they were at once attacked by the Padoucas, coming from the Sand Hills of western Nebraska. Omaha tradition states that the Padoucas protected their horses with armor made of several thicknesses of leather and that the main weapon of the Padoucas was a long-handled stone war club—the same weapon which the Snakes of Montana used with such deathly effect in their attacks on the Blackfeet before the Blackfeet obtained horses. The Omahas and Poncas were without horses and firearms when the Padoucas began to attack them; but within a generation horses and a few guns were obtained, and the Padoucas were thrown on the defensive.

The tide seems to have turned definitely against the Padoucas by the time of the great smallpox epidemic of 1780–81. The tribes on the Missouri now had horses and some guns; the warlike Teton Sioux were on the Missouri, equipped with firearms and thrusting strongly westward. It was time for the Padoucas to go; but just when they went and under what circumstances is a mystery. The French traders, whose information was often faulty, continued to speak of a great Padouca group on or near the Platte even as late as 1800. Truteau put the Padoucas on a branch of the Platte in 1795, and in the same year the trader James Mackay stated, on Omaha Indian information, that the Padoucas still held out in the Sand Hills of western Nebraska. The Collot map of 1796 placed Padouca villages, with symbols indicating permanent settlements, not moving camps, on the South Platte; the Spanish manuscript map obtained by President Jefferson for the use of Lewis and Clark in 1804 also placed permanent Padouca villages on the Platte, but not on the South Platte—on the north bank of the main river, below the forks. The Dismal River branch of Loup Fork was still termed Padouca Fork in 1812, and the South Fork of the Platte was given the same name. It was here between the Loup and the forks of the Platte that the Padoucas vanished, sometime after 1790. Our only clues to the fate of these Indians point to their joining forces with the Kiowas and retiring with that tribe from near the forks of the Platte to the head of the South Platte in the mountains, and thence southward across the Arkansas. As late as 1803, James Pursley found "bands of Padoucahs and

Kyaways" trading horses at the Mandan villages on the Missouri in North Dakota, and he went with them to their camps on the Platte and later on southward to the New Mexican border. This is the last trading expedition of bands of Padoucas to the upper Missouri of which we have any record.[1]

The Snakes seem to have withdrawn from the northern plains about the time of the Padouca withdrawal, but—as in the case of the Padoucas—we do not know just what happened. The northern Snake group that held lands east of the mountains near the Three Forks of the Missouri seems to have been the first to be heavily attacked. Their principal enemies were the Blackfeet, a tribe that now had a regular supply of arms and ammunition; and as the Blackfeet had an insatiable hatred for the Snakes and wanted horses, which were to be obtained most easily by raiding Snake camps, the latter tribe was under constant pressure from Blackfoot war parties.

By 1781 the Piegans, leading the Blackfoot movement westward, had advanced to Red Deer River; but there they were stricken with smallpox, which they asserted they contracted from Snake captives taken by one of their war parties. The Piegans lost a great many people of smallpox; but the Snakes, as they asserted, suffered as heavy losses from the epidemic and began to retreat toward the southwest, closer to the mountains. Both tribes had been badly shattered by smallpox. The Piegans, as they claimed, were contemplating making peace with the Snakes; but now the Snakes sent out a war party and massacred a camp of five lodges of Piegans who were hunting in the mountains near the head of Bow River. This was in the autumn of 1783, and the Piegans at once resumed active warfare against the Snakes. However, that tribe had withdrawn farther toward the south; the Piegan war parties had to go a long distance to find the Snake camps,

[1] Pursley, in Zebulon Montgomery Pike, *The Expeditions of Zebulon Montgomery Pike* (ed. by Elliott Coues), II, 756–58. The Spanish manuscript map is in Meriwether Lewis and William Clark, *Original Journals of the Lewis and Clark Expedition* (ed. by Reuben Gold Thwaites); the Collot map is in Waldo Wedel, "Introduction to Pawnee Archeology," Bureau of American Ethnology *Bulletin No. 112.*

and there were no important fights between the two tribes from 1781 to 1786.[2]

While David Thompson was in the Piegan camp in the autumn of 1787, these Indians moved eighty miles south of Bow River to hunt buffalo in the plains, and from this point they sent a war party of fifty men southward to raid the Snakes. The warriors marched on foot for six days and found a big Snake camp, evidently in the Three Forks of the Missouri district. The Piegans rushed the camp, killed some Snakes, and captured thirty-five horses and fifteen mules.[3]

These contemporary reports of David Thompson are most important. They refute the view of some modern authors, who maintain that the Snakes probably never occupied any extensive area in the plains, for Thompson states that the Snakes after the smallpox epidemic withdrew far to the southwest, and the raid of 1787 shows that they withdrew to the Three Forks of the Missouri. Therefore, we may assume that they had held the plains far to the north of the Three Forks before 1781. The mention of the mules captured in the Snake camp proves that this northern group of Snakes was obtaining horses and mules by trading on the Spanish border, for it was only there that mules were obtainable. Moreover, Alexander Mackenzie reported in 1789 that the Blackfeet had great numbers of horses obtained in raids toward the south, that the Blackfeet were the horse traders of the north, and that numbers of the animals on the Saskatchewan had Spanish brands.

The withdrawal of this northern Snake group and their Flathead and Bannock allies to lands west of the mountains seems to have been forced by Blackfoot attacks on them during the closing decade of the eighteenth century. It was these northern Snakes who told Lewis and Clark in 1804 that within the memory of men then alive their tribe had lived east of the mountains, but their Pawkee[4] enemies had forced them to leave the plains. They

[2] Ewers, *The Blackfeet*, 28–29.
[3] *Ibid.*, 29.
[4] Most authorities state that the Pawkees were Blackfeet; but the name seems to be an abbreviation of the old Cree name for the Atsenas: *Pawaustic-eythin-*

175

still crossed the passes to the plains, usually in September, and advanced cautiously to Three Forks to hunt buffalo, with other bands of Snakes and Flatheads joining them for mutual defense against enemy war parties. These northern Snakes or Lemhis in 1804 had one gun in their camp. Their arms were bows and arrows (the arrows tipped with obsidian, probably obtained from Obsidian Cliff in the present Yellowstone Park), lances, and pogamoggons or long-handled stone war clubs that were used in fighting on horseback. Chief Comeawait of this Snake camp said to Lewis and Clark: "If we had guns, instead of hiding ourselves in mountains and living like bears on roots and berries, we would then go down and live in the buffalo country in spite of our enemies, whom we never fear when we meet them on equal terms."[5]

These Lemhi Snakes were being raided not only by the Blackfeet but by the Atsenas, by the Hidatsas of the upper Missouri River, and probably by the Crow kinsmen of the Hidatsas. With Lewis and Clark was Sacajawea, a Snake girl who had been captured by a Hidatsa war party and who was now the wife of Lewis and Clark's French interpreter. She stated that it was in 1799 that she was captured. Her band of Lemhi Snakes were encamped on one of the three forks at the head of the Missouri when the Hidatsas surprised the camp. At the first gunfire all the Snake men jumped on their horses and made off; the women, children, and old people ran toward the woods, with the Hidatsas pursuing them. The attackers killed a large number of the Snakes, rounded up many young women and older children, and then returned down the Missouri to their own village with a large number of scalps and many captives. Such attacks had been made on the Snake camps in the plains over a long period of years. Armed mainly with bows and obsidian-tipped arrows, the Snake men could not stand against warriors armed with guns, and they lost courage and became thoroughly demoralized.

---

*youwuc*, meaning "Waterfall People." The Lemhi Snakes in 1805 called the enemies who were then harassing them most Pawkees and Minitaris, the latter name referring to waterfall and being the name for both the Atsenas and the Hidatsas of the Missouri River region.

[5] Lewis and Clark, *Original Journals*, I, 450.

Tabeau's reference to Bannocks and Flatheads coming to trade at the Mandan and Hidatsa villages on the Missouri refers to the earlier period, before the Hidatsas and Mandans had firearms in quantity and were therefore not averse to having the Snakes, Bannocks, and Flatheads come to trade with them. The village Indians on the Missouri had maize, dried vegetables, and some European articles to trade to these tribes from the Three Forks of the Missouri. By 1800 this trade at the Mandan villages had come into the hands of the Crows, who went annually to the Mandan and Hidatsa villages to trade horses for British goods, taking with them a camp of Snakes with whom they were on friendly terms.

The middle group of Snakes in the plains, those who held the Yellowstone and Bighorn lands, were probably too far to the south to suffer much from Blackfoot raids in the eighteenth century. Their enemies were apparently the Crows and Atsenas, and the string of prehistoric camp sites extending westward up the Yellowstone probably indicates the Crow movement up the river at some date prior to 1800. The Crow advance was probably close to the date of the smallpox plague of 1781. In 1881, Lieutenant W. P. Clark obtained traditions that the Arapahoes and Cheyennes drove the Kihatsa or Paunch tribe of Crows (the modern River Crows) from the Little Missouri and that these Crows went north and joined the Atsenas. This might have been in the period 1770–80, for the Cheyennes were not with the Arapahoes near the Black Hills until about 1760, and by 1790 the Arapahoes appear to have left the Black Hills and moved farther westward. We might conjecture that it was the Kihatsas or River Crows whose camp sites containing broken pottery have been found along the Yellowstone.

As for the second Crow tribe, the Absarokas or Mountain Crows, we have no definite information about their location before 1800, but Tabeau states that the two Crow tribes were independent until smallpox broke their strength and forced them to live in close alliance. The Absarokas were the Crows who traded at the Mandan and Hidatsa villages, taking a camp of Snakes with them. Larocque, the Canadian trader, met this camp of Absarokas and Snakes at the Mandan villages in 1805 and accompanied them on their return to their own country. These Indians took a trail leading from the Mandans in a southwesterly direction to the Little Missouri, then striking westward across Powder River to Piney Creek and the head of Tongue River, on the eastern flank of the Bighorn Mountains. The Crows and Snakes seemed perfectly at home in the Powder River country, moving their camp with leisurely assurance, stopping for days to hunt buffalo, and no other Indians ever reported. It was their country, and one suspects that the Absarokas or Mountain Crows had advanced westward from the Little Missouri in the eighteenth century and taken these Powder River and Bighorn lands from the Snakes.

As for the camp of Snakes with them in 1805, Larocque reported that they belonged to a Snake tribe that had been destroyed, the survivors joining the Absarokas. A man of this Snake camp went in the spring of 1805 to visit the Snakes in the west, and he rejoined the camp while Larocque was in it, bringing Spanish articles. He had evidently been to visit some southern Snake group that traded in New Mexico. Larocque observed that the Snakes who were with the Absarokas had the same type of bow made of horn that the Flatheads used.

The Crows and their Snake allies in 1805 were evidently blocked toward the south by enemy tribes who prevented their trading on the New Mexican frontier. The horses that the Absarokas traded annually at the Mandan villages were obtained by them from the Flatheads, who had numerous herds of horses in their country west of the Rockies.

This division of the Crows into the River and Mountain tribes is an interesting matter. These Indians appear in the Bighorn and Yellowstone country on the Collot map as Crow Feather Indians. The River Crows seem to have held the Yellowstone Valley and that of the Bighorn, while the Mountain Crows held lands to the south, to the east of the Bighorn Mountains; but each year the two groups met and camped together in late summer on the Yellowstone, above the mouth of the Bighorn. The Atsenas, usually

Uriewici (Jack Tendoy), a Shoshoni chief, about 1880.

Hidatsa earth-lodge village on the upper Missouri. From a painting by George Catlin, 1832.

friendly with the River Crows, had the custom of coming south with all their people on visits, and in the late summer of 1805, Larocque reported that a big camp of Atsenas was on the Bighorn. One suspects that the Atsenas were trading British goods, including some guns, to the River Crows and that they had helped that tribe drive the Snakes out of the Yellowstone and Bighorn country prior to 1790.

The Snakes who had been driven out of the Yellowstone and Bighorn country evidently included the middle group or Pohogues, who after 1800 frequented the Fort Hall district in Idaho —west of the Rockies and immediately west of the present Yellowstone Park, with easy passes through the mountains to the head of the Yellowstone River. The Bannocks were probably with the Pohogues east of the mountains, but the Bannocks were a bold, roving group, and in early times they probably shifted their camps back and forth from one Snake group to another, just as they did after 1800. The fact that Tabeau mentions the Bannocks coming with Flatheads to trade at the Mandan villages on the Missouri indicates that before 1800 the Bannocks were quite at home in the plains east of the mountains, and their wide roving is suggested by the fact that they are mentioned as being intimate with the Flatheads near the Three Forks of the Missouri, while they seem to have been equally at home with the Snakes on the upper Yellowstone and with those farther south in the Green River and Platte country. The amazing fact that these Bannocks had three bands with names identical with those of three Comanche groups (Yamparika, Kotsoteka, and Penateka) strongly suggests that the Bannocks and Comanches were closely associated early in the eighteenth century.

More than any of the Snake groups, the Bannocks after the year 1805 had the appearance of being Plains Indians. They were definitely organized into bands in the plains manner, they were well mounted and armed, and they had the same reputation as the bold Teton Sioux of being robbers and outlaws. About 1832, Nathaniel Wyeth wrote that the Snakes or Shoshonis had no organization. They met in great congregations at the time of the salmon run, but after fishing, they broke up into small groups, each wandering off alone in search of other food supplies. The Bannocks, he stated, were organized into bands which kept together in a single camp the year round. They went east of the mountains in spring to hunt buffalo, coming back across the passes in the autumn, to winter in the Fort Hall district, where there was good pasturage all winter for their horses. From their wintering ground on Snake River, these Bannocks could go through passes that brought them out either on the head of the Yellowstone or into Wind River Valley and to the head of the Bighorn.

The Pohogue Snakes and the Bannocks were camping together at the period 1818–20. Peter Skene Ogden seems to be referring to the Pohogues when he mentions the Plains Snakes in 1820. He estimated this group at fifteen hundred people; the Bannocks were rated at that period at around six hundred. The trader Donald McKenzie had dealings with these Indians at Boise River on Snake River in 1819 and found that he could not get on with them. They were not like the poor and humble Snakes of other groups. They were all mounted and had large numbers of guns; they were like Plains Indians—bold, warlike, afraid of no one, and refusing point blank to hunt beaver for McKenzie, saying that beaver trapping was work for white men and squaws. They told McKenzie that they obtained all the guns and goods they needed by trading with other tribes, evidently in the plains east of the mountains, and that they had no need to hunt beaver like women so that they could trade with him. They were not tied to any white trader. This suggests that they were trading regularly with the camp of Absaroka Crows and Snakes that visited the Mandan villages each year and returned to the plains with British guns and goods obtained from the Mandans.

The third Snake group, farthest toward the south, was on Green River in 1805. The Lemhi Snakes of the north in speaking to Lewis and Clark that year termed the Green River group the southern Shoshonis or Snakes, and the Crows gave the same name to the group. Today ethnologists term this group Northern Shoshonis or Wyoming Shoshonis. They seem to be today a very mixed group, but among them must be the descendants of the old southern Snake group, for they had as late as 1880 a memory that the Comanches had separated from their group and that they had formerly camped with and "run with" the Bannocks. In 1825 this Wyoming Shoshoni group, or part of these Indians, was in the Bear Lake district of northwestern Utah, and General Ashley reported in that year that they claimed the lands east of Great Salt Lake and Utah Lake. In 1850 they claimed lands east of the continental divide, in the Wind River Valley, along the North Platte and in the Medicine Bow country. Since the Mountain Crows or Absarokas claimed and occupied the Wind River country after the year 1815 it would seem probable that the southern Snakes or Kogohols had been driven west of the mountains at a late date, their lands in the east then being occupied by the Mountain Crows. But even after 1805 these southern Snakes ventured east of the mountains to hunt buffalo in the mountain parks and plains, sometimes going with the Bannocks. In 1810 the southern Snakes were a broken and frightened people. They clearly had been subjected to most severe attacks from enemies over a long period. By 1815 they began to obtain firearms and to pick up spirit. A generation or two later a strong chief, Washaki, took control, obtained guns for his men from American traders, and made the Snake warriors once more fit to face any foe, even the fierce Teton Sioux.[6]

It is obvious from the above accounts that by 1805 all the Snake groups had been driven west of the mountains and that they only ventured across the passes into the mountain parks and plains to the east on buffalo hunts, moving cautiously and always ready to flee back across the passes when enemy war parties appeared. Yet, in 1804–1806, Lewis and Clark pictured a great Snake Nation

[6] At the council with government agents in 1852, the southern Snakes (the present Wyoming Shoshonis) made formal claim to the following lands as their old and rightful country: from the summit of the Uinta Mountains north to Wind River Valley; from a north-south line passing through Salt Lake City eastward to a north-south line crossing the North Platte at the mouth of the Sweetwater. This was the same land that the Spanish priests, Escalante and Domínguez, stated in 1776 was held by the Yamparika Comanches.

in the plains, reaching from the Yellowstone south across the Platte and connecting up with the Comanches near the Arkansas. This information concerning the Snakes in the plains was clearly outdated by 1805, and it was vague and confused; but there is enough of historical interest in these accounts to make it worth while to examine them carefully.

Both Lewis and Clark and Tabeau applied to the Snakes the old Caddoan Indian name, variously written as Laytane, Laitan, Alitan, Ietan. Here we have the curious fact that on the upper Missouri after 1800, Ietan was the usual designation for Snakes and Comanches; but when American traders and trappers came among these tribes after 1805, they always termed them Snakes or Shoshonis, applying the name Ietan sometimes to a camp of trading Indians, the Ietans Proper, sometimes extending the name to include all the Comanches.

To the Alitans both Tabeau and Lewis and Clark added a smaller Shoshonean group termed *Têtes Pelées, La Plais,* or "Baldheads," and these were undoubtedly the Baldhead band of Comanches, a group, named for its chief, that after 1805 lived with the camps of trading Indians, among whom the Ietans Proper were a leading band. Here I am applying the name Ietans Proper to the group supposed to have been of mixed Ute-Apache origin, who were evidently not Comanches, although in later years the name Ietan was applied to the Comanches.

Tabeau obtained his information from the Arikara Indians of the Missouri in South Dakota, a tribe akin to the Pawnees of Nebraska. Unlike Lewis and Clark, he did not locate a great Alitan or Snake Nation in the Plains. He made the Alitans and Pelées one group, speaking the same language, a tongue different from that of the Padoucas. He stated that the Cheyennes and their allies warred on the Alitans and Pelées in the lands between the Yellowstone and the Spanish border, defeating them and taking many slaves, and that the Crows, on the other hand, were allies of the Alitans, Pelées, and Serpents, three tribes speaking the same tongue. The Crows met these tribes on the Yellowstone, and every year the Crows and some of these Alitans, Pelées and Serpents went to the Mandan villages to trade horses for British goods, guns, and ammunition. The Serpents had only garments made of beaverskin; some of their children wore robes made by weaving strips of rabbit skins into a kind of furry fabric.[7] At this point Tabeau is obviously referring to the Snakes who in 1805 were going to the Mandan villages with the Mountain Crows to trade horses for British goods; but the Tabeau information suggests a situation some years earlier than that observed by Larocque in 1805. Larocque found only a small Snake camp with the Crows; Tabeau made this Snake group large and added to the group the Baldhead Comanches and evidently their Ietan allies. In truth, Tabeau pictures for us the method by which the Snakes of the Yellowstone, and later the Crows of that district, obtained horses and Spanish goods at the period 1770–90. They were being supplied by camps of trading Indians—Comanches and Ietans—who came up from the south annually to hold a trading fair on the Platte or Yellowstone with the Snakes of the north.

Tabeau explained the origin of the name Baldhead or Tête Pelée by recounting an Arapaho tale. The Kananavich or Arapahoes and the Pelées were once camped near each other without being aware of the fact. They were enemy groups. A scout left each camp. They met and stood watching each other attentively for a time, then laid their weapons on the grass and came together. The Arapaho suggested a gambling game, which the other scout agreed to. The Pelée staked his moccasins and leggings and lost. He then staked the rest of his clothing and his weapons and lost. Taunted by the Arapaho, he staked his scalp and lost it. The Arapaho scalped him, but he lived, and his camp was later called the Tête Pelée or Baldhead band.[8]

Lewis and Clark obtained information concerning the Snake Nation at the Arikara villages on the Missouri, at the Mandan and Hidatsa villages higher up the river in North Dakota, and

---

[7] Tabeau, *Narrative of Loisel's Expedition*, 165, 160.

[8] *Ibid.*, 156–57. This is the earliest known version of a tale that was current among the Plains Indians on into the nineteenth century. Presumably the scalped man belonged to or led the camp of Comanches called Baldheads. This camp does not seem to be mentioned after 1820.

from the Snakes themselves in the country west of the Rockies. The explorers then combined this information. They described the Snakes as a great nation in the plains and west of the Rockies. They gave the tribe's own name as Alitan, which was not correct, and divided them into Alitans of the Plains and of the West. The first group they stated occupied the plains from the falls of the Missouri south to Arkansas River. The Alitans of the West lived in and west of the Rockies, sometimes venturing into the plains near the upper Arkansas River, and had more trade with the Spaniards of New Mexico than the Alitans of the Plains. To these two Snake groups Lewis and Clark added the Pelées or La Plais (Tabeau's Têtes Pelées or Baldhead Comanches), whom they described as a numerous tribe, warlike but badly armed, roving in the plains from the Arkansas south to Red River.[9]

To these Snake and Comanche groups Lewis and Clark added the Castahans, locating the tribe on their map at the head of the Bighorn, extending east beyond Powder River. Tabeau, at the Arikara villages, never heard the name Castahan. Lewis and Clark picked it up at the Mandan and Hidatsa towns, and evidently misunderstood part of the information given to them. They stated that the Castahans spoke the Minitari tongue, the language of the Atsenas and Arapahoes, and that the French called the Castahans *Gens des Vaches*, which was really the French name for the Arapahoes. These Castahans had five thousand people; they roved from the Yellowstone to the Platte, were at war with the Crows, traded with the Kiowas, and sometimes came to the Mandan villages to trade. When William Clark, of the Lewis and Clark party, came down the Yellowstone in 1806, he recorded in his journal the definite statement that the Castahans were Snakes, a tribe that traded with the Spaniards and brought horses and Spanish goods up to the Yellowstone to trade to the tribes there. Here again we seem to have the same group of trading Indians, already referred to by Tabeau and Larocque; but specifically the Castahans were a Snake tribe that occupied the lands from the head of the Bighorn east across Powder River, and by 1805 they had

[9] See statistics, Lewis and Clark, *Original Journals*, VI.

been driven out by enemies. As for their name, it might be an Arapaho designation, as it has the Arapaho terminal *han* or *hani*, meaning "people" or "tribe." Hayden (1862) gave *Catha*, "Many Horses," as the old Arapaho name for the Comanches. *Cathahan* would mean "People with Many Horses." This Lewis and Clark Castahan tribe may have been a part of the Comanche group the Cheyennes and Arapahoes knew as Kwaharis.

Lewis and Clark obtained on the Missouri in 1804–1805 much information concerning the Indians out in the plains from the Yellowstone to the Platte; but the French traders who conveyed this information seem to have had only a vague knowledge of these tribes, and what they did have to say concerning some of the tribes was outdated, as the Indians had removed from the districts in which the Frenchmen placed them. One fact stands out, and that is that before the smallpox epidemic of 1781, the Arikara tribe on the Missouri in South Dakota was the head of a kind of league of tribes. The Arikaras were a strong nation with many villages, some of them fortified; they grew maize, vegetables, and tobacco at their villages, and the tribes out in the plains came regularly to trade, being particularly eager to obtain the native tobacco that the Arikaras always had in quantity. Before 1750 this alliance seems to have embraced the Arikaras, the Gatakas or Padoucas, and the Kiowas; after 1760 the Cheyennes moved from the Missouri to the Black Hills, where they found the Arapahoes, and these two tribes joined the Arikara alliance. But now smallpox attacked the Arikara towns, killing three-fourths of the population before the year 1795. The fierce Teton Sioux then advanced westward and began to attack the Arikaras and their allies.

Before smallpox decimated the Arikaras and the Sioux armed with guns appeared on the Missouri, the tribes of this Arikara alliance must have been actively engaged in raiding the Snakes in the plains and mountain parks west of the Black Hills; indeed, the Verendrye party accompanied an expedition of these tribes against the Snakes in the winter of 1742–43, and the traditions of both the Kiowas and Cheyennes mention their early wars in this district, but they term the enemy the Kwahari Comanches, not

Snakes. Here we may remark again that there was very little to distinguish the Comanches from the Snakes in the lands near the upper Platte and Powder River. These tribes were of the same race, speaking the same language, and whether they were called Comanches or Snakes was a point of little importance.

The Arikaras and their allies were very unfortunate. They feared the Sioux mainly because that tribe had a regular trade for British guns and ammunition at a trading fair held annually on the headwaters of Minnesota River; and, coming from these fairs to the Missouri with new supplies of firearms, the Sioux had the Arikaras and their allies practically at their mercy. At just this time the French traders from St. Louis began to extend their trade up the Missouri. Monier reached the Poncas in northeastern Nebraska about 1789, and the French at once went on up the river to the Arikara villages, trading some guns and ammunition. A few years more and the Arikaras and their allies would have been completely equipped with firearms, but the Sioux were too astute to permit that to happen. They got across to the west side of the Missouri, coming between the Arikara villagers and their allies in the Black Hills region. By 1776 small parties of Sioux had penetrated to the Black Hills, and they now began to war on the tribes of that district. The Sioux picture records, the winter counts, show that in 1786–87 (another count makes the date 1793–94) the Sioux surprised and killed some Cheyennes south of the Black Hills, capturing their camp, which was filled with fresh rawhides, and naming the spot Rawhide Butte. Another winter count records that in 1790–91 the Sioux attacked the Cheyennes again, and in 1798–99 they took many Cheyenne scalps. Kiowa tradition states that at this period the Sioux killed an entire camp of their people. By about the date 1800 the Sioux were in control of the plains west of the Missouri and were fighting the Crows up near the lower Yellowstone and the Kiowas down on the upper Platte.

Thus the old Arikara alliance of tribes was broken up. In the summer of 1795, Truteau was among the Arikaras, and he noted that the Cheyennes, Arapahoes, and Kiowas were hovering far up on the Cheyenne River, wishing to come to the Arikara towns

186

to trade but fearing that they would be attacked by the Sioux if they ventured nearer to the Missouri. The Sioux had actually driven the Arikaras out of their villages in the summer of 1794. Part of the Arikaras fled to the Mandans up the Missouri for protection; part went up White River and camped near the Black Hills, probably close to the Cheyennes. Returning to their villages on the Missouri in the spring of 1795, the group that had been on White River were again driven out by the Sioux, evidently in the fall of 1795 and again in May, 1796. This flight of the Arikaras put a stop to the old trade with the tribes out in the plains; but these tribes had to have trade, and they now began to go to the Mandan villages on the Missouri in North Dakota. In 1796, John Evans went up the Missouri to the Mandan villages and found the Cheyennes and Arapahoes trading there. In 1803, James Pursley found the Kiowas and Gataka Padoucas trading with the Mandans.

About the year 1800 the Arikaras drew the remnants of their tribe together and built three new villages on the Missouri above the mouth of Grand River. Tabeau states that the old allies of the Arikaras out in the plains now attempted to resume trade at the villages. In 1804 or 1805, they formed a big camp near the Black Hills and sent part of the Cheyennes to ask the Arikaras to come out to their camp and trade with them. There were eight camps made up of bands of Cheyennes, Arapahoes, Kiowas, and Gataka Padoucas, and some of these Indians had been all the way to San Antonio in Texas, bringing back horses and Spanish goods. They told of the poor trade the Spaniards gave them: inferior goods at high prices and no guns or ammunition at all.[10] These tribes were eager to visit the Arikaras at harvest time, 1805, for a grand trading fair; but, judging by the Lewis and Clark reports, only a small camp of Cheyennes dared to carry out the plan to go to the Arikara villages.

Wild Indians never remain on friendly terms with other tribes for long, and the tribes out near the Black Hills that had the trading arrangement with the Arikaras were alternately friendly and

[10] Tabeau, *Narrative of Loisel's Expedition*, 137, 158.

hostile. Thus the Cheyennes and Arapahoes were at first friendly toward the Kiowas and Gatakas, but then began to raid them and forced them to retire southward from the Black Hills. Yet, in 1795, the Cheyennes and Arapahoes were on good terms again with the Kiowas and Gatakas, camping and trading with them on Cheyenne River. The Kiowa tradition ignores all this and asserts that their tribe attacked the Kwahari Comanches and followed the retreat of that tribe southward, along the eastern skirts of the Colorado mountains, finally making peace with these Comanches on the Spanish borders, about the year 1790. But apparently only the southern Kiowas were engaged in this movement. The Cold Men or northern Kiowas remained in the north with their Gataka allies, and as late as 1803 they were on the Missouri in North Dakota, trading with the Mandans.

The Arapahoes told Lieutenant W. P. Clark about 1881 that after leaving the Cheyennes in the Black Hills, they moved to the head of the Missouri, where enemies attacked them. They then turned southward, skirting the eastern edge of the mountains. Chief Little Raven told Clark that about 1781 the Arapahoes were ranging as far west as the Bighorn River, and when his father was a child, about 1792, the Sioux attacked them, and they withdrew farther to the south and got into a war with the Utes.[11] Here we have the Arapahoes, by tradition, ranging the country from the Black Hills west to the Bighorn at the period 1782–92, and no mention of any Snake or Comanche group in that region. If this tradition is correct, the Comanches and Snakes had withdrawn from the lands near the upper Platte and the heads of the Bighorn and Powder rivers, but the Snakes were still holding out on the upper Yellowstone and near the Three Forks of the Missouri.

George Bent's Cheyenne traditions asserted that his tribe and the Arapahoes drove the Kiowas and Apaches (Gatakas) from the Black Hills and then turned on the Crows. The Cheyenne war with the latter tribe we know was in progress as early as 1800. Before that date the Cheyennes (as they claimed) had driven the

[11] Clark, *Indian Sign Language*, 39.

River Crows out of the Little Missouri district, with the aid of the Arapahoes, and when the Arapahoes left them, the Cheyennes continued to attack the Crows. In 1804, Lewis and Clark reported that the Cheyennes had recently had a big fight with the Crows, far in the west. The Crows were also being attacked by the Sioux and Blackfeet; indeed, having driven the Snakes from the Bighorn and Yellowstone country, by 1800 the Crows were themselves beset by enemies and were having to battle to keep the lands they had won in the late eighteenth century.

At the period when the southern Kiowas claimed they advanced southward, following the retreating Kwahari Comanches, there were apparently Padouca villages on the Platte, somewhere near the forks, the Spanish manuscript map (1795?) placing them east of the forks, the Collot map of 1796 showing that the Padoucas apparently had moved to the southwest, up the South Platte. The Kiowas of the north were evidently in touch with these Padoucas, who may have been actually the Gatakas, who had been in alliance with the Kiowas as far back as 1740. Lewis and Clark in their statistics (volume VI, page 106) stated that the Kiowas roamed from Loup Fork to Padouca Fork, that is, to the Platte; the Kiowas traded at the villages on the Missouri and then retraded most of the British goods thus obtained to the Castahans and Dotames.[12] Now, the name Castahan seems to have been applied to the Comanches, and Dotame might have been the name of a Kiowa or Comanche camp. At any rate, this Lewis and Clark statement indicates that the northern Kiowas were trying in 1804 to keep up the practice of going to the Missouri with horses and Spanish goods, trading these for British goods and guns, and then trading their British articles to the Comanches for horses and Spanish articles. In fact, the northern Kiowas and Gatakas, having been driven from the Black Hills to the upper Platte, were still trying to keep up the old trade between the tribes on the Spanish border and those on the upper Missouri.

The lost Lewis and Clark map shows the Arapahoes near the

[12] Lewis and Clark, *Original Journals*, VI, 106.

head of the North Platte with the Kiowas south of them, probably on the head of the South Platte.[13] This map gives the earliest hint of the new location of the Arapahoes. They had left the Cheyennes in the Black Hills and advanced westward to near the head of the North Platte. They are reported here after 1810, by Robert Stuart and others, on good terms both with the Snake Indians of Green River and with the Kiowa group on the head of the South Platte. Alexander Henry in 1806 met a camp of Cheyennes with some Buffalo Indians (Bison Path Indians—Arapahoes) at the Mandan villages, and he stated that these two tribes trapped beaver and hunted bears on the heads of two rivers, one of which was a fork of the Platte.

Lewis and Clark were the last writers to attempt to depict a great Padouca Nation in the plains. They stated that this tribe, being warred on by the Indians near the Missouri, withdrew to the Platte, the North Platte being still termed Padouca Fork. Most writers in later years gave this name to the South Fork. At any rate, Lewis and Clark stated that the Padoucas lived on the Platte in villages, the only tribe west of the Missouri that had villages instead of moving camps. They had great numbers of horses and traded in New Mexico. The explorers stated that on the upper Missouri they had failed to obtain definite information concerning the situation, numbers, and condition of the Padoucas and that perhaps the explanation might be that this nation, having been greatly reduced in population, had broken up to form the new groups known as Gatakas, Kiowas, Kunanavich, and so on. This conjecture was of course wrong; for the tribes named belonged to different linguistic stocks, and only the Gatakas were really Padoucas.

And the statement of Lewis and Clark that the Padoucas were hardly known on the Missouri was incorrect. In the very year before Lewis and Clark ascended the river, James Pursley came up to the Mandan villages and there found the Padoucas and Kiowas trading. He went off with these Indians, who moved down to the Platte, where they tried to hold a trading fair with

[13] Lewis and Clark lost map, published in *Science*, November, 1887.

other tribes; but the Sioux came and drove them into the mountains at the head of the South Platte. Pursley went into South Park with about two thousand of these Kiowas and Padoucas, who sent him to New Mexico to ask permission for them to come down and trade; but the Spanish officials held Pursley, and the Indians apparently were not permitted to trade. Pursley was evidently at the trading fair on the North Platte in 1804; he went to New Mexico in the spring of 1805. Meanwhile, Baptiste La-Lande, a French trader, had come up the Platte, joined a camp of Indians, and come down to New Mexico with them; but, like Pursley, he was held or remained in New Mexico.[14]

The significant part of all this lies in the fact that these Padoucas, Kiowas, Arapahoes, and other bands in 1800–1806 were roving and trading between the North Platte and the head of the Arkansas in country that in the late eighteenth century was Comanche and Snake territory, and now, except for the little band known as Baldheads, the Comanches and Snakes were gone. Part of them had died of smallpox or from enemy attacks; the Comanches had withdrawn southward; the Snakes moved westward beyond the Rockies. The Comanches and Snakes were gone by 1800, but they had left some clues as to their former occupation of the lands near the upper Platte.

The Spaniards of New Mexico, as we have seen, termed the northern Comanche tribes the Yamparikas and Yupes, but the Comanches themselves in the nineteenth century termed these old northern groups the Yamparikas and Kwaharis. The Kiowa and Cheyenne statements that late in the eighteenth century the northern Comanches or Kwaharis were still north of the Platte confirms both the Comanche and Spanish information. In 1786 the officials in New Mexico stated that the Yupes and Yamparikas extended from the Arkansas northward, "a little beyond the Sierra de Almagre" or Colorado Front Range. A. B. Thomas, after studying the Spanish documents, was of the opinion that the Comanches extended northward into southern Wyoming, and on his map he placed the Yamparikas in the Green River

[14] Pike, *Pike Expeditions*, II, 756–58, 500, 603.

country, west of the head of the North Platte, extending eastward and south beyond the Arkansas, with the Yupes extending from a point in Wyoming north of the Yamparikas southward to the Arkansas.[15]

Now, Lewis and Clark, while on their expedition, did not obtain any information bearing on this former Comanche occupation of the Wyoming country; indeed, they did not even hear the name Comanche. After the return of the expedition, William Clark became governor of Missouri Territory, in charge of Indian affairs for the whole region west of the Missouri; and, living in St. Louis, he kept in touch with Indian traders with the object of learning more about the tribes near the mountains. He was preparing a map for the forthcoming volume on the Lewis and Clark explorations, and he obtained new material for this map from George Drouillard and John Colter who, in 1807–1808, had trapped beaver in every nook and corner of the lands from Three Forks south to Wind River. In the recently published life of Colter by Burton Harris the sketch maps made by William Clark from this information are reproduced. They show near the head of the Madison Fork of the Missouri, north of Yellowstone Lake, the Ne-moy (perhaps Ve-moy as the initial letter is hard to read), a band of Snake Indians, six hundred souls. Farther south, east of Yellowstone Lake, the maps show Yep-pe Snakes, one thousand souls; west of the Rockies, evidently near the head of Henry Fork, the Po-hah Snakes, one hundred souls. Colter's trail in 1807 is on the map, passing close to these three Snake groups. The French map of Lapie, published in 1821 in *Nouvelles Annales*[16] and evidently copied in part from the William Clark map, sets down Clark's Yep-pe Snake group east of Yellowstone Lake as the Jeupe, which makes it almost certain that this group was part of the Comanche group the Spaniards of New Mexico called the Jupes and who may very well have been the Kwahari Comanches of later times. The Po-hah band of Snakes, placed on this map near Green River, may have been a group of the Pohoi Snakes

[15] Thomas, *Forgotten Frontiers*, 295 and map.
[16] Philip Ashton Rollins, *The Discovery of the Oregon Trail.*

that remained in the north after the rest of the group moved down through the plains to join the Comanches south of the Arkansas. Large numbers of Snakes must have gone south in this manner, most of them joining the Kwahari and Yamparika Comanches, which was the natural thing for them to do, as these two Comanche groups were in the north as late as 1786, and some of their rear bands may have lingered north of the Platte as late as 1800.

The Clark map is extremely interesting, and it gives us a real clue to the place the Kwaharis, alias the Yupes, lived before they retired from their old lands in the north. It indicates that they extended as far north as the Stinkingwater district, east of Yellowstone Lake and near the present town of Cody.

The Ditsakana band of Snakes is said by Comanche tradition to have been among the last Snake groups to join their tribe. They joined the Kwaharis and seem to have merged into that group. Keim in 1868 joined the two together, terming them the Kwahari-Ditsakana band. An older name for the Ditsakanas was *Widyu*, "Awl," probably also the name of their chief. The Comanches are said to have tabooed the names of dead chiefs; thus the Widyu or Awl name (Indian women used awls for sewing leather garments) was altered into a related name, *Ditsakana* or "Sewer." This group was termed Jupe as late as 1857,[17] and here again we have a clue connecting the Jupes and Comanches with an earlier Jupe Snake group in the north.

Frederick Webb Hodge, in the *Handbook of American Indians North of Mexico*, asserts that it was not the Ditsakana but the Detsanayuka band of Comanches that joined the Kwaharis. This does not agree with Keim's earlier information. Detsanayuka was a later name for the old Nokoni Comanche band; for when Chief Nokoni died, his name was tabooed, and his band took the new name of Detsanayuka. However, the Nokonis and Kwaharis were camping together in 1834, and it is possible that the Nokonis were really Kwaharis whose camp had been named for the chief. There is need for further study of the Comanche bands at the period

[17] Hodge, *Handbook of American Indians*, I, 393.

1825-50. The generally accepted notion that during this period the Kwaharis were living in the Staked Plains seems to have little basis except in the fact that no one knows where this group was. It is not reasonable to suppose that this large Comanche group went to live in the Staked Plains desert when they had the fine buffalo plains to the north and east open to their occupation. They did go into the Staked Plains at times to meet the *Comancheros*, who came from New Mexico to trade with them for horses and captives; but the view that the Kwaharis kept in the desert district the year around does not make sense.

The Pohoi or Wild Sage People, who joined the Comanches and moved south with them, seem to have been an offshoot from the Pohogue or Sage Brush People, the Snakes who held the Fort Hall district on Snake River in the nineteenth century. As has been stated, they were probably the Po-hah, placed near Green River on the Lewis and Clark map of 1814.

In reviewing all of this material on the Snakes and Comanches, it is difficult to avoid the impression that there were still large groups of these two tribes in the plains of Wyoming and Montana as late as 1790, and possibly even later. After 1805 they were gone. How many of the Snakes went south and joined the Comanches it is impossible to surmise. Many of them retreated west of the Rockies, where their enemies, armed with guns, pursued them and continued to create panic in their camps; but still the desire for buffalo meat and horses induced Snake bands to venture east of the mountains almost every season, where they risked their lives in the hope of a good hunt. At this period there were buffalo herds west of the mountains on Snake River and Green River; yet the Snakes, Bannocks, and Flatheads longed for their old hunting grounds in the east and continued to take the risk of crossing the passes to hunt in Montana and Wyoming. The Bannocks were particularly persistent in their determination to hunt east of the Rockies. They often wintered in the Fort Hall district on Snake River, close to the Pohogue Snake group, and here we seem to have another link with the Comanches; for in the nineteenth century the present Wyoming Shoshonis, who seem to be in part de-

Yuma men in rabbit-fur robes about 1862.

Diorama of Apache life.

scended from the Pohogues, had a tradition that they formerly camped and roved with both the Comanches and Bannocks. This hints that the northern Comanches—the Yamparikas and Kwaharis or Yupes—with the Pohogue and Kogohol Snakes and the Bannocks formed a powerful group up to 1790, holding lands from Green River and the upper North Platte northward to the Yellowstone. It was the survivors of this old group, the southern Snakes and Bannocks, who after 1805 still persisted in visiting the lands east of the mountains, in the Yellowstone Park country and in the Wind River and upper Bighorn lands, where they hunted buffalo and organized trading parties to go south to the New Mexican border for horses and Spanish goods. This group had not been exposed much to the main attack of the Blackfeet up to the date 1810, and they seem to have kept their morale and organization better than the Lemhi Snakes of the Three Forks of the Missouri, who had been dreadfully mauled by the Blackfeet. These southern Snakes and Bannocks had even formed a kind of alliance with the Arapahoes and probably with part of the Crows; for, as we have seen, the Mountain Crows even had a camp of Snakes living with them and going on trading expeditions to the upper Missouri in 1805.

The Arapaho advance westward as far as Green River west of South Pass at the period 1800–10 is a little-known event in this tribe's history. The Arapahoes made friends with the Snakes and Bannocks and traded with them, the truth probably being that the Kiowas and Gatakas by moving to the heads of the South Platte and Arkansas, about the date 1800, blocked the way of the Snakes going to the New Mexican frontier to trade; and as the Snakes were enemies of the Kiowas and Gatakas, the Arapahoes, who were on friendly terms with both parties, acted as middlemen, obtaining horses and Spanish goods from the Kiowas and Gatakas and trading them to the Snakes and other northern tribes. At this time (1805) the Atsenas, close relatives of the Arapahoes, moved south of the Yellowstone into the Crow lands, bringing British goods and guns with them; and there can be little doubt that they were in touch with the Arapahoes and obtained horses from them in trade.

In 1811 the Astorian expedition, moving westward, met a band of Snakes and Bannocks near the head of the Bighorn River, and these Indians stated that they were going down to the North Platte to trade with the Arapahoes. In the same year an Astorian party was robbed by a band of Arapahoes near Bear Lake, Utah, and in 1812 this same band of Arapahoes met Robert Stuart's party on the North Platte and stated that their camp was on the South Platte. In 1812 Green River was known to the American traders and trappers as "the river of the Spaniards and Arapahos."[18] Ezekial Williams of the Lost Trappers claimed that he was with the Arapahoes south of the Platte in 1812–13 and that when he returned to the mountains in 1814 he found the tribe in the same district. Alexander Ross and his party of trappers are supposed to have found the Arapahoes with the Snakes and Bannocks in the Snake River country west of the Rockies in 1818. Ross divided the Indians he met into Bannocks or Mountain Snakes (bold robbers and outlaws), Ar-are-ree-kas or Fish Eaters (a group of Snakes who had lost courage from being constantly attacked by the Piegans and Blackfeet), and the Shirrydikas or Dog Eaters: a buffalo-hunting group from the plains, whom he termed the real Shoshonis, lean, clean, well-dressed, and brave Indians, quite unlike the other Snakes. Shirrydika (*Saretika*, "Dog Eater") is generally accepted by ethnologists as the old Shoshoni and Comanche name for the Arapahoes; but it seems strange that Alexander Ross and his trappers, who knew the Snakes well, should term the Dog Eaters the "real Shoshonis" if they were Arapahoes. In 1820, Ross mentioned these Indians again, as Buffalo Snakes and Shirrydikas, and stated that the Fort Hall district on Snake River was the center of their range. In 1820 the Arapahoes, or part of them, were south of the Arkansas with the Kiowas, Gatakas, and Ietans, and one suspects that Ross' Shirrydikas were really Snakes and

---

[18] The French fur traders from St. Louis wrote this name as *Rivière des Espagnols et Arapaos* in a report dated July 7, 1812 (Harrison C. Dale, *The Ashley-Smith Explorations and the Discovery of a Central Route to the Pacific, 1822–29*, 34). Spanish traders from New Mexico came at times to Green River to trade with the Snakes; hence, the name, River of the Spaniards. The Arapahoes were frequenting Green River, so their name was also applied to the stream.

not Arapahoes at all.[19] However this may have been, at this period, 1810–20, there was a large group of Snakes and Bannocks west of the mountains, usually found on Snake River, who seem to have been on good terms with the Arapahoes; and they were often in the plains to hunt buffalo and trade. In 1812 the Absaroka Crows were raiding this group, whom they termed Southern Snakes. The trader McKenzie in 1819 considered them the main body of Snakes, evidently meaning the largest organized group still holding together, keeping their horses, and going on buffalo hunts. Ogden in 1820 called them the Lower Snakes. This group clearly knew the country east of the Rockies in the Wind River, Yellowstone, and Bighorn districts; they were hunting in these parts, and they gave the traders and trappers frequent news, such as the report that in 1812 the Absaroka Crows had robbed a party of American trappers in the Yellowstone country. In fact, some of these Snake bands had gone east of the mountains with the trappers and seem to have been present when the Absarokas made their attack.

From a review of the evidence set down in this chapter, it appears that there were still large bodies of Snakes and Comanches in the Wyoming and Montana parklands and plains as late as 1790, perhaps even later. The decision of the last Comanche groups to move south to the Arkansas left the Snakes too weak to hold out, and part of them then followed the Comanches southward; but some groups of Snakes retired west of the Rockies, those camps that managed to keep their horses continuing to visit the eastern parks and plains each year to hunt buffalo. The advance of the Arapahoes westward to Green River and the movement of the Absaroka Crows southward to the head of the Bighorn and to Wind River ended the period of Snake occupation of the northern plains.

[19] An ethnologist obtaining information from modern reservation Indians is often misled by them. They do not know the truth about their people's past, but imagine that they do, and they will tell you, "Our tribe never ate dogs; our people were never called Snakes." They are wrong, usually, but the ethnologist often does not know it and sets down their statements as the truth. The old time Snake Indians ate pretty much everything, and it would not be surprising if some camps that frequented the plains picked up the custom of eating dogs from other tribes and later abandoned and forgot the practice.

The Snakes now for the first time began to obtain firearms from British and American traders west of the Rockies; but the warlike Sioux and Cheyennes, who were even better equipped with firearms, now advanced to the North Platte (1830–35), and any Snake hope that they might recover their old lands east of the mountains was blasted. Furthermore they were soon being raided in their new lands west of the mountains by Sioux and Cheyenne war parties.

# 9. Padoucas, Comanches, and Ietans

WHEN THE UNITED STATES took over the Louisiana Territory the Comanches were almost unknown, and American explorers and traders mentioned the tribe under several names, most often terming these Indians Ietans, at times confusing them with the southern Pawnees of Red River. They were on rare occasions termed Padoucas; but in 1846 the treaty commissioners, P. M. Butler and M. G. Lewis, who were in camp with the Comanches, holding councils with the chiefs, made the bald statement that on the prairies the Comanches were generally known as Padoucas. Indian Agent Neighbors soon after this date repeated the assertion that the Comanches were called Padoucas, adding that the Caddo name for the Comanches was Sowato, a slight error, as Sowato happened to be the Caddo name for the Lipan Apaches, who were really Padoucas. These American officials of 1845–50 seem to have been pretty badly mixed up about who the Padoucas were; but their statements were printed in Schoolcraft's volumes, and for a century later most authors who dealt with Indian matters accepted blindly the assertion that the Padoucas were Comanches. Even today there seems to be no end to this confusion. Frank Secoy made a study of the Padoucas and came to the firm conclusion that they were Apaches; but he added to this that about the date 1750 the French of Louisiana shifted the name Padouca to the Comanches, who now occupied the old Padouca lands in the plains. Mr. Secoy did a fine piece of work on the

199

Padoucas; but it is difficult to follow him when he states that the Louisiana French after 1750 called the Comanches Padoucas. The only Louisiana French we need to consider are the men who were trading with the Indians and in actual contact with the Padoucas, Apaches and Comanches. These men in Kansas in 1723–24 called the Apaches Padoucas, and, in passing, we may note that all the Siouan tribes (later supposed to have known the Comanches as Padoucas did not protest when the French gave that name to the Kansas Apaches. Secoy quotes a letter of La Jonquiere's, September 25, 1751, in which this French officer, evidently quoting the Osages or Frenchmen among the Osages, terms the Comanches Laytanes.[1] In 1772 the French traders on Red River on the Texas border called the Comanches Naytanes and identified the Padoucas as Apaches. In 1804, Lewis and Clark on the upper Missouri learned from the French to term the Comanches Alitans, a corrupt form of Laytanes, and in 1806, Lieutenant Zebulon M. Pike, passing through the Osage country to the plains and accompanied by Frenchmen who spoke the Osage language picked up the habit of terming the Comanches Ietans, another spelling of Laytan. The only Padouca group in the northern plains in later years were the Gataka Apaches, and they were called Padoucas by the French traders down to the year 1805.

It is true that some white men and some Indians did term the Comanches, or a group that lived with the Comanches, Padoucas; but this was not after 1750; it was after 1820; and after a few years this attempt to pin the name Padouca to the Comanches was dropped by men actually in touch with the Indians.[2]

As has been suggested in the earlier chapters of this book, the

[1] Secoy, "The Identity of the Padouca," *American Anthropologist*, N.S., Vol. LIII, 529.

[2] Another mystery is that all the Siouan tribes along the eastern border of the plains seem to have recognized the Apaches as Padoucas in the eighteenth century and then (evidently after 1850) came around to the opinion that the Padoucas were Comanches. They made this change long after all the old men who had met Padoucas were dead and forgotten. Can it be that they were influenced by white men who had read Schoolcraft and who told these reservation Indians that the Padoucas were proved to have been Comanches? This is a curious point, but not a very important one. The late opinion of reservation Siouans does not matter, when it goes against contemporary evidence.

real Ietans seem to have been a small group, perhaps of mixed Ute-Apache blood, and they may have been the mysterious Ae tribe, whom the Comanches were warring on in the lands near the Arkansas River in the middle of the eighteenth century. About 1900, the ethnologist James Mooney gave his opinion that the name Ietan came from an old name for the Utes, *Iata*, and that the terminal "n" indicated a Siouan origin of the name. He was evidently unaware of the fact that the Pawnees of Nebraska always called the Comanches Laytanes, a name probably the same as Ietan, while the southern Pawnees of Red River used the same name, which in their dialect became Naytan. Why the Caddoan Pawnees should have given the name Ietan to the Comanches is another mystery; but perhaps Mooney was right: the name meant Ute, and the Comanches, being very closely related to the Utes, were included under this name by the Pawnees.

Until after 1800 these tribes in the plains were almost unknown to the whites. From 1750 until after 1800, it was so dangerous for white men to venture into the plains that only a few penetrated the region, and most of the information on the plains tribes was picked up from Indians by French traders who had not actually contacted the tribes they spoke of and had only the vaguest ideas concerning the names, languages, and blood relationships of these Indians. The few white men who actually met the Ietans described them as a small tribe.

The first appearance of the Ietans was when the Mallet brothers and their French companions found a camp of these Indians on the upper Arkansas in 1739. They had an Arikara slave from the upper Missouri with them, indicating that they were trading in the north, giving horses and Spanish goods for slaves and northern products. It has been suggested in this book that they were the camp the Verendryes found in 1742 near the Black Hills, a camp that was trading with the Spaniards in the south, taking a route southward that avoided their Snake enemies. But the presence of the Arikara slave suggests that the Ietans may have been trading with the Snakes, who were raiding the tribes near the upper Missouri and taking many captives from them. That would make

Verendrye's trading camp the Gatakas or Padoucas of the Black Hills region. The mystery is deepened by the account of Spanish Louisiana in 1785 which terms the Ietans Apaches. That would make them Padoucas and enemies of the Snakes and Comanches. Truteau, who was on the upper Missouri in 1794–96, termed the Ietans "Halitanes or Têtes Pelées" and described them as a wandering nation in the plains between the Platte and Arkansas and on the Spanish border. This was evidently taken from the Truteau journal by Perrin du Lac (1802), who in his book described the "Halisanes and Baldheads" as roving between the Platte and Arkansas and going as far as the foot of the Mexican mountains.

Thus Truteau, Perrin du Lac and Tabeau confuse the problem still further by introducing the Têtes Pelées or Baldheads, a Comanche or Snake group, and terming them either the Ietans or a band that lived with the Ietans. Tabeau's tale of the Baldhead who met the Arapaho scout and gambled away his own scalp suggests that the Baldheads were in the Wyoming plains about the date 1780–90 and were enemies of the tribes near the Black Hills. From these bits of information it would seem that there were two groups of trading Indians: the Ietan and Baldhead group, trading with the Snakes, and the Gatakas or Padoucas, trading with the enemies of the Snakes. These two trading camps were at times confused, and thus we find a writer reporting in the *Louisiana Gazette* for 1810 that the lands near the head of the Arkansas were occupied by "the Aytans or Padocas."[3] This writer thought these Indians were one tribe; but the names he gave indicate that they were two different groups.

The Gatakas were probably a numerous tribe before the epidemic of 1780–81; but by 1804 they were greatly reduced in numbers and had been driven from their old lands in western Dakota, retiring southward to the Platte. The French traders on the Missouri knew them so little that they informed Lewis and Clark that the Gatakas and Padoucas were separate tribes. In 1803 the Gatakas seem to have made their last trading expedition to the Missouri. They went to the Mandan villages on the river in

[3] Thomas James, *Three Years Among Indians and Mexicans*, 286.

North Dakota, taking their Kiowa allies with them. James Pursley joined these Indians and went with them to a trading fair on the Platte.

We have sufficient evidence to show that at this period northern Kiowas and their Gataka-Padouca allies were on or south of the Platte, holding trading fairs with the northern tribes near the present Nebraska-Wyoming boundary and going at times to trade at the Mandan villages. Formerly enemies of the Ietans and Baldheads, these Kiowas and Padoucas were now forced by circumstances to associate with them and even to camp with them, for mutual protection against the Sioux and other foes. A part of the Arapahoes, who had moved westward and made a peace with the Snakes of Green River, presently joined the trading Indians, obtaining horses and Spanish goods which they took to Green River and traded to the Snakes. Finally, a camp of Cheyennes also joined forces with the trading Indians.

What the trading Indians did after James Pursley left their camp in South Park in 1804 we do not know. Lieutenant Pike's party was on the Arkansas River near the present Pueblo, Colorado, late in the year 1806 and saw many old Indian camps but met no Indians. We may surmise that the trading Indians were all south of the Arkansas. In 1805, 1809, and 1810, parties of American traders left Arkansas and went west into the plains to trade guns and goods to the Indians in the district between Red River and the Arkansas. The trade was mainly with the Comanches; but by this date the camps of trading Indians from the north clearly had an understanding with some of the Comanche bands and were permitted to rove and trade as they pleased in the plains from New Mexico south to San Antonio. It was in these years that the Arapahoes began to trade with the Snakes of Green River, and the Arapaho group thus engaged seems to have developed the practice of going south to camp with the Ietans and Kiowas; they then returned north to the Platte, bringing horses and goods to trade to the Cheyennes, Crows and Snakes. Plenty Poles, a northern Arapaho, told James Mooney that when he was a boy, about the year 1810, the Kiowas came north and traded with the

Arapahoes in a camp on the North Platte, west of the present city of Cheyenne. In the early winter of 1812 a party of Arapahoes came to Robert Stuart's camp on the North Platte, near the present Casper, and stated that their village was due south on the South Platte. About 1810 both the Arapahoes and Kiowas were on the North Platte, west of the present Cheyenne, and about 1815 the Kiowas and other trading Indians came to Horse Creek, east of the present Fort Laramie, where they held a fair with the Cheyennes and other northern tribes; but the Sioux attacked and broke up the fair. The dates in the Sioux winter counts are a little uncertain, and we cannot tell whether this event was in 1814, 1815, or 1816.

As we have seen, Ezekiel Williams left the Arapahoes near the head of the Arkansas in spring, 1813, and went back to Missouri. There he sold the furs he had cached in the Arapaho country to Philibert, who led a party of trappers, including Williams, up the Arkansas. This company trapped in the mountain country, and then Philibert went back to Missouri and sold out to Chouteau and DeMun, who led a big party of trappers up the Arkansas in 1815. This new expedition expected to meet Philibert's trappers at the mouth of the Huerfano, below the present city of Pueblo. The trappers did not turn up; but Indians, whose tribal name is not given, were in the vicinity and gave information concerning the missing trappers. This district on the head of the Arkansas was a favorite haunt of the trading Indians, and in 1820, Major Long's party found log horse pens, in which the Indians kept the great numbers of horses they had for trade, scattered thickly along the Arkansas from the vicinity of the present Pueblo down to the Huerfano. Now, the Chouteau and DeMun trappers scattered through the mountains on trapping expeditions in 1815, and in the following year they continued their trapping. They were also trading with the Arapahoes and other Indians, and in either 1815–16 or the following winter, they were on Grand Camp Creek, a tributary of the South Platte, south of Denver, wintering with the Kiowas, Arapahoes, and a tribe called Kaskaias, who were probably Gatakas or Prairie Apaches. Joseph Bijeau, who was in this camp, stated that the Cheyennes of the Black Hills had recently traded at the Mandan villages on the Missouri, obtaining fine British goods and many guns and they had come down to the South Platte to hold a trading fair with the three tribes mentioned above.

Now, trading fairs were usually held in autumn, and what probably happened was that these trading Indians went up to the North Platte in summer; American Horse's Sioux winter counts give the date as 1814–15, but it was more likely the summer of 1815 or 1816. The trading fair was at a point on the North Platte six miles west of Scott's Bluff, as American Horse asserted, and the trading Indians evidently fled to their favorite camping ground at the head of the South Platte. Part of the Cheyennes went with them, and there they met and wintered with the Chouteau and DeMun trappers.[4]

In the spring of 1817 a force of Mexican troops came up to the head of the Arkansas, arrested Chouteau and DeMun, and seized their property. In this same year, 1817, the trading Indians, who had obtained British goods from the Cheyennes and American goods from Chouteau and DeMun, moved south of the Arkansas, evidently to renew their stock of horses by trading and raiding. From contemporary reports we learn that a large party of Americans traded all winter, 1817–18, with "the northern bands of the Comanches," and on their way home eastward in the spring of 1818, these traders were attacked at the Grand Saline by Skidi Pawnees from Nebraska and Tawehash Pawnees from Red River. Colonel William Bradford reported, March 28, 1818, that these American traders had wintered with the northern tribes of Comanches; he then stated that the Ietans were by far the most numerous tribe in what is now western Oklahoma. Here he seems to be using the name Ietan as a synonym for Comanche. Yet Colo-

---

[4] The Chouteau and DeMun papers are in *American State Papers*, IV, 207ff. DeMun's affidavit says that his party wintered 1815–16 and 1816–17 on the Arkansas near the mouth of the Huerfano; but Joseph Bijeau asserts that his trapping group wintered with three Indian tribes on the headwaters of the South Platte. Clearly, the Chouteau and DeMun party was divided, each group wintering in a separate locality.

nel Arbuckle in 1822 and Thomas James, who traded with the tribe on the Canadian in 1823, termed them Comanches and never mentioned the name Ietan.[5]

Major Long's expedition met the trading Indians on the upper Arkansas in the summer of 1820, and the French traders who were guiding Major Long stated that these Indians were Kaskaias (called Bad Hearts by the French traders), Baldheads, Kiowas, Arapahoes, and a small camp of Cheyennes. Edwin James, who wrote the narrative of the Major Long expedition, stated that these Indians had been south of the Arkansas for three years, had camped with American traders on Red River (really on the upper Canadian), and, to obtain horses to trade to these Americans, had broken their peace with New Mexico and made horse-stealing raids into that province. In the winter of 1819–20, they had a battle with Skidi Pawnees from Nebraska near the upper Canadian, killing most of the Skidis. In his account of this battle, Edwin James stated that it was with the Ietans and their allies; but when these Indians moved up to the Arkansas in late July, 1820, they had no Ietans with them; at least, James did not mention this tribe as being present, nor did Captain Bell in his journal.

The Long expedition first met a man and woman of the Kaskaias on the Arkansas near the mouth of the Huerfano. The French guide, Joseph Bijeau, stated that the language of this tribe was very difficult and few white men knew it. He talked to the Kaskaias in the sign language, and they informed him that some distance down the Arkansas was the rest of their group, six bands: Kaskaias, Baldheads, Kiowas, Arapahoes, Cheyennes, and a small camp of Shoshonis or Snake Indians from Columbia River. They were all heading north toward their old camping grounds on the head of the South Platte, where they had encamped with the Chouteau and DeMun trappers before going south of the Arkansas in 1817. This Kaskaia man also stated that these bands had come together to fight the Spaniards and that early in the summer they had had a fight with a Spanish force on the Canadian.

[5] Bradford and Arbuckle, in Grant Foreman, *Indians and Pioneers*, 46; also, James, *Three Years Among Indians and Mexicans*.

Major Long now divided his party. He led part of the expedition south to the Canadian, where he fell in with a camp of thirty-two lodges of Kaskaias led by Chief Red Mouse. This chief informed Long that his camp had been on the headwaters of the Brazos and Colorado rivers in northern Texas during the past winter and that they were now attempting to open a trade with the Spaniards of New Mexico. He spoke of the Comanches under that name, calling them "Comancias." He did not mention the Ietans.

Meanwhile, up on the Arkansas, Captain Bell led the rest of the expedition eastward, and near the Big Timbers and the mouth of Sand Creek his party found a camp of Kaskaias and Kiowas with a few Arapahoes. The fact that the Kaskaias were camping and moving with the Kiowas supports the general view of scholars that Kaskaias was only another name for the Gatakas or Prairie Apaches. These Indians near the Big Timbers stated that Chief Bear Tooth of the Arapahoes was farther down the Arkansas with the main Arapaho group and a small camp of Cheyennes. Captain Bell did not meet the Bear Tooth group; he also failed to find the camp of Baldhead and Snake Indians that the Kaskaias stated were with the other bands. Much farther east Bell's party, near the Big Bend of the Arkansas, met a war party of "Ietans or Cumanch."

A reasonable interpretation of the information Major Long's party recorded concerning these trading Indians would be that when they went south of the Arkansas about 1817, the Gatakas or Padoucas went down into northern Texas to trade at San Antonio and to be near their Lipan Apache kinsmen in Texas. The Ietan and Baldhead group halted on the Canadian River to be with the northern Comanches, who were their friends, and here they traded with Americans and made raids into New Mexico to obtain horses for that trade. With them apparently were the Arapaho and Cheyenne camps and a small camp of Snake Indians from Columbia River. When they started north in the late summer of 1820, the Kaskaias or Gatakas took a trail that brought them high up the Arkansas; the Arapahoes, Cheyennes, and Snakes took a route

207

farther east; and the Ietans evidently lingered on the Canadian. They were probably the "Ietans or Cumanch" whose war party was met by Captain Bell's group near the Great Bend of the Arkansas, and they were the group usually termed Ietans and Baldheads.

In the next year, 1821, Jacob Fowler and Hugh Glenn led a trading party to the upper Arkansas and actually camped for some weeks with the trading Indians Major Long's party had met. Fowler and Glenn did not mention the Kaskaias—that name was unknown to them—but the Padoucas they found camping with the Kiowas were undoubtedly the Gatakas and Major Long's Kaskaias. On November 19, Fowler and Glenn encountered the first group of Indians, whom they termed Kiowas and Padoucas, at a point on the Arkansas near the mouth of the Apishapa, below the present city of Pueblo. There seem to have been 50 lodges of these Indians; but more bands came in every day, and on the twenty-second, 350 lodges of "Highatans" or Ietans arrived. The chief stated that Major Long had promised in 1820 to send government presents to him; he demanded these gifts from Hugh Glenn, and when Glenn denied that he had any government goods for the chief, there was a violent scene. The chief suspected that Glenn was keeping the goods from him; but later he was convinced that this was not true, and he was then more friendly. Meanwhile other bands came in, camps of Arapahoes, Cheyennes and Snake Indians, and when Glenn and Fowler took a count, they found over 700 lodges. Most of these Indians had been down on the Texas frontier making raids to get horses, and they had one Spanish boy captive in the camp who had been taken near San Antonio. They were on friendly terms with the Spaniards of New Mexico, had been trading with them, and actually had some Taos Indians in their camps. The Arapahoes during the past summer had been up on the Platte, trading horses to the Cheyennes, and they had very few horses left. The other bands in the camp had large numbers of fine horses, which they kept at night in log pens in the center of the big camp. The Crow Indians were encamped on the Platte, about two days' travel away;

208

but almost nightly parties of bold Crow warriors slipped into the center of this camp on the Arkansas, led horses out of the log pens, and got away safely with their plunder.

It is obvious that the Padoucas referred to in Jacob Fowler's journal in this camp of trading Indians were Major Long's Kaskaias. They were close allies of the Kiowas and, therefore, were the Gatakas, later termed the Kiowa-Apaches. Today they have merged into the Kiowa tribe. Fowler's Ietans were a large camp and were probably the group known in past years as Ietans and Baldheads. Their connection with the northern Comanches is suggested; yet they evidently were not regarded as real Comanches.

While Glenn and Fowler were with the trading Indians on the head of the Arkansas, Thomas James with another large trading party of Americans was down on the Canadian with the Comanches. He termed them Comanches, and he made no mention of the Ietans or Padoucas. The assertion by Butler in 1846 that in the prairies the Comanches were commonly termed Padoucas just does not appear to have any support from these records covering the period 1800–35. Tixier, in *Travels on the Osage Prairies*, did term the Comanches "Patokas," which is an apparently clearcut identification; but this French traveler stated that Patoka was the Comanche name for their own people which is an absurdity that makes one wonder just how little Tixier's informants knew about the Comanches and Padoucas. Again, one of Chouteau's traders told Tixier that Chouteau was the only white man who had ever actually met the Patokas. If the tribe Tixier called Patoka was really Comanche, this statement is wildly inaccurate; for we know that numerous parties of American traders, coming up Red River or going westward through Indian Territory, had met and traded with the Comanches from about 1800 on, and the military expedition of Colonel Henry Dodge had met and camped with the Comanches in 1834. It is obvious that Tixier's informants regarded the Patokas as an almost unknown group, never seen by any white man but Chouteau. This description does not fit the Comanches, but it would fit fairly well the Padoucas who belonged to the camp of trading Indians and who were probably met by Chouteau on the head of the Arkansas in 1815–17. In fact, Tixier's Patokas were most probably the Padoucas James Pursley had met in 1803, that Major Long had met in 1820, and Fowler and Glenn in 1821. Chouteau might thus have been termed the first trader who had seen the Padoucas on the upper Arkansas (1815–17), and Tixier, misunderstanding, might have turned this into a statement that Chouteau was the only white man who had ever met this tribe. Both Tixier and Butler later in 1846 seem to have been misled by interpreters who were either too ignorant to know the Comanches and Padoucas apart or—more probably— did not go to the trouble to make their exact meaning clear. If they said baldly that the Comanches were Padoucas, that was not true. The real situation, perhaps, was that the Comanches were sometimes called Ietans, that the real Ietans lived in a camp with the Padoucas, the two tribes being sometimes termed Ietans *and* Padoucas, at other times being confused and termed one tribe, Ietans *or* Padoucas. Thus, it was easy for ill-informed men to think the Comanches were Padoucas, because the Comanches were sometimes called Ietans and the Ietans were sometimes confused with the Padoucas they were camping with.

What happened to the camps of trading Indians after 1821 is unknown. Conditions in the plains had altered significantly since 1790; new tribes equipped with firearms had come into the plains; American trading companies had established themselves on the Missouri, Yellowstone, Platte, Arkansas, and Red River. The old tribe-to-tribe trade in poor grade Spanish articles was no longer worth the trouble and danger of making long journeys from Texas up to the Black Hills and Yellowstone. The trade in slaves was dead; the old trade in horses was dying. The new tribes preferred to obtain the horses they required by raiding other tribes, a method more satisfactory and much cheaper than the older custom of actually paying for the animals. The Comanches stole the horses they required in Texas and Old Mexico; the Pawnees of Nebraska and the Cheyennes sent war parties southward and stole the horses from the Comanches; the Sioux and Crows sent out parties and stole the horses from the Pawnees and Cheyennes, and as likely as not the Blackfeet on the Saskatchewan then stole them from the Crows. This was a much better method than the old humdrum process of meeting the trading Indians and bartering for horses. It gave a zest to life, with every young Indian in the northern plains striving to make a reputation as a bold and skillful horse thief.

After 1821 there are no further references to Ietans and Padoucas making trading journeys north of the Arkansas. Those camps of Arapahoes and Kiowas that had been living with the trading Indians up to 1821 made an effort to continue the old trade, going up to the Platte occasionally to hold a trading fair, but their ventures usually ended in their being attacked and robbed by some northern tribe. In the autumn of 1824, General Ashley led a trapping party up the Platte and was told by the Skidi Pawnees that these Arapahoes and Kiowas were encamped on the Arkansas, with one hundred Arikaras in the same camp.[6] We find no further reference to Indians going up to the Platte on trading visits. Indeed, from about 1826 on, the Cheyennes, instead of trading for horses, were sending war parties to the Canadian and even to Red River to steal herds from the southern tribes. The result was war and an advance of half of the Cheyenne tribe southward to the upper Arkansas.

What may be the last report of the Padoucas as an existing tribe was written by Paul of Württemberg in 1823. He went up the Missouri, and among the Skidi Pawnees he purchased a Padouca scalp with long luxuriant hair resembling, he said, the hair plaits of the Arapahoes, which were lengthened by attaching additional lengths of hair with resin.[7] The last mention of the Ietans as a separate group seems to be that of the English traveler Charles Murray. He was told in the Pawnee camp in 1835 that the Pawnees were sending trading parties south of the Arkansas every summer

[6] Dale, *Ashley-Smith Explorations*, 126. The Arikaras, attacked by the Sioux and Americans, had fled from their villages on the Upper Missouri and were roving in the plains of western Nebraska, Kansas, and eastern Colorado, some of them camping with the trading Indians, as recorded here, on the Arkansas in 1824.

[7] Paul Wilhelm, Herzog von Württemberg, *Erste Reise nach dem Nördlichen Amerika in den Jahren 1822 bis 1824*, 373.

to trade guns and other articles to the Ietans, *a small tribe*, for horses.

The old names, Padouca, Ietan, and Kaskaia, were embalmed for a number of years in the government Indian statistics published in Schoolcraft's volumes. These government reports continued year after year to present these bands of trading Indians, met by Major Long on the Arkansas in 1820. In 1829 and 1834, Schoolcraft listed three thousand Kaskaias and two thousand Padoucas Proper; he listed the Ietans among the Snakes, keeping alive the Lewis and Clark report of 1806 that all the Snakes were Alitans or Ietans. In 1835, Colonel Dodge was on the Platte and Arkansas and failed to find these tribes; so at last, in 1836, the government reports buried the Padoucas, Ietans, and Kaskaias.

The Bent brothers established a trading post on the upper Arkansas in 1826 and continued to trade there for over thirty years. There is no record that they ever mentioned the Padoucas or Ietans. In all the voluminous historical narratives of the Southern Cheyenne Indians, there is not one reference to Padoucas or Ietans. These groups seem to have gone south of the Arkansas in 1822 and then to have vanished. The Bents called the old Gataka or Padouca group the Prairie Apaches, and William Bent stated that about 1830 these Apaches had some twelve hundred people. Colonel Dodge, who evidently obtained his figures from Bent, gave the same number for these Apaches in 1835.

Vanishing as the Padoucas and Ietans did after 1822, it is not reasonable to assume that they became suddenly extinct. In all probability they joined the Comanches and Kiowas and were known under new names. It should be borne in mind that, when the large Kwahari Comanche tribe moved south of the Arkansas, it was lost. There is not one clear reference to this tribe until after 1860, when it suddenly emerged again as a most powerful Comanche group. If the Kwaharis could have been hidden in this fashion from 1800 to 1860, the Ietans, a much smaller group, may have been similarly concealed.

There was a chief named Shaved Head who was well known on the Arkansas as late as 1860. He and Bull Hump were leaders of the northern Comanches at the period 1825–50, and it is possible that he was the son of the old chief of the Baldhead camp. That might have been, if the Baldheads were so named for their chief, who was the man who gambled and lost his scalp. With his death, his name might have been tabooed, and his son might have taken the similar name of Shaved Head; but this is pure conjecture.

Additional information concerning the ultimate fate of the Ietans, Padoucas, and other Indians of the old trading group may come to light in future years, with the discovery of manuscript material written by Indian agents and other men interested in Indian affairs in the country between the Arkansas and the Texas borders. Some new material of this type turns up every few years. At present we can only surmise that the Ietans, after 1835, merged into the Comanche tribe; that one of the last Padouca groups may have been those Esikwita Apaches who went to live in Mexico, returning to Texas about the year 1846 to join the Lipan and Mescalero Apaches; and that the Baldheads, who were the trading Indians in 1820, joined the northern Comanches.

# Bibliography

Alter, J. C. "Father Escalante and the Utah Indians," *Utah Historical Quarterly*, Vol I (1928).

*American State Papers*, edited by Walter Lowrie *et al.* 38 vols. Washington, 1832–61.

Bancroft, Hubert Howe. *History of Arizona and New Mexico*. San Francisco, 1889.

———. *History of the North Mexican States and Texas*. 2 vols. San Francisco, 1890.

———. *History of Nevada, Colorado, and Wyoming*. San Francisco, 1890.

———. *History of Utah, 1540–1887*. San Francisco, 1891.

Benavides, Fray Alonso de. *The Memorial of Fray Alonso de Benavides 1630*. Annotated by Frederick Webb Hodge. Albuquerque, 1945.

Bishop, M. *The Odyssey of Cabeza de Vaca*. New York, 1933.

Blair, Emma H. *Indian Tribes of the Great Lakes and the Mississippi Valley*. 2 vols. Cleveland, 1911.

Bolton, Herbert Eugene (ed.). *Athanase de Mézière and the Louisiana–Texas Frontier, 1768–80*. Cleveland, 1914.

———. (ed.). *Spanish Explorations in the Southwest*. New York, 1916.

Bryce, George. *The Remarkable History of the Hudson's Bay Company*. Toronto, 1904.

Burpee, L. J. *The Search for the Western Sea*. New York, 1908.

Carrington, Margaret I. *Ab-sa-ra-ka, Home of the Crows*. Philadelphia, 1869.

Champe, J. L. *Ash Hollow Cave*. Lincoln, Nebraska, 1946.
———. "White Cat Village," *American Antiquity*, Vol. XIV (1949).
Chittenden, Hiram M. *The American Fur Trade of the Far West*. 2 vols. New York, 1925.
Clark, W. P. *The Indian Sign Language*. Philadelphia, 1885.
Dale, Harrison C. *The Ashley-Smith Explorations and the Discovery of a Central Route to the Pacific, 1822–1829*. Cleveland, 1918.
Davis, W. H. *The Spanish Conquest of New Mexico*. Doylestown, Pa., 1869.
DeMun, Jules. "Journals," *Missouri Historical Society Collections*, Vol. V. (October, 1927–June, 1928).
Denig, Edwin T. "Indian Tribes of the Upper Missouri" (ed. by J. N. B. Hewitt), Bureau of American Ethnology *Forty-sixth Annual Report* (1928–29). Washington, 1930.
Dunbar, John. "The Pawnee Indians; Their History and Ethnology," *Magazine of American History*, Vol. IV (1880).
Dunn, William E. "Apache Relations in Texas, 1718–1750," *Texas State Historical Association Quarterly*, Vol. XII (1910).
Espinosa, J. Manuel (trans.). *First Expedition of Vargas Into New Mexico, 1692*. Albuquerque, 1940.
Ewers, John C. *The Blackfeet: Raiders on the Northwestern Plains*, Norman, 1958.
———. "The Story of the Blackfeet." Haskell Institute, Lawrence, Kansas, 1952.
Fletcher, Alice C., and Francis La Flesche. "The Omaha Tribe," Bureau of American Ethnology *Twenty-seventh Annual Report* (1905–1906). Washington, 1911.
Foreman, Grant. *Indians and Pioneers*. Norman, 1937.
———. *Advancing the Frontier*. Norman, 1933.
Fowler, Jacob. *The Journal of Jacob Fowler*. New York, 1898.
Gebow, J. A. *A Vocabulary of the Snake or Sho-sho-nay Dialect*. Green River, Wyo., 1868.
Griffin, James Bennett (ed.). *Archaeology of Eastern United States*. Chicago, 1952.
Grinnell, George Bird. *The Cheyenne Indians*. 2 vols. New Haven, 1923.
———. "Who Were the Padouca?" *American Anthropologist*, New Series, Vol. XXII (1920).
———. *The Fighting Cheyennes*. Norman, 1956.

Gunnerson, Dolores. "The Southern Athabascans: Their Arrival in the Southwest," *El Palacio*, Vol. VI (1956).

Haines, Francis. "The Northwest Spread of Horses Among the Plains Indians," *American Anthropologist*, Vol. XL (1938).

Hammond, George P., and Agapito Rey. *Don Juan de Oñate, Colonizer of New Mexico, 1595–1628.* 2 vols. Albuquerque, 1953.

——. *Expedition into New Mexico made by Antonio de Espejo, 1582–1583, as Revealed in the Journal of Diego Pérez de Luxán.* Los Angeles, 1929.

——. *Narratives of the Coronado Expedition.* Albuquerque, 1940.

Harrington, John P. "Southern Periferal Athapaskawan Origins, Divisions, and Migrations," *Smithsonian Miscellaneous Collections*, Vol. C. Washington, 1940.

Harris Burton. *John Colter: His Years in the Rockies.* New York, 1952.

Harris, William Richard. *The Catholic Church in Utah.* Salt Lake City, 1909.

Hebard, Grace R. *Washakie.* Cleveland, 1930.

Henry, Alexander, and David Thompson. *New Light on the Early History of the Greater Northwest.* Ed. by Elliott Coues. 3 vols. New York, 1897.

Hill, A. T., and George Metcalf. "A Site of the Dismal River Aspect in Chase County, Nebraska," *Nebraska History*, Vol. XXII (1941).

Hill, J. J. "Spanish and Mexican Exploration and Trade Northwest from New Mexico," *Utah Historical Quarterly*, Vol. III (1930).

Hill, W. W. "Some Navaho Culture Changes During Two Centuries (with a Translation of the Early Eighteenth Century Rabal Manuscript)," *Smithsonian Miscellaneous Collections*, Vol. C. Washington, 1940.

Hodge, Frederick Webb (ed.). *Handbook of American Indians North of Mexico.* Bureau of American Ethnology *Bulletin No. 30.* 2 vols. Washington, 1907.

Hoijer, Harry. "Southern Athapaskan Languages," *American Anthropologist*, New Series, Vol. XL (1938).

Hyde, George E. *The Pawnee Indians.* Denver, 1951.

——. *Rangers and Regulars.* Columbus, 1953.

——. *The Early Blackfeet and Their Neighbors.* Denver, 1933.

——"The Mystery of the Arikaras," *North Dakota History*, Vol. XVIII, No. 4 (1951) and Vol. XIX, No. 1 (1952).

Irving, Washington. *Astoria*. New York, 1849.

James, Edwin. *Account of an Expedition from Pittsburgh to the Rocky Mountains, 1819-20*. Philadelphia, 1823.

James, Thomas. *Three Years Among Indians and Mexicans*. St. Louis, 1916.

Jenness, D. *The Sarcee Indians of Alberta*. National Museum of Canada *Bulletin 90*. Ottawa, 1938.

Keim, DeBenneville Randolph. *Sheridan's Troopers on the Border*. New York, 1870.

Kivett, Marvin F. "The Woodruff Ossuary," Bureau of American Ethnology *Bulletin No. 154*. Washington, 1953.

Laut, Agnes. *Conquest of the Greater Northwest*. 2 vols. New York, 1908.

La Verendrye, Pierre G. V. *Journals and Letters of Pierre Gaultier de Varennes de la Verendrye and His Sons*. Ed. by L. J. Burpee. Toronton, 1927.

Leonard, Zenas. *Narrative of the Adventures of Zenas Leonard*. Ed. by Milo M. Quaife. Chicago, 1934.

Lewis, Meriwether, and William Clark. *Original Journals of the Lewis and Clark Expedition, 1804-1806*. Ed. by Reuben Gold Thwaites. 8 vols. New York, 1904-1905.

Lockwood, Frank C. *The Apache Indians*. New York, 1938.

Lowery, Woodbury. *The Spanish Settlements Within the Present Limits of the United States, 1513-1561*. Ed. by Philip Lee Phillips. Washington, 1912.

Margry, Pierre. *Découvertes et établissements des français dans l'ouest et dans le sud de l'Amérique Septentrionale (1614-1754). Mémoires et documents originaux recueillis et pub. P. Margry*. 6 vols. Paris, 1879-88.

Martin, P. S., G. I. Quimby, and D. Collier. *Indians Before Columbus*. Chicago, 1947.

Mooney, James. "Calendar History of the Kiowa," Bureau of American Ethnology *Seventeenth Annual Report*, Part I. Washington, 1898.

———. "The Cheyenne Indians," American Anthropological Association *Memoirs*, Vol. I (1905-1907).

Mott, M. "The Relation of Historic Indian Tribes to Archeological

Manifestations in Iowa," *Iowa Journal of History and Politics*, Vol. XXXVI (1938).

Mulloy, W. "A Prehistoric Campsite near Red Lodge, Montana," *American Antiquity*, Vol. IX (1943–44).

———. "Some Ancient Caves in the Yellowstone Valley. MS in Missouri Valley Project, University of Nebraska, Lincoln, Nebraska.

Nasatir, A. P. *Before Lewis and Clark*. St. Louis, 1952.

——— (ed.). "An Account of Spanish Louisiana in 1785," *Missouri Historical Review*, Vol. XXIV (1930).

Ogden, Peter Skene. "Journal of the Snake Expedition, 1825–26," *Oregon Historical Society Quarterly*, Vol. X (1909).

———. "Journal of the Expedition of 1826–27," *Oregon Historical Society Quarterly*, Vol. XI (1910).

Paul Wilhelm, Herzog von Württemberg. *Erste Reise nach dem nördlichen Amerika in den Jahren 1822 bis 1824*. Stuttgart and Tübingen, 1835.

Pike, Zebulon Montgomery. *The Expeditions of Zebulon Montgomery Pike to the Headwaters of the Mississippi River, Through Louisiana Territory, and in New Spain, During the Years 1805–6–7*. Ed. by Elliott Coues. 3 vols. New York, 1895.

Pool, R. J. "A Study of the Vegetation of the Sandhills of Nebraska," University of Minnesota *Botanical Studies*, Vol. IV (1914).

Quaife, Milo M. (ed.). "Extracts from Captain McKay's Journal," *Wisconsin Historical Society Publication* (1915).

Renaud, Étienne Bernardeau. *Archaeological Survey Reports, 1934, 1936, 1937, 1943*. Denver, 1934–43.

Richardson, Rupert Norval. *The Comanche Barrier to South Plains Settlement: A Century and a Half of Savage Resistance to the Advancing White Frontier*. Glendale, Calif., 1933.

Schoolcraft, Henry R. *Historical and Statistical Information Respecting the History, Condition, and Prospects of the Indian Tribes of the United States*. 6 vols. Philadelphia, 1857.

Secoy, Frank R. *Changing Military Patterns on the Great Plains*. Locust Valley, N. Y., 1953.

———. "The Identity of the Padouca," *American Anthropologist*, New Series, Vol. LIII (1951).

Snow, W. J. "Utah Indians and the Spanish Slave Trade," *Utah Historical Quarterly*, Vol. II (1929).

Steward, Julian H. "Basin-Plateau Aboriginal Sociopolitical Groups,"

Bureau of American Ethnology *Bulletin No. 120.* Washington, 1938.

———. "Ancient Caves of the Great Salt Lake Region," Bureau of American Ethnology *Bulletin No. 116.* Washington, 1937.

———. "Native Cultures of the Intermontane (Great Basin) Area," Smithsonian Miscellaneous Collections, Vol. C. Washington, 1940.

Strong, W. Duncan. "Introduction to Nebraska Archeology," *Smithsonian Miscellaneous Collections,* Vol. XCIII. Washington, 1935.

Stuart, Granville. *Forty Years on the Frontier.* Cleveland, 1925.

Stuart, Robert. *The Discovery of the Oregon Trail: The Journal of Robert Stuart.* Ed. by Philip Ashton Rollins. New York, 1935.

Swanton, John R. "Source Material on the History and Ethnology of the Caddo Indians," Bureau of American Ethnology *Bulletin No. 132.* Washington, 1942.

Tabeau, Pierre-Antoine. *Tabeau's Narrative of Loisel's Expedition to the Upper Missouri.* Ed. by Annie Heloise Abel. Norman, 1939.

Teit, James A. "The Salishan Tribes of the Western Plateaus: The Flathead Group," Bureau of American Ethnology *Forty-fourth Annual Report.* Washington, 1930.

Thomas, Alfred Barnaby. *Forgotten Frontiers.* Norman, 1932.

——— (ed.). *After Coronado: Spanish Exploration Northeast of New Mexico, 1696–1727.* Norman, 1935.

——— (trans. and ed.). *Teodoro de Croix and the Northern Frontier of New Spain, 1776–1783.* Norman, 1941.

———. *Plains Indians and New Mexico.* Albuquerque, 1940.

Thompson, David. *David Thompson's Narrative of his Explorations in Western America, 1784–1812.* Ed. by J. B. Tyrrell. Toronto, 1916.

Truteau, J. B. "Journal," *South Dakota Historical Society Collections,* Vol. VII (1914).

Villagra, G. P. de. *History of New Mexico.* Los Angeles, 1933.

Villiers, Baron Marc de. *La Découverte du Missouri et l'histoire du Fort d'Orléans (1673–1728).* Paris, 1925.

———. *La Louisiane.* Paris, 1929.

Wedel, Waldo R. "Culture Sequence in the Central Great Plains," *Smithsonian Miscellaneous Collections,* Vol. C. Washington, 1940.

———. "An Introduction to Pawnee Archeology," Bureau of American Ethnology *Bulletin No. 112.* Washington, 1936.

———. "Culture Chronology in the Central Great Plains," *American Antiquity,* Vol. XII (1946–47).

Will, G. F. "Archeology of the Missouri Valley," American Museum of Natural History *Anthropological Papers,* Vol. XXII (1924).

———. "Tree Ring Studies in North Dakota," North Dakota Agricultural College *Bulletin 338* (1946).

———, and T. C. Hecker. "Upper Missouri River Valley Culture in North Dakota," *North Dakota Historical Quarterly,* Vol. XI (1944).

Willson, Beckles. *The Great Company.* London, 1900.

Wissler, Clark. *North American Indians of the Plains.* New York, 1927.

# Index

Williams, Ezekial, trapper: 196
Woodland culture: 3
Wyeth, Nathaniel, trader:
125, 179

Yampa plant, as food: 57

Záldivar, among Apaches: 9–11

## THE CIVILIZATION OF THE AMERICAN INDIAN SERIES

of which *Indians of the High Plains: From the Prehistoric Period to the Coming of Europeans* is the fifty-fourth volume, was inaugurated in 1932 by the University of Oklahoma Press, and has as its purpose the reconstruction of American Indian civilization by presenting aboriginal, historical, and contemporary Indian life. The following list is complete as of the date of publication of this volume:

1. Alfred Barnaby Thomas. *Forgotten Frontiers:* A Study of the Spanish Indian Policy of Don Juan Bautista de Anza, Governor of New Mexico, 1777–1787. Out of print.
2. Grant Foreman. *Indian Removal*: The Emigration of the Five Civilized Tribes of Indians.
3. John Joseph Mathews. *Wah'Kon-Tah:* The Osage and the White Man's Road. Out of print.
4. Grant Foreman. *Advancing the Frontier, 1830–1860.* Out of print.
5. John Homer Seger. *Early Days Among the Cheyenne and Arapahoe Indians.* Edited by Stanley Vestal.
6. Angie Debo. *The Rise and Fall of the Choctaw Republic.* Out of print.
7. Stanley Vestal (ed.). *New Sources of Indian History, 1850–1891.* Out of print.
8. Grant Foreman. *The Five Civilized Tribes.* Out of print.
9. Alfred Barnaby Thomas. *After Coronado*: Spanish Exploration Northeast of New Mexico, 1696–1727. Out of print.
10. Frank B. Speck. *Naskapi:* The Savage Hunters of the Labrador Peninsula. Out of print.
11. Elaine Goodale Eastman. *Pratt: The Red Man's Moses.* Out of print.
12. Althea Bass. *Cherokee Messenger*: A Life of Samuel Austin Worcester. Out of print.
13. Thomas Wildcat Alford. *Civilization.* As told to Florence Drake. Out of print.

14. Grant Foreman. *Indians and Pioneers*: The Story of the American Southwest Before 1830. Out of print.
15. George E. Hyde. *Red Cloud's Folk*: A History of the Oglala Sioux Indians.
16. Grant Foreman. *Sequoyah*.
17. Morris L. Wardell. *A Political History of the Cherokee Nation, 1838–1907*. Out of print.
18. John Walton Caughey. *McGillivray of the Creeks*.
19. Edward Everett Dale and Gaston Litton. *Cherokee Cavaliers*: Forty Years of Cherokee History as Told in the Correspondence of the Ridge-Watie-Boudinot Family. Out of print.
20. Ralph Henry Gabriel. *Elias Boudinot, Cherokee, and His America*.
21. Karl N. Llewellyn and E. Adamson Hoebel. *The Cheyenne Way*: Conflict and Case Law in Primitive Jurisprudence.
22. Angie Debo. *The Road to Disappearance*.
23. Oliver La Farge and others. *The Changing Indian*. Out of print.
24. Carolyn Thomas Foreman. *Indians Abroad*. Out of print.
25. John Adair. *The Navajo and Pueblo Silversmiths*.
26. Alice Marriott. *The Ten Grandmothers*.
27. Alice Marriott. *María*: The Potter of San Ildefonso.
28. Edward Everett Dale. *The Indians of the Southwest*: A Century of Development Under the United States. Out of print.
29. Adrián Recinos. *Popol Vuh*: The Sacred Book of the Ancient Quiché Maya. English version by Delia Goetz and Sylvanus G. Morley from the translation of Adrián Recinos.
30. Walter Collins O'Kane. *Sun in the Sky*.
31. Stanley A. Stubbs. *Bird's-Eye View of the Pueblos*.
32. Katharine C. Turner. *Red Men Calling on the Great White Father*.
33. Muriel H. Wright. *A Guide to the Indian Tribes of Oklahoma*.
34. Ernest Wallace and E. Adamson Hoebel. *The Comanches*: Lords of the South Plains.

35. Walter Collins O'Kane. *The Hopis*: Portrait of a Desert People.
36. Joseph Epes Brown. *The Sacred Pipe*: Black Elk's Account of the Seven Rites of the Oglala Sioux.
37. Adrián Recinos and Delia Goetz. *The Annals of the Cakchiquels*. Translated from the Cakchiquel Maya, with *Title of the Lords of Totonicapán*, translated from the Quiché text into Spanish by Dionisio José Chonay, English version by Delia Goetz.
38. R. S. Cotterill. *The Southern Indians*: The Story of the Civilized Tribes Before Removal.
39. J. Eric S. Thompson. *The Rise and Fall of Maya Civilization*.
40. Robert Emmitt. *The Last War Trail*: The Utes and the Settlement of Colorado.
41. Frank Gilbert Roe. *The Indian and the Horse*.
42. Francis Haines. *The Nez Percés*: Tribesmen of the Columbia Plateau. Out of print.
43. Ruth M. Underhill. *The Navajos*.
44. George Bird Grinnell. *The Fighting Cheyennes*.
45. George E. Hyde. *A Sioux Chronicle*.
46. Stanley Vestal. *Sitting Bull: Champion of the Sioux, A Biography*.
47. Edwin C. McReynolds. *The Seminoles*.
48. William T. Hagan. *The Sac and Fox Indians*.
49. John C. Ewers. *The Blackfeet*: Raiders on the Northwestern Plains.
50. Alfonso Caso. *The Aztecs*: People of the Sun. Translated by Lowell Dunham.
51. C. L. Sonnichsen. *The Mescalero Apaches*.
52. Keith A. Murray. *The Modocs and Their War*.
53. Victor W. von Hagen (ed.). *The Incas of Pedro de Cieza de León*. Translated by Harriet de Onis.
54. George E. Hyde. *Indians of the High Plains:* From the Prehistoric Period to the Coming of Europeans.

UNIVERSITY OF OKLAHOMA PRESS : NORMAN